CAMBRIDGE LIBRARY COLLECTION

Books of enduring scholarly value

Classics

From the Renaissance to the nineteenth century, Latin and Greek were compulsory subjects in almost all European universities, and most early modern scholars published their research and conducted international correspondence in Latin. Latin had continued in use in Western Europe long after the fall of the Roman empire as the lingua franca of the educated classes and of law, diplomacy, religion and university teaching. The flight of Greek scholars to the West after the fall of Constantinople in 1453 gave impetus to the study of ancient Greek literature and the Greek New Testament. Eventually, just as nineteenth-century reforms of university curricula were beginning to erode this ascendancy, developments in textual criticism and linguistic analysis, and new ways of studying ancient societies, especially archaeology, led to renewed enthusiasm for the Classics. This collection offers works of criticism, interpretation and synthesis by the outstanding scholars of the nineteenth century.

The Alps of Hannibal

Controversial for centuries, the route across the Alps taken by Hannibal, his Carthaginian army and his famous elephants in 218 BCE formed the basis of an extended scholarly dispute between William John Law (1786–1869) and Robert Ellis (1819/20–85). Fought in the pages of books and the *Journal of Classical and Sacred Philology*, their exchanges lasted several years. Ellis' *Treatise on Hannibal's Passage of the Alps* (1853) and *An Enquiry into the Ancient Routes between Italy and Gaul* (1867) are also reissued in this series. Published in 1866, this two-volume work was Law's major contribution to the debate, examining the various theories and historical accounts. Modern scholarship has questioned, however, whether either man was right. Volume 1 examines the accounts of Polybius, using numerous modern measurements to try to gauge their accuracy. It also evaluates the reliability of previous suggestions for Hannibal's route at each stage of the journey.

T0382421

Cambridge University Press has long been a pioneer in the reissuing of out-of-print titles from its own backlist, producing digital reprints of books that are still sought after by scholars and students but could not be reprinted economically using traditional technology. The Cambridge Library Collection extends this activity to a wider range of books which are still of importance to researchers and professionals, either for the source material they contain, or as landmarks in the history of their academic discipline.

Drawing from the world-renowned collections in the Cambridge University Library and other partner libraries, and guided by the advice of experts in each subject area, Cambridge University Press is using state-of-the-art scanning machines in its own Printing House to capture the content of each book selected for inclusion. The files are processed to give a consistently clear, crisp image, and the books finished to the high quality standard for which the Press is recognised around the world. The latest print-on-demand technology ensures that the books will remain available indefinitely, and that orders for single or multiple copies can quickly be supplied.

The Cambridge Library Collection brings back to life books of enduring scholarly value (including out-of-copyright works originally issued by other publishers) across a wide range of disciplines in the humanities and social sciences and in science and technology.

The Alps of Hannibal

Volume 1

WILLIAM JOHN LAW

CAMBRIDGE
UNIVERSITY PRESS

CAMBRIDGE
UNIVERSITY PRESS

University Printing House, Cambridge, CB2 8BS, United Kingdom

Cambridge University Press is part of the University of Cambridge.

It furthers the University's mission by disseminating knowledge in the pursuit of
education, learning and research at the highest international levels of excellence.

www.cambridge.org
Information on this title: www.cambridge.org/9781108079495

This edition first published 1866
This digitally printed version 2014

ISBN 978-1-108-07949-5 Paperback

THE ALPS OF HANNIBAL.

IN TWO VOLUMES.

THE ALPS

OF

HANNIBAL.

BY

WILLIAM JOHN LAW, M.A.

FORMERLY STUDENT OF CHRIST CHURCH,

OXFORD.

IN TWO VOLUMES.

VOL. I.

London:

MACMILLAN AND CO.

1866.

LONDON :
R. CLAY, SON, AND TAYLOR, PRINTERS,
BREAD STREET HILL.

THESE PAGES ARE INSCRIBED

TO THE MEMORY OF

MY REVERED GRANDFATHERS,

EDMUND LAW, BISHOP OF CARLISLE,

AND

WILLIAM MARKHAM, ARCHBISHOP OF YORK ;

MEN OF LEARNING AND PIETY,

AND SINCERE LOVERS OF TRUTH.

W. J. L.

PREFACE.

SOME apology will be expected for treating at large this very old topic of dissension. A few facts must plead my excuse. At the end of July, 1854, I was sent for health to Aix-les-Bains, in Savoy; and I took with me Mr. Ellis's "Treatise on Hannibal's Passage of the Alps," then lately issued from the Cambridge University press, a work in which the march is carried over the Little Mont Cenis. At Aix I met with another new work by a savant of that country, who launches the invaders into Italy from the Col de la Seigne. A further circumstance presently kindled my interest in a subject which had been familiar to me: that an indication of one reputed track was in sight from the garden of my house. I borrowed from my physician the volumes of De Saussure, to help me in my French and in my Alps, and amused myself during August with some comments, which I printed at Chambéry, on the speculations of M. Replat.

I left Aix on the 17th September with renewed impulse to a favourite theme, proposing for my daughter and myself a week's absence from my family, that we might cross the Little St. Bernard and return by the Col de la Seigne and the valley of Beaufort. The result was calamitous: I made my first and last descent into Italy in a state of serious illness: for nine weeks I lay within gunshot of the great precipice, without a hope of contemplating it. To avoid being snowed up for the winter at Courmayeur, I was at last moved slowly down the valley to seek a more favouring climate. So began and so ended the chance of contributing by personal investigation to a knowledge of the disputed track.

In my progress to convalescence at Nice, I found myself without employment; and a resource offered itself in the examination of Mr. Ellis's theory. I weighed its merits, and sifted them as well as I could under the circumstances; and on my return to England in April, immediately published the results. In 1856 Mr. Ellis defended himself in two numbers of the " Cambridge Journal of Classical and Sacred Philology; " and I replied promptly to each through the same channel. That warfare was to be excused; I was only criticising a new theory. If now I maintain a theory myself, and strive to overthrow all the rest, it may be asked, why further stir this worn-out controversy; has not too much been said already?

That sentiment would accord with a remark made by the last English writer of eminence who has touched the subject. Dr. Liddell says, " The con-" troversy will probably last for ever : the data " seem insufficient to enable us to form a positive " judgment." This feeling of despair may be alleviated if the inquiry shall enable us to account for the failure of a few marked men, whom the world would have expected to command assent on the question. Such were D'Anville and Gibbon. But improvement has been slow, and error obstinate. Many a year has passed since the very learned Thirlwall, reviewing the efforts of a distinguished commentator, spoke of " the enormous mass of " literature which has been already piled upon " this theme." Mass, indeed, there is; but it is

accounted for in the remark of Niebuhr, "that
" even ingenious and learned men have opposed the
" most palpable evidence." The theme is not worn
out: men of learning continue to embarrass truth
in their professions to illustrate it: popular and
plausible arguments hold their credit, because unanswered; and reputed difficulties are looked upon
with dismay, as if they were real ones. The subject is not exhausted, and the fact that it has
been worked so much is the best proof that it
needs to be worked more.

When one comes to interfere in a dispute which
has lasted so long, the great discouragement is, that
a fit treatment of it threatens to be too copious
for the patience of a reader: and I expect censure
for my prolixity. But who can have the vanity to
hope that inveterate error may be exterminated
with a few pages? Heresies must be attacked
which took root in the first days of the Roman
empire, which have been cultivated in various forms
to the present time; nourished by men who have
adorned the literature of modern Europe. Few
there are who take pains to scrutinise what is
plausible, or to sift what is obscure. The laborious
effort of novelty, which I have mentioned as

inviting me to the combat, has succeeded, as I know, in unsettling the faith of able minds.

In meeting with the strange contrivances offered for solving this question, one is apt to pause and say, " Must we consume time in combating such a notion as this? " But, if the notion which suggests the scruple should be countenanced by men like Schweighæuser, or Gossellin, or Letronne, or Arnold, or Ukert, there is no alternative: the unresisted sanction of such names governs the opinion of the world: and, though an error may in itself seem unworthy of refutation, the friend of truth cannot leave it unassailed. In this controversy there is nothing so extravagant that you may pass it by: the most perverse fancies are found in writers of formidable reputation. All obstacles then must be encountered: we dare not despise what the world esteems: the consequence is, that the subject must not be treated shortly, if it is to be treated safely.

Fortunately those very circumstances make the pursuit of it exceedingly entertaining. The strangeness of conceptions, whether in history, geography, logic, or grammar, which offer themselves to notice, provoke a never-ceasing interest, and entice you by degrees into the full current of the dispute. Such

has been my fate: and I offer, though not ripened
as it should be, the fruit of my temptation. I have
endeavoured to perceive the drift of each hostile
argument: and, dealing freely with the opinions of
others, may be thought not to bespeak indulgence
for my own. But, in truth, I bespeak it earnestly.
An old man, returning to Greek after long absence,
cannot possibly be exempt from error; and when
he finds, in the great names he has to deal with,
none that he can in all points follow, he constantly
has to apprehend error in himself. The danger is
felt and acknowledgéd: but the fear of it will
not deter from the utterance of thoughts honestly
entertained. Whilst, among the varieties and
complications of our subject, we are differing from
those whom we greatly respect, in the process
which discloses the errors of such men, we
become convinced of the fallibility of all, and most
conscious of the indulgence needed for ourselves.

CONTENTS OF VOLUME ONE.

PART I.

THE CONTROVERSY.

PART II.

ON THE AUTHORITY OF POLYBIUS.

PART III.

POLYBIUS INTERPRETED. PASSAGE OF THE RHONE.

PART IV.

POLYBIUS INTERPRETED. THE BEGINNING OF ALPS.

PART V.

THE MOUNTAIN MARCH. ASCENT.

PART VI.

THE MOUNTAIN MARCH. SUMMIT.

PART VII.

ERRATA.

Page 71, line 2º, *for* "equæ" *read* "aquæ."

„ 93, „ 3, *for* "agreement" *read* "argument."

„ 118, „ 18, *for* "nom" *read* "nomme."

„ 122, „ 33, *for* "equivocal" *read* "equivalent."

„ 156, „ 29, *for* "marching" *read* "reaching."

„ 158, „ 10, "from Valence" *to be omitted.*

„ 221, „ 14, *for* "hushing" *read* "hashing."

„ 304, „ 2, *for* "but" *read* "best."

„ 319, „ 24, *for* "Vin" *read* "Viu."

The material originally positioned here is too large for reproduction in this reissue. A PDF can be downloaded from the web address given on page iv of this book, by clicking on 'Resources Available'.

THE ALPS OF HANNIBAL.

PART I.

THE CONTROVERSY

CHAPTER I.

The Controversy : Progress and State of it.

SEVEN cities contended to be the birth-place of Homer. As many mountains contend to be the Alps of Hannibal. Great and good men have toiled to fix the death-hour of Alexander, and the landing-spot of Cæsar in Britain. There are who hold such labours to be vain and unprofitable : and it is true that, in the variety of objects which provoke curiosity and research, the interest which they excite is not regulated by their importance. But the value of the thing pursued is alone not a test of the merit of the pursuit : the scrutiny of a question which it hardly imports us to solve may nevertheless be deserving of praise : an examination of evidence, as in the case before us, can vindicate an interest far surpassing that of the thing to be proved ; and it is enough to say, that a subject which has engaged Letronne and Ukert and Arnold, bespeaks itself worthy to be explored. When we regard the various matters which such inquiries will embrace, we make better estimate of their value ; and see danger in a doctrine which, condemning them as useless, would confine our exercise of thinking to the exigencies of the passing day. Efforts of retrospect, even such as these, are conducive to the interests of society.

But in our subject is there need of effort? Remains there a question to discuss? Has not error been removed: and the evidence of truth been submitted to and confessed? There is no such acquiescence. The lamented Arnold, whose loss we cease not to deplore, studied the subject among the Alps themselves: in 1825 he was on the spot with Polybius in hand; in 1835 he wrote, "I have been working at Hannibal's passage of the Alps:" zealous in the tracing of military movements, he hardly reached a firm opinion on this subject, and to the last declared Polybius an unintelligible guide. Letronne and Ukert are among the later lights on geography and history; one invites us to the Genèvre, the other to the Cenis: while Arneth, director of the Museum at Vienna, has taught that the Carthaginians descended from the Simplon. So late as 1851, a savant of Savoy discovered their track through the Allée Blanche, hailing Mont Blanc as the λευκόπετρον; and Mr. Ellis in 1854 proclaims the Rock of Baune as the representative of that landmark, and the little Mont Cenis as laid down in the Chart of Pentinger. So long as there are such doubts and such difficulties among learned men, the question is not closed; truth is not established; search is still reasonable: nec modus est ullus investigandi veri, nisi inveneris.

Progress and State of the Controversy.

More than eighteen hundred years ago, Livy brought forward the course of Hannibal as a matter of controversy: and it is controverted to this day. In our own times books and pamphlets innumerable have been written upon it, exhibiting various degrees of labour and merit. The subject indeed has been agitated from time to time for the last three

hundred years, in works which the curious who have leisure
may explore. A considerable list is given with Dr. Ukert's
Dissertation, in his second volume, Part II. p. 563 ; and many
are enumerated in a preface to the work of. M. le Comte de
Fortia d'Urban, 1821.

The earliest of modern authors, whose opinion I can quote,
is Mr. Breval, Fellow of Trinity College, Cambridge. In his
Travels, published 1726,* he named the Little St. Bernard as
the Pass of Hannibal. But, though he saw some essential
points correctly, his suffrage is of no value; for, referring to
Polybius, he says that Hannibal passed the Rhone at Lyons.
Then, doubting whether the site of that city between the
Saône and the Rhône could represent the district called the
Island, he finds relief in the work of Menetrier, the historian
of Lyons, whose antiquarian researches had brought him
acquainted with an old canal cut from one river to the other
—which, says Mr. Breval, " makes the third side of an island
in every respect like that described by Polybius ! "

Soon after Mr. Breval's short notice of the matter, the
voluminous and wearisome commentaries of the Chevalier
Folard appeared, encumbering the translation of Polybius by
Dom Vincent Thuillier, which is in six quarto volumes ; our
subject occurring in the fourth, published in 1728.

D'Anville's notions were, I believe, first shown in a map
which he published in 1739 to illustrate the march of
Hannibal. I saw it for the first time on the 31st December,
1863, at the British Museum : it is entirely founded on his
apprehension of Livy, and there is nothing in correction of it
in his " Ancienne Gaule," published 1760. The labour of
interpreting Polybius does not appear to have been undertaken
by him, nor the necessity of such a task recognised. The

* " Remarks on several parts of Europe," 2 vols. by J. Breval,
Esq. late Fellow of Trinity College, Cambridge. Vol. I. 228, and
Vol. II. 2.

remarks of Gibbon on the subject of our inquiry, which he states to be the result of his reading and careful reflection, are dated 1763 : they appear in his miscellaneous works, published since his death, (Vol. iv. pp. 355, 418). No man could be better qualified to solve such a question : he possessed every advantage; nevertheless he made a poor business of it, and is without excuse for his abandonment of the question.

It was some years later that General Melville, on an investigation of the Alps made in 1775, came to a conclusion in favour of the Little St. Bernard. He did not publish his views on the subject, nor were they ever placed before the public till forty-three years after that date. It appears that Mr. Hampton, a translator of Polybius, must have already held the same opinion on the track ; for there was a third edition of his work, published in 1772, containing a map, where the march is traced in the very line which General Melville conceived. The author calls it " A map for the expedition of Annibal, engraved, with some difference in the route, from the map of Mr. D'Anville."

In 1794 came forth an elaborate work in favour of the Great St. Bernard, which exhibits, for some purpose or other, almost every old text that is applicable to the question. " The Course of Hannibal over the Alps Ascertained. By John Whitaker, B.D. Rector of Ruan Lanyhorne, Cornwall." 2 vols. 8vo. And in 1812 was produced the work of General Vaudoncourt, " Histoire des Campagnes d'Annibal en Italie. Par Frédéric Guillaume, Général de Brigade," 3 tomes 4to. Milan. I conceive that neither D'Anville in 1760, nor Vaudoncourt in 1812, were aware of the rival pretensions of the Little St. Bernard ; but the intermediate writer knew them well. Mr. Whitaker had the advantage of General Melville's notes ; but he did not condescend to be a copier ; his taste was to be original, and he took no benefit from the assistance.

Fortunately the General imparted his notes also to M. De Luc, of Geneva, who in 1818 laid the matter of them before the world in a very able and convincing manner. "Histoire du Passage des Alpes par Annibal. Par Jean André De Luc. Genève, 1818." There was a second edition in 1825. This writer also made a correction of General Melville's line, which is of the utmost importance, and essential to a just view of the subject. General Melville fixed the main pass of Alps. De Luc cleared the way for arriving at it.

From the time when M. De Luc's work appeared, this old controversy has been pushed with vigour : the learned in Germany and France, not without auxiliaries in England, have carried on a lively hostility against the Graian Alp, or Little St. Bernard. M. De Luc was first attacked by M. Letronne, in the "Journal des Savans," Janvier, 1819; and the same publication, in the following December, contained an answer from M. De Luc, with M. Letronne's reply to it. The theory was supported in 1820 by the Dissertation of my friends Wickham and Cramer,* who first came forth anonymously as "a member of the University of Oxford," and published a second edition in 1828. Their Dissertation ably elucidated the subject on many points, though in one matter I consider them to struggle against the juster interpretation of De Luc.

These are the two works which, in my opinion, support the truth. And yet, great as is their merit, adverse hypotheses have been insisted upon more strenuously than ever. That which, with these two works, I shall acknowledge as the line of march described by Polybius, is not advocated in any work since published on this particular subject ; and our construc-

---

* Henry Lewis Wickham, Esq. late Chairman of the Board of Stamps and Taxes; and the Rev. John Antony Cramer, late Dean of Carlisle, and Professor of Modern History in the University of Oxford.

tion of his text on the progress to the first Alps, which is
perhaps the clearest point of any that are litigated, has been
blinked by all other writers, without exception. I know not
how numerous the hostile list may be. I have myself met
with the following :—

> Criticism by M. Letronne. Journal des Savans. Janvier
> 1819. P. 22.
>> Do.   do.   Décembre, 1819. P. 783.
> Dissertation sur le Passage du Rhône et des Alpes par
> Annibal. Par M. le Comte de Fortia d'Urban.
> Paris, 1821.
> Hannibal's Zug über die Alpen : in the Jahrbücher der
> Literatur for July, August, September, 1823. By
> Arneth, Director of the Museum, Vienna.
> Histoire Critique du Passage des Alpes par Annibal.
> Par feu M. J. L. Larauza. Paris, 1826.
> Hannibal's Passage of the Alps. By a Member of the
> University of Cambridge. London, 1830.
> The March of Hannibal from the Rhone to the Alps.
> By Henry Lawes Long, Esq. London, 1831 (Author
> of "A Survey of the Early Geography of Western
> Europe," 1859).
> Hannibal's Zug über die Alpen. By Dr. Fr. A. Ukert.
> In the Second Part of Second Volume of his work,
> Geographie der Grechen und Romer, p. 559. Weimar,
> 1832.
> Notice sur le Passage des Alpes par Annibal, ou Com-
> mentaires du récit qu'en ont fait Polybe et Tite-
> Live. Par le Général St. Cyr Nugues. 1837.
> Récherches sur l'Histoire du Passage d'Annibal d'Espagne
> en Italie, à travers les Alpes. Par M. Baudé de
> Lavalette. Montpellier, 1838.
> Géographie Ancienne des Gaules. Par M. le Baron
> Walckenaer. Paris, 1839.

Note sur le Passage d'Annibal. Par Jacques Replat,
    Chambéry, 1851.
A Treatise on Hannibal's Passage of the Alps, in which
    his Route is traced over the Little Mont Cenis.
    By Robert Ellis, B.D., Fellow of St. John's College,
    Cambridge, 1854.
Two papers by the same author. Journal of Classical
    and Sacred Philology. Vols. II. and III. Cam-
    bridge, 1856.

All these writers disclaim the scheme of march, as corrected
by De Luc and the Oxford Dissertation, from the mouth of the
Isère into Italy: for the partial acquiescence of my friend,
H. L. Long, is not more acceptable to the truth of history
than the full defiance of the rest. In this list of adversaries
there is much of literary reputation, and in their zealous
labours much that calls for a reply. Among them is an
author of celebrity, enjoying the high commendation of one
whose praise is strength. In an admirable work, unhappily not
long continued, the "Philological Museum," the very learned
Dr. Thirlwall, reviewing, in 1833, the Dissertation of Dr.
Ukert, pronounces a deliberate eulogium on him as a geographer and a man of learning : and this is an antagonist whom
I resist throughout. He is the champion too of the new
doctrine—that the invaders crossed the Rhone at or near
Tarascon ; which is a matter of importance, in that it affects
the construction of the Greek narrative from one end of the
controverted line to the other. The sceptics on this head
have appeared only since the last edition of the Oxford Dissertation ; and they remain unanswered.

These persevering hostilities, to which let me add the
gravely-expressed doubts of Dr. Arnold, may give excuse to
the present attempt. In making the attempt, I abstain from
the formula with which some modern commentators wind up

their preface. Seventy-two years ago the learned Whitaker proclaimed himself the source of "so clear a sunshine as no mistakes can veil, and no wilfulness can darken for ever again :" and among the newer theorists, my friend who sojourned at Grenoble stands convinced that his proofs " have set this long pending discussion at rest for ever." I am taught to resist the fond delusion. Seeing how the most learned have yielded to error, I cannot expect to extinguish a question that has proved so provoking to conjecture, and so seducing into paradox. Still there is hope : we are encouraged to look for the triumph of truth, if ever the causes of her confusion shall be exposed—πολὺν χρόνον ἐπισκοτισθεῖσα, τέλος αὐτὴ δι' ἑαυτῆς ἐπικρατεῖ, καὶ καταγωνίζεται τὸ ψεῦδος. Polyb. xiii. 5.

CHAPTER II.

The Subject proposed, and Method of treating it.

IN the year 218 before Christ, being the 536th year of Rome, Hannibal marched from Carthagena in the month of May ; he crossed the Rhone towards the end of September ; and, clearing the Alps, touched the plain of Italy at the end of October.

The dates rest on the following grounds. The Greeks, as we learn from Polybius and Strabo, used to mark the seasons by the rising and setting of the Pleias or Pleiades. When Polybius in his narrative has brought the Carthaginian army to the summit of the Alps, he remarks that the setting of the Pleias is at hand ; which setting is known by a recognised calculation to have been in that year, on the 26th October. Accordingly, as they actually reached the plain of Italy in five days from the summit, we must consider that crisis of the season to have passed, and may place their arrival in the plain at the very end of October.

The crossing of the Rhone was performed fully a month before they reached the plain; for the march proceeded on the second day after crossing the river; it lasted fourteen days to the Alps ; and had occupied fifteen days in the Alps when they touched the plain. Accordingly the Rhone was crossed at the end of September.

In the same sentence where Polybius states the Alps to have been traversed in fifteen days, he says that the entire march from Carthagena was performed in five months ; and, as it was completed at the end of October, we may place its commencement in the latter part of May. Moreover, the setting forth of the expedition is alluded to by Polybius in his introduction to the affairs of Greece at the beginning of the fifth book, where he draws attention to many contemporaneous events. Having said that the prætorship of the younger Aratus expired at about the rising of the Pleias, he states that about the same time, as summer was coming on, Hannibal began his march.

Livy ascribes the expedition to the same season of the year ; he states the same duration of the march, and gives the same date to the end of it. On the march through the Alps, he says, nearly in the terms of Polybius, that the summit was reached on the ninth day; that the encampment there was for two days; that the constellation of the Pleiades was then setting; that the passage of the Alps was completed on the fifteenth day ; and that they arrived in Italy in the fifth month from Carthagena.

If a stranger to the subject should ask to be shortly informed upon the region which is principally concerned in the controversy, the answer might be this :—Imagine Hannibal with his army about half-way between Orange and Lyons,

near to the confluence of the Rhone and Isère; you have to
trace him thence to the plain of Italy. Now you can hardly
draw a line from that confluence to the Po, which has not
been favoured as the line of the Carthaginian march. Almost
every pass from Viso to the Simplon, with almost every route
for reaching it, has found an advocate. The Chamouni valley
has, I believe, escaped the views of criticism; not so the
shores of Lago Maggiore, nor the Col de Bonhomme, nor the
vale of Viu.

Such is the chief, but not the only question made on the
track. In the march from the Pyrenees to the Rhone, all
have been satisfied that it proceeded through Nîmes, excepting
Mr. Whitaker, who carried it through Carcasone, Lodeve,
Le Vigan and Anduse, coming upon the Rhone near Loriol, a
place about nineteen miles below the influx of the Isère. In
the period which has elapsed since that course was proposed, I
believe that no one has adopted it, unless it was Mr. Tytler,
who promptly published an eulogium of Mr. Whitaker's
discoveries. When the history comes to be explained, that
notion will appear inadmissible; although Mr. Whitaker
considers it demonstrated, and performs the process with his
usual accuracy of facts. All are now agreed, that the army
passed through Nemausus, Nîmes.

But in the first movement from Nîmes there is matter for
consideration. A new doctrine has lately been put forth, and
supported by an authority much commended, as to the part
where Hannibal, coming from Nîmes, effected the passage of
the Rhone before he marched up to the Isère; so that our
first business must be with his course from Nîmes to the
Rhone. The crossing need not, indeed, have been effected
from the point where the march first touched the river; nor
is it quite necessary that the whole force should have proceeded from Nîmes to the river in one line. Still the question,
where did Hannibal cross the Rhone, is not only interesting in

itself, as represented in the powerful descriptions of Polybius and Livy, but it bears importantly on matters of ulterior inquiry.

Method of treating the Inquiry.

As Polybius and Livy are the two writers whose histories of the Carthaginian invasion have come down to us, the point which it is sought to determine necessarily calls upon all who pretend to understand those historians to consider whether they concur in the Pass of Alps by which Hannibal came to Italy : and, if they shall be found not to concur, to say which is entitled to our belief.

Modern interpreters of these ancient narratives of Hannibal's march may then be ranked in two classes : those who maintain that the Greek historian and the Latin historian concur on the Pass of Alps by which the invasion was effected, and those who maintain that they do not concur. It is apparent that they who would identify the two tracks are far more numerous than those who insist on their disagreement : and one has to consider whether the former opinion is entitled to respect, by reason that it is the opinion of the majority. I find reason to say that it is not : for, while so many are ready to declare that Polybius and Livy favoured the same line, they rarely agree upon what that line was.

What then can have provoked so prevailing a persuasion ? Has a conviction of the identity been arrived at by a separate examination of each, followed by a comparison : or has the identity been presumed, and the effort been an attempt at expedients for smoothing differences and reconciling contradictions ? The latter has been the case ; and many authors would have escaped the conclusions which they profess, if they had only examined Polybius as if there were no Livy, and Livy as if there were no Polybius. Instead of this, they embark in the subject, determined to make the two agree.

M. Letronne tells us, " Polybe et Tite-Live sont necéssaires à l'explication l'un de l'autre. Dans Tite-Live, il n'y a pas un seul mot à changer pour faire coincider son texte avec celui de Polybe." In the same spirit, Général St. Cyr Nugues writes : " Il faut expliquer et concilier ces deux récits : voilà le problème." M. Baudé de Lavalette : " Il faut concilier Polybe et Tite-Live : tel est l'œuvre qui doit, en définitif, être le but de nos efforts." M. le Baron Walckenaer : " On a cru qu'il y avoit, entre le récit de Tite-Live et celui de Polybe, une contradiction ; on a cherché à se déterminer pour l'un des deux : tandis qu'il fallait trouver les moyens de les concilier."

How shall we account for this predilection ? Can it be that a first perusal of the two narratives produces the impression that they intend the same track ? I am fully persuaded that this has never happened : no one, on tracing the outlines of the two stories, can be impressed in favour of their geographical coincidence. Whence then the prejudice ? I apprehend the cause to be this : Both historians being held in great repute, both are presumed to relate the truth ; and, as truth is one, to relate the same thing : and a repugnance is felt to the notion that they intend different things, unless as a last resource, on failure of the expedients of conciliation.

This principle is unsound. It assumes that which need not in any case be true, and which in this case is notoriously otherwise. The greatest historians will sometimes be in error. The wisest man, recounting facts of which he has no proper knowledge, must be liable to error. Further, on this question men celebrated in ancient times are known to have differed ; and we are inquiring whether two among them did differ or not. To presume either solution of such a question is unreasonable. Livy is himself the example that there was diversity of opinion between authors of the highest credit. Writing two centuries after the invasion, he cites the historian Coelius, one whom he held in respect, as having named a pass of Alps different from that in which he himself believed. One of these must have been in error. Whether Livy intended to follow Polybius, or to contradict him, is a question to be solved : he has not professed to solve it : he does not allude to Polybius : he adopts a large part of his events, but seems to vary the places to which he would assign them; whether he intended to vary them is a question on which it is foolish to lean to either alternative without inquiry.

Seeing how so many critics have embarked in this inquiry under the trammels of a false prepossession, let us avoid it. Also, when great modern names are adduced, when we are told of D'Anville, Gibbon, Ukert, and others, let us answer that we will heed their arguments, not their names. No human judgment stands above scrutiny. Labour and learning cannot ensure a freedom from error. Arnold imagined the elephants to be three or four nights above the snow-line; Cramer and De Luc conceived the Carthaginians marching along the Ticino ; Niebuhr asserted that they crossed the Po below Piacenza ; and Napoleon III. says that Scipio, landing at the mouth of the Rhone, learned that Hannibal had already entered the Alps.

Many writers are seen to confuse the two histories by applying the narrative of the one author to supply the deficiencies of the other. I approve a different principle ; that, antecedent to any comparison of the histories, a separate examination must be made of the matter of each ; not disturbing the scrutiny of one by blending with it notices of the other. When this has been fairly done, the similarity or dissimilarity of the results may be viewed : then only shall we be qualified to estimate the practicability of conciliation.

But, while it is necessary to keep distinct our examination of the ancient authorities, it is requisite that we should set forth the views of modern commentators together with our own. We are not to presume that the reader is already aware

of the diversities of interpretation; and it is our business to
lay them fairly before him. A very false commentary may
make an impression, which it would fail to make if the rival
explanation were presented with it. It is proposed, therefore,
to combine defence and attack where it shall aid a comparison
of one theory of construction with another.

I hope now to be excused if, in treading the way from
Nîmes to the Italian plain with the first of our two great
historians, I defer for a while the dissection of his evidence,
that I may call attention to the value of his authority.

THE ALPS OF HANNIBAL.

PART II.

ON THE AUTHORITY OF POLYBIUS.

CHAPTER I.

His Journey through the Alps.

POLYBIUS explored in person the Alps of Hannibal. We know not who may have been his companions, and there has been a difference of opinion as to the time when he made the journey. He was born in the fourteenth year of the war: in the vigour of life he was withdrawn from the service of his country, as one of the hostages extorted by the grasping violence of the Roman Republic ; and about seventeen years of his mature manhood were passed in a forced separation from Greece. This gave a cast to the part which he had to act as a citizen of the world. When his liberty was regained, the crisis had almost arrived which was to ensure the universal tyranny of Rome : Cato had pronounced the doom of Carthage ; and the downfall of Greece was not to be averted by those few of her citizens who were at the same time wise and honest.

Polybius was about thirty-seven years old at the time of the Achæan exile. He had filled important posts in the state of which he was a distinguished member ; he had become

acquainted with Roman generals and Roman warfare in
Thessaly and Macedonia, and such a man might already have
travelled westward in search of truth.   But this has never
been suggested; and we may assume that his visitation of
Gaul and Spain through the Alps was performed after
167 B. C.[1], the date of his removal to Rome.   How soon then,
after this, may we suppose him to have made the journey?
Was it before or after the return of the exiles?   His own
words are—"I shall explain these things with confidence,
because I have obtained my information of the events from
those who themselves belonged to the times, and have viewed
the scenes of those events, and myself performed the journey
through the Alps, that I might see and know" (iii. 48. 12).

Whether such information was sought in Rome or elsewhere, it would become every day more difficult to obtain,
by the deaths of witnesses.   It appears that, from the first
arrival of Polybius in Italy, he had the peculiar indulgence of
residing at Rome, while the other hostages were scattered in
distant towns (xxxii. 8. 5).   Being so in favour, he might
after a time have permission to travel beyond the confines of
Italy.   The Roman purpose, of separating such a man from
his country, was equally answered, whether he was within or
without the Alps.   He would not be more tempted to violate
his faith as an hostage; for such a course would have
brought speedier destruction upon all that was dear to him.
Neither would the faculty of escape have been readier than
in the full personal freedom which he enjoyed at Rome : he
could at any time have contrived his own escape, as he promoted that of Demetrius.   For himself the Alpine enterprise
had its attraction; and, while he was peremptorily cut off
from his own country, his duties to her suffered no worse
suspension by a wandering into the west of Europe.   The
time too was favourable: for some years the rage of war was

[1] 587 U.C. of the Varronian period.

lulled in those quarters, and that embarrassment of a traveller was removed. Looking at these circumstances, and remembering that Polybius was not less than fifty-three years old when he regained his liberty in 151, we may reasonably believe that he had before that time traced Hannibal through the Alps.

A later period is far less probable. When the liberation came, the first impulse would probably lead him to seek the shores of Greece. I am not aware that there is any record of his immediate transactions: but he appears to have been in Greece early in 149, when the consul Manilius, ordered to act against Carthage, wrote to the Achæans, urging that Polybius might join him at Lilybæum: accordingly he set out, but receiving intelligence at Corfu, from which he concluded that hostilities were at an end, he returned to Greece.*

Some have imagined that the journey was made on the termination of the exile; and have conceived the friend and preceptor accompanied by his illustrious pupil Scipio, the younger Africanus. I see great improbability in this. The one, as well as the other, had had better leisure for such an enterprise at an earlier period, whether before or after the death of Scipio's father in 160. I doubt that there is any authority for saying that they ever went through the Alps together. It would no doubt have been agreeable to both, that Polybius should have attended Scipio at the time mentioned; as afterwards at the age of seventy he attended him to Numantia. The discharge of the Greek hostages tended to cement the friendship between them: it was through Scipio's intercession with Cato, that the Achæans were permitted by the Senate to return to their country; when that venerable man settled the matter with his well-known remark, that the dispute was whether a few old Greeks should be carried to their graves

---

* Fast. Hellen. iii. 99. Mr. Clinton quotes Polyb. Fragm. Vatican. p. 447.

by Roman corpse-bearers or their own.* Scipio then went
to Spain, to serve under Lucullus : but did he go through the
Alps ? In taking the office of Legate he courted a respon-
sibility which others had declined, and had the credit of
making a sacrifice to public duty in an unpopular service.†
The occasion was pressing : he would not at such a time have
exposed himself to the delays and risks of a tour of curiosity
in the Alps. No Roman force had ever then crossed the
Rhone : and this young officer, like other servants of the
state, must have gone to Spain by sea.

M. Gossellin, (Récherches, ii. p. 6) speaks of Scipio and
Polybius travelling together from Carthagena to the Rhone,
as a fact related by Polybius himself; and he refers to Polyb.
Historiar. lib. iii. 39. This is a mistake : no such thing
is mentioned there, nor I believe anywhere. M. Gossellin
imagines their companionship not in going to, but in returning
from the Celtiberian war. But that notion is as improbable
as the other, and cannot be accepted without evidence.
Scipio was still too full of weightier business : he only joined
the camp in Spain in 151 ; and in 149 we see him serving
in the first work of the war against Carthage, the author of
every wise movement under an inefficient leader. And note
the busy interval : he rapidly gained a reputation in Spain,
though holding an inferior command. On one occasion his
duties carried him into Africa, where he witnessed the battle
between Asdrubal and Masinissa, and returned to Spain with
a supply of elephants, the professed object of his mission.
When he returned to Rome, as when he left it, the times
were teeming with great events ; and there was no leisure for
such a man to strike away from the theatre of Roman interests
for exploits on his own account in unknown Gaul and unknown Alps. I allow that Polybius's attendance on Scipio
was at any time a probable result of their friendship; but if

* Polyb. Reliq. lib. xxxv. 6.   † Polyb. xxxv. 4.

we assume such an incident in that space of two years, the scene of it would be Spain and Numidia, not Gaul and the Alps. Appian records their being together before Carthage at the close of the last Punic war; but does not name Polybius as being concerned in the Celtiberian war, nor notice him as present at the great battle in Numidia.

When we consider that the return of the Greeks was in 151 ; that Carthage was destroyed in 147, and that the fall of Corinth immediately followed ; and, if we observe the extreme activity of the political interval, that interval cannot be thought a probable time for Polybius's journey through the Alps, or for the facts supposed by M. Gosselin. Still more improbable would be that later time, when the independence of his country was gone, and his own duties in assuaging her misfortunes had been fulfilled. All things considered, the historical probability seems to be that Polybius explored the tract before his exile was relieved. Gibbon may have been near the truth, when he spoke of him as " examining the country with his own eyes, where he might " collect the precious remains of tradition, which the period of " sixty years had not been able to efface, and where he might " converse with some of the old men of the country, who had " in their youth either resisted Hannibal's invasion, or followed " his standard." Sixty years after the invasion denotes seven years before the termination of the Achæan exile.

Beside the probabilities which rest on the transactions of the times, on the better opportunities for active inquiry and literary employment, which Polybius enjoyed during his domicile at Rome, and the utter disturbance of such advantages in the events which succeeded his liberation, we gather evidence to the date of his journey from his own writings. The invasion of Italy by Hannibal is an early fact in that period of history which he first proposes to record, beginning in the 140th Olympiad. And his own exploration of the

Alps is announced as having been made before he wrote his account of that invasion. Niebuhr says (transl. by Smith and Schmitz, iii. 42), that the first edition of Polybius is to be placed about the beginning of the seventh century; which, (601 U.C.) was before the return of the exiles. He says also (21st Lecture, published by Dr. L. Schmitz, i. 283) that that edition ended with the carrying away of the Achæan hostages, and that a second edition was published afterwards, with the subsequent history. It is curious to notice how the historian incorporated the new matter of his further history with that of the earlier one.

He announces his history in the outset as one of fifty-three years, the matter of the two first books not belonging to that period, but containing so much of earlier events as may serve for introduction. He says, at the beginning of the first book, that he has thought it necessary to compose that and the next, in order to prepare his readers for the history : and, at the end of the second, he speaks of having completed the opening and preface of his whole history. In the opening of the third book, the fifty-three years are again announced as beginning with the 140th Olympiad, and ending with the subversion of the Macedonian empire : in fact that period, beginning from 220 B.C. was completed with the defeat of Perseus in 168, and the seizure of the Achæan exiles in 167. As we read on, the next paragraph shows that those events are not now to close the work, and that the design is enlarged. Though the limitation to fifty-three years remains in the text, we are informed that new events have arisen so momentous, events of which the author has been himself concerned in many, and an eye-witness of nearly all, that he shall undertake the task of relating them, and begin as it were another history. Pointing out the leading features of this further history, he names the Celtiberian war of Rome, the wars between Carthage and Masinissa, the wars between Attalus and Prusias, the wars of Cappadocia and Syria, the return of the Achæan exiles, the last war between Rome and Carthage, and the events which have consummated the misfortunes of Greece. Further on, when he vindicates the minuteness of his inquiry into the causes of Hannibal's war, he speaks of his work as now intended to comprehend the destruction of Carthage and the battle of the Isthmus, and to be comprised in forty books.

There is still further evidence in the tone of the historian's remarks, showing that his original work must have been composed during the tranquillity of his residence in Italy ; some things are such as he cannot have produced after the last fatal troubles of Greece had begun. When he is about to explain the institution of the Achæan confederacy in the second book, he takes occasion, c. 37, to allude to the fortunes of the Macedonian kingdom, and those of that republic ; to the utter destruction of the one, and the unlooked-for growth and harmony of the other—περὶ μὲν ταύτην ὁλοσχερὴς ἐπαναίρεσις, περὶ δὲ τοὺς 'Αχαιοὺς παράδοξος αὔξησις καὶ συμφρόνησις. In the sketch of Achæan annals which follows, the same feeling of the writer is exhibited ; and this not in the introductory books only ; for, having closed the third book with the battle of Cannæ, he refers in the fourth to the scheme of his history ; and taking up the affairs of Greece in the 140th Olympiad, notes the remarkable advance which has been made by the Achæan state. Who will believe that Polybius should thus express himself after or shortly before the last convulsion of Greece ? The pride of country struggled hard to make the exile hide her degradation under some eulogium, at a time when he must in his own person have been deeply sensible of it : but that he should have poured forth those praises after the fall of Corinth, is impossible He uttered those sentiments, not in the period of distraction and strife which followed the crushing of his country's

liberties; but when, in his Italian banishment, he would
quietly and fondly indulge in some contrast between her
fate and that of Macedonia.

Whatever was the precise time at which Polybius investigated the track of Hannibal, on which I have pointed
out what appear to me the best grounds of argument, it
seems clear that the journey was performed by him; and
that, if we can rightly interpret his narrative, we thereby
know the course of Hannibal. But that narrative itself is
in innumerable particulars interpreted in different ways by
learned men. It is natural therefore to suppose, that there
is difficulty in making a right interpretation: and we have
to search for the cause of this difficulty; a task which is the
more necessary, as some have suggested a cause, by imputing
to the historian a singular deficiency in geographical knowledge and the faculty of acquiring it. We cannot feel safe
in interpreting his geographical matter, without noticing
the reasons of those who declare his incompetency to deal
with it.

It is true that this disparaging opinion is not general; and
that some consider Polybius to have been eminently qualified
for ascertaining and transmitting truth, as a politician, a
soldier, and a man of learning. These are further influenced
by knowing that, within forty years after the Carthaginians
had evacuated Italy, he was living in familiar intercourse
with distinguished Romans; that he conversed freely with
those who in their youth had served against Hannibal; that
his friendship was sought and adhered to by the celebrated
Scipio Æmilianus and his brother, to whom the minutiæ of
those campaigns and the memorials of their own illustrious
ancestors must have been matter of interesting concern; also
that his study of the course through the Alps took place
while there may have been upon it still living witnesses of
the invasion.

But, though these notions seem to be true, and, being true, to recommend Polybius as one of the safest historians of any times ; still, as in this inquiry importance will be attached to his designation of countries and of rivers that run through them, also to measurements of space where the termini are litigated ; and since, among those who impeach him in these respects, are men themselves celebrated for geographical and historical acquirements, I must sustain an authority on which I purpose to rely. How shall we not fear that that authority may be despised, when such a man as Dr. Arnold, himself so commended for the geographical instinct, has imputed to him " a total absence of geographical talent," and that in his labours "he laboured against nature ? " How shall we not fear the depreciating tone of the German critic, who is pronounced by Dr. Thirlwall " to come to the discussion of the question with all the light that profound geographical learning can throw upon it ? " Some of the disparaging comments I delay to notice, until the examination of our subject shall have made the matter of them easier to be understood. Some I will advert to now ; examining, as briefly as I may, the reasonings by which they dissuade us from a confidence in the Greek historian.

CHAPTER II.

Strictures of Dr. Ukert.   Italy and the Alps.   The Rhone.
Direction of the March.

DR. FR. A. UKERT, the eminent professor and librarian at Gotha, is author of a work published at Weimar on the Geography of the Greeks and Romans : and he is, I presume, the most learned man among those who have maintained that the course of Hannibal was over the Mont Cenis ; a

doctrine which he supports in the 2d division of his second
volume, published in 1832. The recommendations of him
to our notice in this matter of criticism are from an authority
which is recognised as the most eminent in this country :
and I will without scruple refer to a report made by one
so highly qualified to make it justly. I speak of an article
on Hannibal's passage, signed C. T.,* in the Philological
Museum of May, 1833. I may say here that this review
was mentioned in 1854 by Mr. Ellis, in his Treatise, p. 18,
where he says that the reviewer adopts the supposition of
Dr. Ukert that Hannibal crossed the Rhone near Beaucaire.
I conceive that Mr. Ellis must here have mistaken the
opinions imputed to Dr. Ukert for the opinions of Dr.
Thirlwall himself ; who says, " Ukert conceives that Hannibal
crossed the river near Beaucaire." I cannot so easily account
for another thing which is asserted ; namely, that " in many
" material points the views advocated in his, Mr. Ellis's treatise,
" receive the sanction of the learned writer of the article."
This proposition is, as far as I can judge, quite erroneous ;
and I find nothing to qualify the error.

It is said in the Philological Museum, " Our object is
" not to describe the march, but to explain the nature of the
" arguments by which Ukert supports his hypothesis." The
learned writer thus introduces the German geographer to the
attention of the reader. " Ukert has defended an hypothesis
" which had been adopted by many learned men, and within
" these few years by a French author, Larauza, whose book I
" have not been able to meet with ; that Hannibal crossed the
" Mont Cenis. Ukert has the advantage of coming last to
" the discussion of this question, with a thorough knowledge
" of all that has been done by his predecessors, and with all
" the light that profound geographical learning can throw upon
" it : so that a review of his arguments may exhibit, though

* Connop Thirlwall, Lord Bishop of St. David's.

" not the history of this controversy, yet the latest stage which
" it has reached. There are, it is well known, four main points
" on which the whole controversy depends. 1. The passage
" of the Rhone. 2. The position of the Island and Hannibal's
" movements in it. 3. His march to the foot of the mountains.
" 4. The passage of the Alps. These we will consider in their
" order. We must however premise that Ukert takes a different
" view of the relative authority of Polybius and Livy from
" that which has been adopted by many, perhaps by most, pre-
" ceding writers, and particularly by the advocates of General
" Melville's hypothesis. He observes that, though the zeal
" with which Polybius laboured to ascertain the truth is in-
" disputable, his means were not exactly proportioned to his
" good will. As the Alps in his time were inhabited by fierce
" and unconquered tribes, it was not in his power to explore
" them with the same calmness and undivided attention as the
" modern travellers who have visited them with his book in
" their hands. Notwithstanding his travels, the geographical
" knowledge which Polybius had acquired was very imperfect :
" his conception of the direction of the Alps, and the course
" of the Rhone, erroneous : and his errors in this respect led
" him to say, that Hannibal, after crossing the Rhone, marched
" away from the sea eastward, as if he had been making for
" the midland parts of Europe (iii. 47) ; when, if he had
" been correctly informed, he would have spoken of the north.
" With regard to Livy's relation to Polybius, Ukert observes
" that, though the Roman frequently took the Greek author's
" description as the foundation of his own, yet, as the countries
" of which Polybius wrote were much better known in the
" time of Augustus, he also drew more accurate accounts from
" other sources, with which he supplied the defects of his
" predecessor, but sometimes without perceiving that he was
" framing his narrative out of statements which were irrecon-
" cileably discordant." *Phil. Mus.* May, 1833, C. T.

Such are reported to be the views of Dr. Ukert concerning
the authority of Polybius in the question of Hannibal's
march. With due respect for one so laudatus laudato, I
cannot perceive that his depreciation of the Greek historian
rests on valid grounds. It is most true that, whatever Alps
Polybius explored, he explored regions which were independent of Rome, and whose inhabitants, notwithstanding
the mitiora ingenia which Livy ascribes to them in the
twelfth year of the war, were still rude and fierce. But to
what tends this exposition of the traveller's danger? It may
help to account for the want of the poetic and the pic-
turesque which some think should identify the pass of
Hannibal. But, as to finding in the barbarism of the Alpine
tribes a circumstance that lowers his authority, it only makes
us to admire the zeal and daring that incurred the danger,
and to estimate the man by his devotion of those powers to
the observation and gathering of truth. The question is
between the authority of him who made that effort, and of
those whom no such thing has qualified. The proposition
that he could not explore the Alps with the same calmness
as modern travellers who may visit them with his book in
their hands, is most true. If it were not, this controversy
would not exist. If Polybius had journeyed with the advantages of a modern tourist, the Alps and the district beyond
them reposing under the well-established protection of civilised government, instead of being still unexplored by the
Romans, the places which lay in the march would have been
enjoying recognised names; these names would have been
found in his work; and neither Livy nor Ukert would have
had a question to litigate.

It is indeed the modern traveller who has so explored
with Polybius in hand. This task was first performed by
General Melville in the latter part of the eighteenth century.
If this had been done in the days of Augustus, that age

would not have founded a controversy, nor created the difficulties which we are even now endeavouring to solve. For
why does the traveller explore the Alps with that book in
his hand? In order that he may ascertain the track which
Polybius intends; that he may know how to apply his narrative. This is our endeavour; to interpret rightly that which
is acknowledged to contain the truth.

Dr. Ukert having exhibited the disadvantages under which
Polybius must have travelled, proceeds, as we have seen, to
expose the inaccuracy which resulted from them. He dwells
on his erroneous conceptions concerning Italy and the Alps,
as a ground on which we should à fortiori distrust his
geography beyond the Alps; saying this,—" His description of
" that country, which from his long residence in it he was
" able leisurely to investigate; a task for which, through his
" acquaintance with the most distinguished and enlightened
" Romans, he enjoyed every advantage, may serve as a scale
" by which we should estimate his statements concerning less
" known and less frequented countries. According to him, the
" whole of Italy is a triangle; an opinion already censured by
" Strabo." He then exposes the descriptions of Italy and the
Alps as made by Polybius, with a criticism of what he has
said on the course of the Rhone and the course of the Po:
and we are invited to the conclusion that the geography of
his history is not to be relied on.

Strictures, which chiefly import, that one who wrote before
the last Punic war was not precise upon north, south, east,
and west, are sufficiently disarmed, when we view the errors
of a later age, whose improvements it is the policy of those
criticisms to extol. But retaliation is not enough. Let us
sift the value of the strictures themselves, as they affect
three subjects of attack; the Alps; the Rhone; and the
direction of the march. The Po must be reserved for a
future chapter.

Italy and the Alps.

IT is perfectly true that Polybius, ii. c. 14, has described
Italy as a three-sided figure, of which one side is the Adriatic
and Ionian seas, another the Tyrrhenian and Sicilian seas, and
the third the range of Alps: also that he has described the
northern plain of Italy as another three-sided figure, of which
the Alps form the north side, the Apennine the south side,
the base being the Adriatic from the end of the gulf to
Sena. Strabo censured these triangles, saying, τρίγωνον δὲ
ἰδίως τὸ εὐθύγραμμον καλεῖται σχῆμα· ἐνταῦθα δὲ καὶ αἱ
βάσεις καὶ αἱ πλευραὶ πειφερεῖς εἰσίν,—" a figure, to be
" rightly called a triangle, must be rectilinear: but there both
" the bases and the sides are curved." Then, in objection to
the eastern side of Italy, he says, πλευρὰν γὰρ λέγομεν τὴν
ἀγώνιον γραμμήν—"for we call a side that which is a line
without angles," v. 210.

These dogmata, not enforced by Strabo when more necessary, are pronounced here, not against the knowledge nor the
judgment of the writer, but against his style. Polybius is
not charged with believing the lines which he calls sides of
Italy to be straight, but with calling them sides when they
were not straight; he knew them not to be straight, for he
speaks of one as turned partly to the south, partly to the
west: as to the other, Strabo himself relieves him of the
suspicion; for he cites Polybius (vi. 261) on the distance
from the Lacinian promontory to the Iapygian across the
entrance of the gulf of Tarentum, and (v. 211) reports from
him the unequal distances of a land journey and a sea
journey from the Iapygian to Messana.

Are then these rough descriptions given by Polybius to be
called erroneous? Precision is not sought, and is not requisite. In these bold outlines he fulfils his avowed purpose

of writing, which is to communicate ideas by well-known symbols. These are to be found in the larger features and more notorious marks of a country. He reminds us that mere unexplained names do not give geographical impressions. When he uses the word Τρανσάλπινοι, ii. c. 15, he takes care to inform his readers that τρᾶνς is Latin for πέραν. He is not compounding the topography of departments for the Italian student: he is providing by large outlines a notion of entire Italy for those who knew it not. In the very beginning of his work, i. c. 3, he announces that he writes for the instruction of Greeks : and again, after he has brought Hannibal into Italy, iii. c. 59, he speaks of his own travels in Spain and elsewhere with the object of them —"that, correcting the ignorance of our predecessors in these " matters, we may bring these parts also of the habitable earth " within the knowledge of Greeks."

If there existed not these excuses for the roughness of the Polybian delineations, the spirit of fair play would rise against the attack that is made. In the vice of applying the name of a rectilinear figure to that which is really not one, or of making a crooked and curved line to be a side to such figure, Polybius is not a solitary offender. Strabo himself, the sage whose corrections are appealed to, indicates in his own practice the foibles which in others he condemns. He rejoices in parallelograms, not triangles : he gives, p. 177, as the boundaries of Gaul, the Pyrenees on the west, the Rhine, as their parallel, on the east: the ocean on the north ; the Mediterranean and Alps on the south. As parts of this large figure, he exhibits three other parallelograms : one, p. 178, has, for west and east, the Pyrenees and the Alps ; for north and south, the Cevennes and the Mediterranean : another, p. 189, has, for west and east, the Pyrenees and the Garonne, for north and south, the ocean and the Cevennes : another has, for west and east, the Garonne and the Loire,

having also the ocean and the Cevennes for north and
south.

Let me ask whether, in the broad definitions of Polybius
there is anything which so conflicts with the proprieties of
modern geography as these specimens of the Augustan. At
least let the indulgence which is claimed for the licentious-
ness of a parallelogram be extended to the extravagance of
a triangle. But if there belongs to the former figure some
peculiar privilege, then be it remembered that Strabo too, iv.
199, has his triangle, the Island Brittannia : and she, too, has
her πλευραί. Are these ἀγώνιοι γραμμαί? M. Gossellin
says with much gravity, Récherches, ii. 15, "Au temps
"de Polybe l'Italie n'avoit pas plus une forme triangulaire
"qu'elle ne l'a aujourd'hui." He might have added, "La
"Grande Bretagne n'avoit pas plus une forme triangulaire
"qu'elle ne l'a aujourd'hui:" the Bristol channel and the
Solway derogate as much from the εὐθύγραμμον σχῆμα as
does the gulf of Tarentum. It is most true that Polybius
was addicted to the pourtraying of triangular forms : it is
seen, i. 26, 14, in his account of naval manœuvres. But
there was excuse for the rudeness of those forms, which
Strabo, not an illiberal critic, might have acknowledged. If
Polybius had called Italy a parallelogram, he would have
earned the applause of his illustrious successor.

The Rhone and the Alps.

Polybius, iii. 47, thus instructs his readers. "The Rhone
"has his sources above the Adriatic gulf, which fall to the
"westward in those parts of the Alps which slope away to the
"north : his course is to the winter sunset; and he discharges
"himself into the Sardinian sea. He is carried for a consider-
"able way through a valley, to the north of which dwell the

" Ardyes* Celts, while the whole southern side of it is bounded
" by the mountain sides of the Alps, which slope northwards :
" the higher Alpine chain separating the plains of the Po,
" of which I have often spoken already, from the valley of the
" Rhone, and spreading as it were from Marseille to the head
" of the Adriatic gulph—which higher chain Hannibal, having
" surmounted from the country on the Rhone, invaded Italy."

Men of our day, having their map of the Alps, may be
startled at the introduction of Marseille and the Adriatic into
this description. But we are to remember, that the aim of
the writer was to bring his Greek readers to a notion of that
which he described, by naming things which already existed
in their minds; thus enabling them ἐφαρμόττειν τὸ λεγόμενον
ἐπὶ τὶ γνώριμον, iii. 36, 4. They knew the Adriatic : they
knew Marseille : they knew not that which intervened :
accordingly the Alps are described by reference to those
known objects, and the Rhone by reference to the Alps.
Precision could not attend this method of instruction : he
teaches here that the first springs of the Rhone are away to

* This word Ἄρδυες is not explained. Αἴδυες has been suggested. May it not be corrected to Ἐλουήττιοι? In a passage of
Strabo, p. 192, we find Αἰτουάτιοι, which it is pretty clear should
be Ἐλουήττιοι. Strabo, enumerating the accolæ of the Rhine, seems
to take them from Cæsar. Both place Nantuates on the lake of
Geneva near the Rhone. Cæsar's text, iv. 10, carries the Rhine
per fines Nantuatium, Helvetiorum, Sequanorum, Mediomatricorum,
Tribocorum, Trevirorum: and Strabo, probably having Cæsar before
him, writes, " The first of all, πρῶτοι τῶν ἀπάντων, upon the Rhine
are Αἰτουάτιοι." Then he notices the source, length of stream,
mouths, &c.; and resumes the accolæ in this way ; " Μετὰ δὲ τοὺς
Ἐλουηττίους Σηκοανοὶ καὶ Μεδιοματρικοὶ κατοικοῦσι τὸν Ῥῆνον ;" then
he names Τριβόκχοι and then Τρηούιροι. This leads one to
suppose that Ἐλουήττιοι were meant to be πρῶτοι τῶν ἀπάντων, and
that Αἰτουάτιοι is a corruption. Kramer has put Ἐλουήττιοι in
the text. The word Nantuatium in Cæsar's 4th book may perhaps
be struck out.

the north-east, among the Alps : more than this was not within his reach. He had no materials by which to speculate on the longitudes of those fountains : no civilised eye had seen the glacier of the Rhone : he conceived its direction, not its place. The Romans then had no acquaintance with Transalpine Gaul save by the access of Marseille : while he lived, their only military performance between that place and the Pyrenees was in Scipio's few days near the Rhone's mouth. The addition which the researches of Polybius gave to a knowledge of that river may have been limited to the line of the Carthaginian march. It cannot be asserted that he ever visited the lake of Geneva, or the town of Lyons. Some may infer his non-acquaintance with the lake from his silence upon it : and they are welcome to do so : if he was never there, neither was Hannibal. Not that the mere absence of particulars warrants us to presume a want of information : for, if the lake of Geneva lay not in the march, it would have no place in this narrative. Polybius expressly excuses himself from introducing into historical statement more of geography than is necessary for understanding the story which he is relating, iii. 56.

In the time of Strabo, 140 years later, conquest had made the Rhone a familiar feature in the geography of Gaul : it was known in his earliest days through the efforts of Julius Cæsar to purge from obstruction the main route between Italy and the heart of the Helvetian territory. And yet Strabo's Rhone has its errors : speaking of the Rhone, the Doubs, and the Saone, he says, iv. 186, " It happens that each of these three rivers flows in the first instance to the north, and then to the west : and then they all fall into one stream, which by another bend is carried southward to the sea." Thus the Rhone of Strabo begins at Martigny. He could only relate what he had heard. He relates that the Rhone runs into and through the lake of Geneva, and that his stream refuses the commixture of other waters : but he knew not of the river above Martigny : so there he conceived the source. The source of Polybius, though less specific, is more correct.

The direction of the March.

Dr. Ukert charges Polybius with making Hannibal to march eastward, when in fact he marched northward. This criticism also asserts the improved knowledge of countries in the days of Augustus; and it would again be enough to answer, that Strabo's north side of Gaul, iv. 177, is from Bayonne to the mouths of the Rhine. The twist which he gives to the countries of the world might well belong in some degree to earlier geography : and Polybius, who deals in general rather than minute instructions, needs little justification if, in dividing his subject, he deemed the march from Carthagena to the Rhone to bear northward, and the march from the Rhone to Italy to bear eastward. This, after all, would be found the sum of his offence ; but the criticism before us is more feeble than it at first appears : the critic misapprehended the author.

The notion which is impeached is contained in the following sentence, iii. 47, which I give from the edition of Schweighæuser. Περαιωθέντων δὲ τῶν θηρίων, ἀναλαβὼν Ἀννίβας τοὺς ἐλέφαντας καὶ τοὺς ἱππεῖς, προῆγε, τούτοις ἀπουραγῶν, παρὰ τὸν ποταμόν· ἀπὸ θαλάττης ὡς ἐπὶ τὴν ἕω ποιούμενος τὴν πορείαν, ὡς εἰς τὴν μεσόγαιον τῆς Εὐρώπης. " The elephants having been brought over, Hannibal, taking " with him these and the cavalry, led forward, bringing up " the rear with them, along the river ; making his march " away from the sea as it were towards the east, as if into the " midland of Europe."

We know that, immediately after crossing the river, the inclination of the march was, for some way, northward.

But it is not to that first inclination that the idea of eastward is applied. It is applied to the scope of march which
was before them to the plain of Italy. The first moving
forward is seen in the word προῆγε. The making a march
is seen in ποιούμενος πορείαν, words which import a large
stretch of the expedition, or the whole of it. Παρὰ τὸν
ποταμὸν belongs to προῆγε: but ὡς ἐπὶ τὴν ἕω belongs to
ποιούμενος πορείαν. Dr. Ukert desires to annex this idea of
eastward to προῆγε: and he would alter the usual punctu-
ation by removing the stop from ποταμόν, and placing it
after ἕω. This may also be inferred from the reviewer's
report of the criticism,* where the sentence is badly divided
into two parts, for telling the progress: the words προῆγε
ἀπὸ θαλάττης ὡς ἐπὶ τὴν ἕω are translated "marched away
from the sea eastward:" and the remaining words ποιούμενος
τὴν πορείαν ὡς εἰς τὴν μεσόγαιον τῆς Εὐρώπης are translated
"as if he had been making for the midland parts of Europe."
The comma after πορείαν is rejected.

This notion of fixing "eastward" upon προῆγε, and dis-
connecting it from the scope of the march, I take to be
erroneous. Such frame of sentence as we have here, with
the verb and participle and an object of movement, is very
usual with Polybius: and it seems to me that, when a word
like προῆγε represents the idea of setting out or leading
forward, with another word of larger sense expressing the
idea of making an expedition or voyage, the words which
give the object of movement (as here ἐπὶ τὴν ἕω) cannot be
annexed merely to the former, and disconnected from the
term of larger sense. We read i. 29, i. ἀνήγοντο ποιού-
μενοι τὸν πλοῦν ὡς ἐπὶ τὴν Λιβύην—"they set sail making
their voyage as for Africa." In the same way, iii. 17, ἀνα-
ζεύξας ἐκ τῆς καινῆς πόλεως προῆγε ποιούμενος τὴν πορείαν
ἐπὶ τὴν Ζ᾽κανθαν—"having disencamped from Carthagena

* See beginning of this chapter.

he led forward, making his march for Saguntum." In such instances ἐπὶ with its substantive must belong chiefly, if not exclusively, to the word which denotes the making a voyage or expedition.

It seems equally clear, that, in the sentence before us the other idea, " from the sea," must be subject to the same appropriation; that it fixes itself upon ποιούμενος πορείαν. There would be no force in saying that Hannibal set out from the sea; especially if, as is believed, he was already above Avignon. But there is good sense in describing the scope of march that was now before him, as tending from the sea : it was here that, having hitherto advanced, as it were, parallel with the sea-coast,* he turned away from it, and pursued his march from the Rhone to the plain of the Po as the object: especially as the next sentence gives a south-west direction to the course of the Rhone. If he had said that the march from Carthagena to the Rhone had been ὡς πρὸς ἄρκτον, and that now it would be ὡς ἐπὶ τὴν ἕω, the distinction would not have been objected to.

The rejection of the comma after πορείαν is also sub-servient to the error of Dr. Ukert's criticism. The stop is in its proper place. In fact, the sentence was complete with πορείαν, and without the words which follow. The idea which those last words express, serves to enforce the purport of the sentence, by suggesting an object of movement in addition to that which is already expressed ; the addition occurring, as is not unusual, to a writer or speaker, just as he is completing his sentence.

Some have conceived a low estimate of the early authority of Polybius, on the ground that geographical accuracy must

---

* He had brought his forces from the Pyrenees to the place where they crossed the Rhone, "having the Sardinian Sea on right hand." Lib. iii. c. 41.

have been improved in the long interval which followed him, giving to the Romans an increased acquaintance with the countries of the world.   Hence the distrust of ancient authority seems not to extend to Strabo.   This geographer was precisely the contemporary of Livy.   I only advert to his errors, because others on the faith of his superiority criminate his predecessor.   Dr. Ukert will deduce a fact of actual distance from the loosest data of Strabo, rather than accept it from the most direct and safe evidence of the present day.

The fourth book of Strabo was not completed till sixty years after the death of Julius Cæsar.   This able and accomplished man bears in matters of geography an authority analogous to that of Polybius: he related things which had come under his own observation, being most competent to judge of them and to explain them: but, as he was not infallible, the geographer by profession, coming after him, might have corrected his faults.   When the latter wrote, there had been opportunity of improving upon the knowledge of Gaul and Britain which had belonged to Cæsar.   Strabo professes to have read the Commentaries: he observes that Cæsar had passed twice into Britain, and soon returned, having done no great things, nor penetrated far into the island; but that in later times some of the British chiefs had cultivated the favour of Augustus, and brought nearly the whole island to be in familiar intimacy with the Romans; that they yielded small duties on exports and imports, but needed not a garrison to control them.*

We are entitled to expect some geographical improvement. Note the amount of it.   Cæsar wrote that of the three sides of Britain the side opposite to Gaul was the shortest: Strabo writes that it is the longest.   Cæsar wrote that Ireland was to the west of Britain: Strabo writes that it is to the north.

* iv. p. 200.

Cæsar wrote that the side of Britain opposite to Gaul was in length 500 miles: Strabo writes that it is 5,000 stadia = 625 miles. One is surprised that he did not make it more; considering that he reports the coast of Britain to face the coast of Gaul, with their extreme points corresponding both east and west.—Cæsar de Bell. Gall. v. c. 13. Strab. i. 63—iv. 199.

In the passage last referred to, Strabo thus expresses himself—" Britain is in figure triangular: her longest side is " that which is spread opposite to Gaul, being in extent " neither more nor less: each is as much as 4,300 or 4,400 " stadia; that is to say, the Gallic coast from the mouths of " the Rhine to the northern extremity of the Pyrenees in " Aquitania; and the British coast from the most easterly " point where Kent lies opposite the mouths of the Rhine, to " the western head which is over against Aquitania and the " Pyreneau. This too is the shortest distance from the Pyre- " nees to the Rhine, as the greatest has been called 5,000 " stadia: but there is probably some convergence from the " parallel position of the river and the mountain, a bend " taking place in each line near its termination at the ocean."

Thus does the authority of the Augustan day, writing nearly a century and a half after Polybius, instruct the world that the coast from Margate to Penzance is parallel to and of equal length with the coast from the Brill to the Bidassoa; and that this is the shortest way, from the course of the Rhine to the chain of the Pyrenees, by reason that these two lines rather converge as they approach the ocean.

CHAPTER III.

The Polybian Map of M. Gossellin. His reference to Pliny for confirming it. His theory on the Stade.

NOTHING can be more injurious to the fame of Polybius than the map of the celebrated French philosopher, M. Gossellin, which professes to represent the Mediterranean of Polybius, with the positions of places according to his writings. This map is annexed to M. Gossellin's great work, " Récherches sur la Geographie systematique et positive des Anciens," where it is called " Polybii Internum Mare ;" also to the well-known translation of Strabo, where it is called " Mer Interieure selon Polybe." Such a map ought to be according to the authority of the imputed author.

Let us suppose a course along the south of the Mediterranean in three instalments: Gibraltar to Tunis : Tunis to Cape Passaro : Cape Passaro to Rosetta at the mouth of the Nile. These four places represent, sufficiently for our purpose, the Pillars of Hercules, Carthage, Pachynus, and Canopus. Now the first distance, from Gibraltar to Tunis, is in fact more than three times as great as the second, from Tunis to Cape Passaro : and the last, from Cape Passaro to Rosetta, is greater than the first. The Polybian chart of M. Gossellin exhibits the second or middle distance as being the greatest of the three : it places Carthage farther from Pachynus than from the Pillars of Hercules ; and Pachynus nearly twice as far from Carthage as from the mouth of the Nile. Equally monstrous and foreign from fact are the distances pourtrayed from the coast of Carthage to the coast of Sicily and to Marseille : the former of these two is in fact not a fourth of the latter : M. Gossellin, on behalf of Polybius, represents it as more than double of the latter.

M. Gossellin's map represents Italy with a straight line of Mediterranean coast from Narbonne to Policastro. Now Polybius distinctly recognises the great bend of Italy, when he says that the Tyrrhenian and Sicilian seas bound that side which faces the south and the west—τὴν πρὸς μεσημβρίαν καὶ δυσμὰς τετραμμένην, ii. 14. His apprehension of the bearings appears too in what he says on the chain of the Apennine; he ranges it along the southern border of the great plain. He says that Ligurians dwell on either side of it as far as Pïsæ on the seaside, and the lands of the Arretini on the side towards the plain; that you then have the Etrurians on one side and the Umbrians on the other: that the Apennine bears away from the great plain to the right, and through the middle of the rest of Italy reaches to the Sicilian sea. As to the other coast, he speaks of the side of Italy which is bounded by the Adriatic and the Ionian strait as the eastern side—τὴν πρὸς ἀνατολὰς κεκλιμένην: and he names the promontory of Cocynthus as separating the Ionian strait from the Sicilian sea. Lib. ii. 14, 5.

One who is acquainted with Polybius, knowing his Italy, and his position of Sicily in relation to Italy and to Africa, will promptly condemn much of the map we speak of as a delusion. But numbers have seen, and will see, M. Gossellin's Mediterranean of Polybius in one or other of his celebrated works, who have not read Polybius himself: and these will be misled.

I believe that not one of the disproportions apparent in this map is based upon anything found in the works of Polybius. The chief attempt to fix an extravagant measurement on him is by an inference drawn from Strabo, through which M. Gossellin imputes to Polybius an estimate of 18,766 stadia as the length of a direct sea-line from the Pillars of Hercules to the Sicilian strait. If that numeral were found expressed by Strabo, such authority is surely not safe for what was

written by one who preceded him by nearly a century and a
half : especially when we remember Strabo's own report of
the Mediterranean, and that from the entrance at Gibraltar
he carried a parallel up the Mediterranean, as lying midway
between the coast of Europe and the coast of Africa, distant
2,500 stadia from each.

But we are not quite without evidence from Polybius himself to show that he would not have so given the line from
the strait to the Pillars. We read, in lib. iii. 39, 2—" At this
" period (Hannibal's invasion) the Carthaginians were masters
" of all parts of Libya which are towards the inner sea, from
" the Altars of Philænus which stand above the Great Syrtis,
" as far as the Pillars of Hercules : and this length of coast
" was above sixteen thousand stadia." Can we believe that
Polybius conceived the Sicilian strait to be at a greater distance from the Pillars than the Altars of the Philæni were :
that, while he reckoned this south-eastern part of the Syrtis
to be distant 16,000 stadia from the Pillars by the coasting
line, he reckoned the Sicilian strait to be in a direct line
18,766 ? He explored those countries : his history exhibits
his information upon them along the whole coast : he tells the
operations of the fleets during the first Punic war :* and at a
later period the encroachments of Masinissa on the Carthaginian possessions : † he knew that the boundary of dominion
was far eastward of the district of Carthage herself : ‡ and it
was in his time, and before his own eyes, that this empire
passed into the hands of the Romans, when his great pupil
Scipio brought these very tracts into the condition of a Roman
province. Did he then, of all men, after he had recorded the
much longer line, a coast-line too, to be 16,000 stadia, did he
wade through a trigonometrical argument for proving the
much shorter line to be 18,766 ? In truth this 16,000 fairly
corresponds with other rational estimates made by him, and

* Polyb. ii. 19. 2.　　† *Ibid.* xxxii. 2.　　‡ *Ibid.* x. 40. 7.

gives a cogent disproof of the extravagant numeral on which M. Gossellin relied.

In the same region of the same map is another very palpable misrepresentation, where nothing can be said in mitigation of it. I mean the Polybian distance between Carthage and Lilybæum ; that is to say, between Tunis and Marsala, represented by M. Gossellin as 8,000 stadia. These are the words of Polybius himself—τὸ δὲ τρίτον (ἀκρωτηρίον) τέτραπται μὲν εἰς αὐτὴν τὴν Λιβύην, ἐπίκειται δὲ τοῖς προκειμένοις τῆς Καρχηδόνος ἀκρωτηρίοις εὐκαίρως, δίεχον ὡς χιλίους σταδίους· νεύει δ' εἰς χειμερινὰς δύσεις, διαιρεῖ δὲ τὸ Λιβυκὸν καὶ τὸ Σαρδῷον πέλαγος, προσαγορεύεται δὲ Λιλύβαιον. This is in all points true : the Lilybæan promontory does look south-west towards the forelands of Carthage, distant about a thousand stadia, dividing the Libyan and Sardinian seas. And in all the proper works of Polybius not a word can be found to excuse M. Gossellin for substituting 8,000 for 1,000.

No excuse of ignorance or mistake is made; the thing professes to be a misrepresentation. These words (Réch. ii. 19) avow it :—" Cependant, il existe une grande erreur dans cette
" partie de la Carte de Polybe. En partant de la Sicile, il
" place la promontoire Lilybée au couchant, et dit qu'il est
" éloigné de mille stades des caps qui sont près de Carthage ;
" dans notre carte, le distance entre ces deux points se trouve
" être d'environ 8,000 stades. Une différence si considérable
" ne peut provenir que de deux causes ; ou d'un faux emploi
" que nous aurions fait des grandes distances de Polybe dans
" la Mediterranée, ou d'un défaut d'ensemble dans le système
" général des mesures adoptées par cet historien. Pour ce
" qui nous concerne, le doute ne peut tomber que sur la
" correction que nous avons faite au texte de Pline." *

Does the erroneous exhibition of geography become a fair

---

* For this, see the next head.

proceeding by M. Gossellin's confessing the discrepancy between the real Polybius and his own? His arguments and his confessions are no doubt accessible to those who will get them and read them ; but how many will see the map and not study the comments ! The knowledge of a published map is far more than commensurate with that of the work to which it belongs. The student may contemplate this "Internum mare Polybii," without exploring the four quarto volumes on ancient geography: he may be attracted by the same geographical portrait, "Mer Méditerranée selon Polybe" belonging to the five volumes of Strabo, translated by Du Theil, Coray, and Letronne, not scrutinising the principles on which it was framed, but relying on the name of Gossellin for its truth. It is awkward, under any circumstances, to represent a man as having said eight, when you know that he said one ; and the more so, when you know that, in saying one, he spoke deliberate truth. M. Gossellin was well-informed of the facts from which Polybius's acquaintance with all the ground of Sicily must be inferred ; his description of the long wars in which every foot of land had been won and lost, and every village subjected to the violence of contending parties. He knew of Polybius's crossings into Africa, and his study of that continent from the Nile to the Atlantic. In some leading distances the historian had spoken plainly for himself, even if Pliny had said nothing to illustrate him. Yet, M. Gossellin, clinging to that loose and half-told story of Strabo, constructs upon this basis a system for Polybius, holds him answerable for all results, and bids him bear the blame. One can understand that a man, wanting to make a map for ancient times, may feel himself embarrassed in the "défaut d'ensemble" among the authorities that lie before him. But in pourtraying the geography of some one author, if any measurements can claim to be observed, they are the measurements of that author himself ; and one, who could only make a Polybian map by sacrificing those, might have abstained from the attempt.

His appeal to Pliny.

I must be content with my protest against this map. One who ventures to be dissatisfied with M. Gossellin on ancient measures of space, should be prepared to canvas the new doctrines of the Stade, for which he was so great an advocate. I am not armed for such encounter. I may recommend the perusal of what Dr. Ukert has written in vol. I. of his geography, 2d division, p. 51—77: also of Col. Leake's paper on the Stade in the Journal of the Royal Geographical Society, vol. ix. However, as in M. Gossellin's words above quoted, he refers to his own alteration of Pliny's text, and in Récherches, ii. p. 12, acknowledges the propriety of showing the enormous distance which he is imputing to Polybius to be confirmed by other authority, and there commends us to Pliny, I will submit to those who are more competent than I am to deal with such matters, that Pliny does not confirm M. Gossellin's imputation on Polybius, but plainly dissents from it.

M. Gossellin adduces two passages of Pliny,* one from the 5th book, c. 6, the other from the 6th book, c. 38. The earlier passage attributes to Polybius 1,100 miles from the Pillars to Carthage : and this is unequivocally hostile to the notion that he estimated 18,766 stades = 2,345¾ miles from the Pillars to the Sicilian Strait. The passage in the 6th book M. Gossellin amends, so that it may answer his purpose; altering the received version of Pliny before he applies it.

Pliny quotes from Polybius the length of the Mediterranean ; a sea-line, from the Pillars to Seleucia Pieria, in six instalments, making a total of 2,440 miles. They are

* Récherches, tom. ii. pp. 8, 9, 13.

stated thus : à Gaditano freto ad orientem recto cursu Siciliam : Cretam : Rhodum : Chelidonias : Cyprum : Syriæ Seleuciam Pieriam—which M. Gossellin thus presents in translation, with the distances—*

Du détroit de Gades, au détroit de Sicile	1260½ m. p.
Du détroit de Sicile, à l'île de Crète . .	375
De l'île de Crète, à Rhodes	183½
De Rhodes, aux îles Chelidoniæ . . .	183½
Des Chelidoniæ, à l'île de Cypre . . .	322
De Cypre, à Séleucie en Piérie . . .	115½

2,440 m. p.

As the total 2,440 m. p. is confessedly inadequate, one or
more of the parts must require to be increased beyond the
amount so imputed to them. M. Gossellin thinks the total
too short by 1,000 miles, and says it should be 3,440. But,
though it is in six parts, he bestows the whole increase on
one part ; not saying a word upon the other five. He ratifies
his favourite exaggeration à Gaditano freto Siciliam ; and,
bestowing the additional 1,000 miles on the 1,260½ miles of
the text, brings out for that interval 2,260½ miles, alias 18,837
stades ; which keeps 18,766 in countenance.

Now it may be doubted, whether by Siciliam Pliny meant
the first land of Sicily, or, as M. Gossellin renders it, the
Strait. If the former, 1,260½ m. p. would need no correction,
being 10,084 stades. M. Gossellin, however, construing Siciliam "to the Strait," includes in the 1,260½ m. p. the length
of Sicily : and for that, the stated distance would certainly
not be enough : as 12,000 stades (1,500 miles) was the commonly accepted distance from the Pillars to the Strait. But
why add the whole 1,000 miles (8,000 stades) to this first

* There are various readings. It is convenient to quote as
printed in Récherches, ii. 8.

instalment? Supposing the deficiency of the total to have been 1,000 miles, why add it all to this particular portion of the length of the Mediterranean, without inquiring whether some of the other component parts may not require correction? Manifestly the next instalment requires increase; Cretam, 375 m. p. This is very much below what it should be. The mere sea-line between those great islands must be more than 500 miles; and, if the first distance was to embrace the length of Sicily, the second would, according to M. Gossellin, embrace the length of Crete, about 200 more. If Siciliam means, as he says, "to the eastern end of Sicily," Cretam must mean "to the eastern end of Crete." On the other hand, if Siciliam meant, "to the first land of Sicily," the next distance, "to Crete," should include Sicily itself. The thing told is the whole length à Gaditano freto Seleuciam; and the length of those islands cannot be omitted.

And now, what is the result of the reference to Pliny? Does it give countenance to the monster sea-line which M. Gossellin imputes? does it confirm it and rectify it into 18,837? It happens that, when Pliny had this 2,440 miles of Polybius under consideration, 3,440 was offered to his attention as more correct, being a distance stated by Agrippa between the same termini. But Pliny questioned this amendment as erroneous, and declined to accede to it. If he had listened to so large an addition to the total, it would not follow that M. Gossellin's favourite instalment should enjoy the whole of it. However, all difficulty is met with complacently assuring us, that Pliny had a bad edition of Polybius—" Il faut en conclure, que l'erreur que Pline entrevoyoit, étoit dans l'exemplaire de Polybe, qu'il avoit sous les yeux, et non dans celui d'Agrippa, comme il le conjecturoit."—Géog. des Anciens, ii. p. 10.

New Theory of the Stade.

To those who may not be aware of this controversy on the
stade, I am safe in saying, that a leading principle of M.
Gossellin's theory is, that the apparent errors in distances
expressed by the early philosophers, and which were deemed
so by one another, were not actually errors : that if one man
pronounced the circumference of the earth to be twice as
long as another man, they were probably both right, and
that the cause of the apparent difference was the difference
of stades in which the measurements had been originally
computed. M. Gossellin exhibits many of these varieties in
the total perimeter from 180,000 to 400,000 stadia, and from
500 to 1,111⅓ stadia in the degree.

I will only observe, that it is easy to imagine that in very
early times men might differ, even by two to one, on the
size of the earth; but not so easy to believe it as to small
superficial distances between one place and another. Here
some approach to truth would be perceptible to observation
and experience, not in the other case. But M. Gossellin
accounts in the same way for differences in measurements on
the largest scale and the smallest. When he blames Strabo
for censuring those who differed on the large distances in
India, he pronounces all their measurements to be "iden-
tiques, quoiqu' exprimées en modules différens :" that Patro-
cles had expressed himself in stades of 666⅔ to the degree ;
Megasthenes in those of 1,111⅓; and Eratosthenes in those
of 833⅓—and, when he finds in Strabo, iv. 178, that from
Aix en Provençe to the Var it is 73 miles, he explains
that this distance had been calculated at the rate of 500
stades to a degree. When presently Strabo reports 200 stadia
along the Rhone from Vienne to Lyon, M. Gossellin interprets them by the standard of 833⅓. Notes to Strabon, tom. ii.
pp. 7. and 27.

Among the instances given by M. Gossellin as examples of his method of explaining supposed differences, none is more remarkable than that of the direct sea-line from the Pillars to the Strait. He says that one philosopher treated it as expressed in stades of 500 to the degree; another in stades of 1,111⅓ to the degree; another in stades of 700 to the degree : that Eratosthenes happened to adopt an estimate made on the footing of 180,000 to the circumference; that Polybius hit upon a computation resulting from 400,000; and Strabo had the good fortune to find one founded upon 252,000.

He insists that all these reckonings were right, though the philosophers were not aware of it themselves. These are his words,*—" Cet ancien, (Eratosthenes), comptoit, en ligne " droite, depuis le détroit des Colonnes jusqu'au détroit de " Sicile, 8,800 stades; Polybe vouloit qu'il en eût 18,837; " et Strabon, critiquant ces deus auteurs, prétend qu'il s'en " trouve 12,000."

" La grande dissemblance de ces dernières mesures feroit " croire, au premier aspect, qu'il est impossible de les con- " cilier, et que l'une on l'autre, ou toutes les trois peut-être, " renferment des erreurs considerables. Cependant, on les " trouvera assez justes, si l'on soit distinguer le module " du stade qui appartient à chacune d'elles." But I am warned to pause. Our subject is historical ; not pre-historical. And, though a theory which involves the incidents of unrecorded times may tempt to amusing speculations, I will, without further running out of the course, proceed to business in the persuasion that the stade of Herodotus was the stade of Aristotle and Eratosthenes. A few words are wanted touching the stade of Polybius.

* Rech. tom. iv. p. 315.

CHAPTER IV.

On the Stade of Polybius, and his Distances.

POLYBIUS reckons distances from place to place, commonly by the stade, a Greek measure ; sometimes by the mile, a Roman measure. The one was not a precise multiple of the other ; but the mile was almost equivalent to eight stades, wanting about 22 English feet. Eight stades to a mile is the rate by which Livy adopts distances from Polybius : and Polybius himself sanctioned this ratio, in saying that the Romans had marked their roads with indications of distance at intervals of eight stades. If ever there was a man in the world who knew rightly what a stade was, and what a mile was, one would think that Polybius had that knowledge. But here again there is controversy. M. Gossellin, in 1798, propounded that Polybius had a stade of his own ; and Dr. Ukert, notwithstanding what he had written on measurements in 1816, became a convert to the notion in 1832.

The notion that Polybius treated the Roman mile as equal to $8\frac{1}{3}$ stades rests only on a few words of Strabo, lib. vii. p. 322. The passage translated is this :—" From Apollonia, " the Egnatian way is eastward into Macedonia, stepped by " the mile ; and furnished with columns as far as Cypselus " and the river Hebrus, 535 miles. Reckoning the mile at " 8 stades, as men usually do, this would be 4,280 stades. " But if, like Polybius, you add to the eight stades two plethra, " the third of a stade, the number will be increased by 178, " being a third of the number of miles."

Here Strabo has been thought to impute to Polybius that, in opposition to the rest of the world, he reckoned the mile as equal to $8\frac{1}{3}$ stades. In D'Anville's Traité des mesures Itinéraires, p. 54, he says this :—" Quand on lit dans Strabon

" que selon la comparaison que faisait Polybe de l'intervalle
" des colonnes milliaires à des stades sur cette voie, il comp-
" toit 8 stades et un tiers pour un mille, il ne s'ensuit pas
" qu'on soit dans l'obligation de prolonger le mille d'un tiers
" de stade, pour suffire en rigueur à cette évaluation; et il
" n'y faut voir qu'une méprise, qui peut procéder de la pro-
" portion du pied Grec au pied Romain, comme 25 est à 24."

Whatever brought Strabo to make the allusion to Polybius,
it was probably caused by ʻa confusion between the Greek
and Roman foot. The stade is a Greek measure, consisting
of 600 Greek feet : the mile is a Roman measure, consisting
of 5,000 Roman feet—that is to say, 1,000 steps of five Roman
feet : thus, 5,000 Roman feet being a mile, the eighth is 625.
And, if a man should imagine such a thing as a stade of 600
Roman feet, and make his mile with eight of such false stades,
one should say to him, " If you employ a stade like that, you
must take not 8, but $8\frac{1}{3}$ of them to make a mile." The
blunder would require that correction : but Strabo's words
intimate that Polybius, in his own estimation of a Roman
mile, added to eight stades the δίπλεθρον, which is the third
of the Greek measure. Now there is nothing in the works
of Polybius, or any other author, where such an idea is to be
traced : and one may prefer the κατὰ σταδίους ὀκτώ of Polybius himself to the ὡς Πολύβιος of Strabo.

Strabo does not introduce this observation as appropriate
to the matter that he is speaking of in the seventh book,
namely, the length of the Egnatian way : it would equally
have suited any other assertion of milliary distance in any
part of his works ; nothing shows why it has come in here.
Macedonia may have been the first conquered state in which
the Roman mile was employed, and indicated by columns ;
and, if any such blunder as a Roman stade had occurred,
which does not appear, Polybius was a likely man to notice
it. But a greater improbability was never suggested than

that he himself made the mile 200 Greek feet longer than
the rest of the world; he had the best opportunity of understanding both Greek and Roman weights and measures; and,
if such a man, one so much referred to by those who came
after him, had so estimated a measure which he has to mention in almost every page that he writes, this one oblique
reference to it in Strabo's seventh book would not be the
only clue. If the fact were true, Strabo would have disclosed
the notion in a less questionable manner. But the notion is
supported by nothing, either in Strabo or any other author:
it is contradicted by Livy when he translates the stades of
Polybius into miles, as in the case of Hanno's march up the
Rhone, 200 st. = 25 m. p.; it is contradicted by Polybius
himself. When he says in a parenthesis, iii. 39, that the
Romans marked their distances along the Iberian coast at
intervals of eight stadia, do we not see that the intervals
were Roman miles?

M. Gossellin does not admit this notion of Polybius, though
reported by himself, but twists it into another shape by the
aid of Strabo. Noticing the Polybian intervals of 8 stadia,
between "les pierres milliaires que mesuroient et ornoient les
voies Romaines," he had said reasonably, "D'après ce passage
" il paroîtroit que Polybe auroit reconnu que le mille Romain
" valoit huit stades juste."—Récherches, ii. p, 6. But in the
next page he turns away from those appearances, and sub-
mitting himself to "le témoignage positif d'un auteur aussi
grave que Strabon," clings to the 8⅓ with a permanent devotion. All his calculations are made on that footing.

Dr. Ukert, in his elaborate disquisition on ancient measures
of length, which occupies twenty-six pages in the second part
of his first volume published in 1816, and in which he com_
bats M. Gossellin's doctrines on the stade, notices the addition
of two plethra to eight stadia which Strabo is said to impute
to Polybius: and then says, " In the writings of Polybius

" which remain to us, we find him to report the relation of
" the stade to the mile, the same as others." However, in the
volume published in 1832, p. 578, this learned man, taking
part in the Hannibal controversy, condemns the passage in
Polybius as spurious, and asserts him to reckon 8⅓ stadia to
the mile. He might as well have saved his consistency. It
will appear in a future chapter (Part iii. ch. 3), that he shifted
into error on this point without any adequate temptation.
He is treating " Roman measurements in Gaul and Spain."

And now a few words on the distances of Polybius. No
one will claim for his measurements that they are minutely
accurate : for they are commonly expressed in round hundreds
of stades ; and it would be idle to suppose that the length of
each space had amounted to a precise multiple of an hundred.
Others wrote in the same way. Strabo cites the opinions of
his predecessors in hundreds of stades : and in the Roman
Itineraries every space is given in entire miles, the mile being
5,000 Roman feet : no fractions are ever mentioned.

But, while precision is disclaimed, reasonable accuracy is
fairly to be supposed in Polybius. The rudeness of science
made calculations of space across the ocean a matter of much
difficulty : there was not the same difficulty in a measurement from Rome to Milan, or from Nîmes to Valence. In
the spaces that we must deal with, we have to trust to Polybius alone : they had not been registered from prior investigation : he is responsible ; and the truthful intention, which is
conceded to him by all, gives a presumption of accuracy
where error is not apparent. The importance of his distances
is peculiar, for the usefulness of his evidence depends upon
them. The struggle, as we proceed from point to point, is to
identify his termini : when he describes a portion of the line
of march from an ascertained point, the disputation is, whether
it should end at this or that place ; accordingly, the length
which he gives to the interval is a criterion towards de-

termining what that place was, and the trustworthiness of
such a narrator becomes more than usually important, as there
are not the conclusive means of checking his accuracy.

A country travelled, is ordinarily shown by naming in
succession the places through which a traveller has passed.
Such is not the index to Hannibal's route through Gaul and
the Alps : we find our way by description of regions traversed,
with allegation of time and space. In telling the story of the
invasion, there is a point in the progress where Polybius lays
aside the usual notices, the names of places and peoples.
While the march was yet in Spain, the names of nations who
resisted the Carthaginians have been freely told : Hannibal
subdued in succession the Ilergetes, the Bargusii, the Ærenosii,
the Androsini. The country spoken of had long been the seat
of war, and, in naming the nations, he gave an intelligible
clothing to his ideas : all readers might know the points of
distance from Carthagena to the Ebro, and from the Ebro to
Emporium. But from the Pyrenees to the plain of Italy he
was employed on a line of movement which, when he wrote,
was untrodden by the armies of Rome from one extremity to
the other. Scipio had advanced a little way from the eastern
mouth of the Rhone, and visited the site of the Carthaginian
encampment ; but he returned to his ships, not having
trodden one stadium of Hannibal's route.

Polybius felt the risk of error which there would be in
attempting here the usual memorials of a track ; and sought
a safer method of instruction. In that whole course, from
the Pyrenees to the plain of Italy, we do not find one name
of place : to the time when the invaders are actually descending into the plain, one people only has been named, and one
river besides the Rhone. Of the march from the Pyrenees to
the Rhone it was enough to say, that they performed it,
having the sea on their right hand ; and the point where they
first touched the Rhone, is to be perceived only by its distance

from natural objects, the sea below it, and a confluent river, the Isère, above it. In the onward march along the Rhone from that confluence to and through the Alps, we are helped by no names save that of the people called Allobroges : no further name assists us to understand the tale of events, till we come to the Insubres of the plain : the instruction is by local character, with circumstances of opposition and difficulty, and allotment of time and space to operations performed. The incidents of each day are thus offered to our attention; and, by such notification of things without names, the historian hoped to show the course of the invasion in a way that should be recognised in after times.

A plain assurance of this is given in the author's own words. When Hannibal is on the eve of forcing the passes of the Pyrenees, (iii. 36,) Polybius writes as follows—" But " that my narrative carrying you through unknown countries " may not be altogether obscure, I must state from whence " Hannibal set out, what and how great regions he traversed, " and into what parts of Italy he arrived. I am not going to " set forth the proper names of districts, and rivers, and cities; " which some writers do, supposing this part of the business " to be all-sufficient for making things intelligible and clear. " I allow that the citation of names in known countries very " greatly contributes to cause a recognition of the objects : " but in countries utterly unknown, a detail of names has " but the effect of words that give sound without sense : for " so long as the mind has nothing to lay hold of, and cannot " apply the words to any known ideas, the narrative is with- " out order and without point. Wherefore a way is to be " shown by which, though speaking of unknown things, it is " practicable to bring one's hearers in some measure to con- " ceptions that have truth and knowledge. The first and " main thing to know, and which all men may know, is the " division and arrangement of the firmament which surrounds

" us ; by the perception of which all of us, that is all in
" whom there is usefulness, comprehend East, West, South,
" and North. Next is that knowledge by which, apportioning
" the several regions of the earth according to those distinc-
" tions, and always in our minds applying what we hear to
" those distinctions, we come to have clear and familiar
" notions about places unknown to us, and unseen.".

Explanations follow touching the great divisions of the
earth, and the greater or less acquaintance which had been
arrived at with the several parts of the world : the discussion
ends thus—" For, as we are used, for the purpose of seeing,
" to bend our faces towards an object pointed out by the
" finger ; so must we, for the purpose of understanding, make
" the effort to bend our thoughts to places that are from time
" to time pointed out by the story told."

The observations from which these extracts are given, are
made in peculiar application to that small portion of the
earth's surface which is the theatre of this controversy. The
tale, which for good reasons is weak in names, assumes an
increased strength in its other features : for these I claim
attention, because they are so characterized as important by
the special announcement of this admirable historian.

THE ALPS OF HANNIBAL.

PART III.

POLYBIUS INTERPRETED. PASSAGE OF THE RHONE.

CHAPTER I.

Introduction. Division of the March. Three points to be fixed : the Passage of the Rhone ; the beginning of Alps ; the exit into the Plain.

SAGUNTUM fell during the winter of 219 B.C. Thereupon the Romans sent an embassy to Carthage, demanding the surrender of Hannibal and other chiefs, with war as the alternative. We may collect from Polybius, that the Consul had completed his successes in Illyria and returned to Rome before the siege of Saguntum was brought to a conclusion. The Romans had despatched Æmilius with his army to Illyria at the opening of the season ; and Hannibal marched from Carthagena against Saguntum about the same time. His designs were fully understood by the Romans ; but it does not appear that they knew his operations to have been commenced when the Illyrian expedition was sent out. We read, c. 20, that Æmilius returned and entered Rome in triumph on the close of the summer, ληγούσης ἤδη τῆς θερείας. Now the siege of Saguntum lasted eight months : so that, before the fall of that place, the winter may have been far advanced.

After the news of this event was received, the embassy was
sent to Carthage; and Hannibal was then in his winter
quarters.

The Carthaginian senate having accepted the declaration
of war, Hannibal, being at Carthagena, immediately gave
leave to his Spanish soldiers to go home for the remainder
of the winter: he framed regulations, for the administration
of affairs in Spain during his absence by his brother Asdrubal: and with a view to the security of his own country, and
to produce a mutual confidence, he transferred a large body
of Spanish troops into Africa, bringing in their place African
troops into Spain. He had taken great pains to inform himself on the nature of the country of the Gauls, of their population, and character, and especially on their feelings towards
the Romans; knowing that his hopes of success must rest
mainly on their co-operation. In this view he had made communication to the Celtic chieftains, both those of Italy and
those in the Alps themselves; and was now anxiously expect-
ing emissaries from them. At length the desired intelligence
was brought: it was in all points favourable; and towards
the spring Hannibal drew his troops together from their
winter quarters: he had also received the last news from
Carthage. Elated and confident, he announced to the army
his resolution to invade Italy, and named a day for marching
from Carthagena.

Having made all his arrangements during winter quarters,
on the appointed day he led forward about ninety thousand
infantry and about twelve thousand cavalry: he passed the
Ebro, and, after great resistance of the nations whom he had
now to bring into subjection, and great loss of men, he
reached the Pyrenees. Here the heavy baggage was laid
aside: he left a sufficient force from his own army to keep
the newly-conquered peoples in subjection; and, as a matter
of policy, freely discharged an equal number of his Iberian

troops. Taking with him the rest of his army, fifty thousand foot and nine thousand horse, lightly equipped, he led them forward in march through the Pyrenees for the passage of the Rhone.

At this stage of the narrative the historian digresses into comments (c. 36, 37, 38,) which contain very sound advice to the compilers and the readers of history, from which I have already exhibited extracts. The narrative is resumed with the 39th chapter, and the text will thence be given in translation,* till the invaders reach the plain of Italy in ch. 61, where the Roman and Carthaginian leaders will be seen mutually advancing in the valley of the Po, each conscious of and wondering at the presence of the other.

The thirty-ninth chapter claims especial notice, and should be always under attention during our consideration of the subject. The line of march, from Carthagena to the Italian plain, is broken into five parts : the termini being Carthagena, the Ebro, Emporium, the passage of the Rhone, the beginning of Alps, the end of Alps. The last three are the peculiar subjects of question in this controversy.

1. Where was the passage of the Rhone ?

2. Where was the first ascent of Alps ?

3. Where did the invaders escape from the Alps and touch the plain ?

This line of march being our subject throughout, it may be set forth in the author's own words, according to the edition of Schweighæuser.

Having said that the καινὴ πόλις, whence Hannibal began his march to Italy, is distant 3,000 stadia from the Pillars of Hercules, he states the five sections of the march thus—

1. ἀπὸ δὲ ταύτης εἰσὶν ἐπὶ μὲν τὸν Ἴβηρα ποταμὸν, ἑξακόσιοι στάδιοι πρὸς δισχιλίοις.

---

* See Appendix.

2. ἀπὸ δὲ τούτου πάλιν εἰς Ἐμπορεῖον, χίλιοι σὺν ἑξακοσίοις.

3. καὶ μὴν ἐντεῦθεν ἐπὶ τὴν τοῦ Ῥοδανοῦ διάβασιν περὶ χιλίους
ἑξακοσίους (ταῦτα γὰρ νῦν βεβημάτισται, καὶ σεσημείωται
κατὰ στάδιους ὀκτὼ διὰ Ῥωμαίων ἐπιμελῶς).

4. ἀπὸ δὲ τῆς διαβάσεως τοῦ Ῥοδανοῦ, πορευομένοις παρ᾽ αὐτὸν
τὸν ποταμὸν ὡς ἐπὶ τὰς πηγὰς ἕως πρὸς τὴν ἀναβολὴν
τῶν Ἄλπεων τὴν εἰς Ἰταλίαν, χίλιοι τετρακόσιοι.

5. λοιπαὶ δὲ αἱ τῶν Ἄλπεων ὑπερβολαί, περὶ χιλίους διακο-
σίους· ἃς ὑπερβάλλων ἔμελλεν ἥξειν εἰς τὰ περὶ τὸν Πάδον
πεδία τῆς Ἰταλίας.

The words in parenthesis have been objected to by Dr.
Ukert, not, that I am aware of, by other writers. There is
good ground of objection; and he has proposed a remedy.
I shall propose a different one, which I hope will be deemed
preferable.

CHAPTER II.

*Passage of the Rhone near Roquemaure indicated by the distance
from the Sea ; by the distance from the Island ; by the single
Stream.*

AN inquirer into the subject will propose to himself this
question :—" Did Hannibal, coming from the region of Nîmes,
" proceed to cross the Rhone, above or below the confluence of
" the Durance?" At whatever part the passage should be
effected, a good stretch of river, unbroken by islands, was to
be desired. A flotilla qualified to transport so large an
armament demanded a considerable extent of shore to arrive
at. In so broad and rapid a current, much distance would
be lost in crossing, each boat reaching the opposite bank

much below the point which it had parted from: so that a great stretch of unembarrassed stream, not often found in the lower Rhone, was to be looked for.   This idea is expressed by Polybius, in the words κατὰ τὴν ἁπλῆν ῥύσιν.

On observation of the river, and the country about it, all will believe that the passage was effected, either at the nearest convenient part above the influx of the Durance, or at some convenient part below that point.   Those who lean to the former opinion have usually fixed upon a part of the river between the villages of Roquemaure and Montfaucon, being about five miles from the town of Orange.   The few who place the crossing below the Durance have fixed upon the stream at, or just above Beaucaire, in Languedoc, the ancient Ugernum, being opposite to Tarascon, a well-known place in Provence.   To decide between these, we look for evidence in the history.   As Dr. Ukert has taken pains to prove a crossing near Tarascon, and has received no answer, the question must be sifted.

Two data guide us to the Passage near Roquemaure.

Polybius has made statements which serve the purpose of giving to his readers a fair apprehension of the place: 1, that Hannibal undertook this operation, where he was not quite four days' march, or journey, from the sea : 2, that from that place he reached the district called the Island, by a march of four successive days.   We have thus a double clue to find the place: its relation to a point lower down the stream, and its relation to a point higher up the stream: nearly four days' march from the sea, and four days' march to the Island.

The entire distance from the Isère down the Rhone to the sea may be exhibited in these successive measurements : to the reach between Roquemaure and Montfaucon, about 75 Roman miles ; thence to Tarascon and Beaucaire, about 29 miles : thence to the eastern, or Massiliotic mouth of the Rhone about

36 miles—total 140. If we recognise, as the place of crossing, the parts near Montfaucon, we assign about 75 miles to the four days' march of Hannibal, and about 65 to the nearly four days' journey below. If we make the passage at Beaucaire and Tarascon, we give about 104 miles to the four days' march, and about 36 to the nearly four days' journey. Whether the distances are apprehended through ancient authorities or modern, this must be admitted : that, if 140 miles of Rhone are to be divided into two portions, of about four days' work each, it is more probable that the higher portion should be to the lower as 75 to 65, than as 104 to 36. For the distances themselves, I will refer to the labours of those who have preceded me in the inquiry.

Distance of the Passage from the Sea.

If we seek ancient authority for showing the distance from the sea to the part where Hannibal crossed the Rhone, the nearest point on the coast that offers itself in any known writings seems to be a place denoted Fossæ Marianæ, the Canal of Marius, probably at the sea mouth of the canal. This place is one of the stations in the Via Aurelia, stated there as at 48 miles from Marseille. D'Anville (notice de Gaule) looks upon Foz as the place named Fossæ Marianæ in the Itineraries, where we find it to be 33 miles to Arles, and thence 27, through Avignon to Sorgues (Cypresseta) ; beyond which you come in 6½ miles to the part vis-à-vis to Roquemaure, according to De Luc ; making that place 66½ from Fossæ Marianæ.

By modern measurements, the distance appears much the same. M. De Luc states the lengths of which it is composed, as measured now on the Great Map of France, thus—" Depuis " l'embouchure orientale du Rhône jusqu' à Arles, 26 milles " romains; Tarascon, 10 ; Avignon, 15 ; Sorgues, 7 ; vis-à-vis "de Roquemaure, $6\frac{1}{2} = 64\frac{1}{2}$ miles." But he conceives that the ancient mouth was to the east of the present mouth, and not carried so far to the sea ; he also points to the village of Foz as on the ancient limit of the land against the sea ; the river stream being now compressed by the atterrissemens which Nature has formed in 2,000 years.

M. Laranza, adopting Foz as a probable terminus from which to estimate a four days' journey, gives the route in toises, varying little from M. De Luc's estimate, considering that he measures to rather a higher point ; his statement is : "To Arles, 19,000 toises ; to Tarascon, 7,500 ; to Avignon, " 11,500 ; to Sorgues, 5,000 ; to Montfaucon, sur la rive qui " est en face, 6,400 = 49,400 toises = $65\frac{1}{3}$ milles."

Some have suggested that, in ancient times, a distance from the sea at the Rhone's mouth was greater than now : this shall be noticed presently. In the meantime, I will consider that the distance from the sea to the part where we conceive the army to have crossed the Rhone, namely, between Roquemaure and Montfaucon, was about 65 miles.

Distance of the Passage from the Island.

This distance is still less open to question than the other. All but a short space at either extremity is exhibited in the ancient registers. The six stages from Orange to Valence appear in the Jerusalem Itinerary as 66 miles = 49,896 toises. Laranza adds, from the Passage to Orange, 3,600 ; and from Valence to the Isère, 3,800 ; making the whole distance from the Passage of the Rhone to the island, 57,296 toises, which is $75\frac{3}{4}$ miles, or 606 stadia. De Luc computes the two spaces at the extremities so as to bring out a precise 75 miles, or 600 stadia. Both these writers, who are quite hostile to each other in most points of our subjects, try other tests for the length of the line in question : one referring to an old

livre de Poste used before the new metrical system was in
force : the other, measuring on the Great Map of France
according to the scale.   The result is, that they bring it so
near to the 75 Roman miles, that they concur in deeming
the space to be 600 stadia, and to be part of the 1,400 of
Polybius.

While we contend for a place of crossing the Rhone which
is 75 miles = 600 stadia below the influx of the Isère, it is
plain that Polybius would have recognized the same interval ;
for, though he does not assert it, it necessarily results from
distances which he does assert.   He states that it is 1,400
stadia from the passage of the Rhone to the beginning of
Alps.   When he has brought Hannibal to the Island, there is
a pause in the narrative of progress while certain incidents
are told.   When the tale of progress is resumed, Hannibal
marches 800 stadia to the beginning of Alps.   Thus the prior
portion had required 600.

Critics the most hostile to our theory, whatever sites they
have conceived, either for the διάβασις or the ἀναβολή, have,
with two exceptions, agreed in accepting 600 stadia as the
length of the first four days' march from one to the other :
and all agree that this was the distance from Roquemaure to
the Island.

Mr. Whitaker, boldly pronouncing the Island to be the
ground on which the city of Lyons stands, says this (p. 8) :
" Polybius states the place of Hannibal's passage over the
" Rhone to be seventy-five miles below Lyons :" and, in a
note, he says, " Polybius, iii. 39, tells us that Hannibal's
" march, from his crossing the Rhone to his mounting the
" Alps, measured 1,400 stadia ; and in iii. 50, tells us addi-
" tionally that, of this distance, 800 stadia, or 100 miles, was
" the length from Lyons to the Alps !"

M. Letronne says:—" Polybe compte quatorze cents stades
" depuis le passage du Rhône jusqu' à la montée des Alpes :

" il dit qu' Annibal a parcourir huit cents stades depuis l'île
" dont il s'agit et la montée des Alpes : c'est donc six cents
" stades depuis le passage jusqu' à la rivière, ou 75 milles
" Romains."—Journal des Savans, Janv. 1819, 26–7.

M. Laranza says :—" Nous voyoni dans Polybe lui-même
" qu'il compte quatre jours de marche pour les 600 stades, ou
" 75 milles, qu'il fait parcourir à Annibal depuis le passage
" du Rhône jusqu' à l'Ile."

Général St. Cyr Nugues, expounding Polybius, says :—" La
" distance du point de passage du Rhône à celui ou l'armée
" s'arrêta le quatrième jour, etoit de 600 stades, 75 milles
" Romains."—Notice, p. 33.

So M. Baudé de Lavalette, Récherches, " Polybe fixe à
" 600 stades la distance parcourir dans ces quatre jours de
" marche."

Even Dr. Ukert, though his crossing is at Tarascon, has a
sentence which bears testimony to the same truth :—" Poly-
" bius später erklärt, von dem Uebergangesorte bis zur Insel
" hätten die Karthager, in vier Tagemärschen, 600 Stadien
" zurückgelegt."—" Polybius afterwards says, that from the
" place of crossing, to the Island, the Carthaginians had
" traversed 600 stadia in four days' march."—Geographie, iii.
580 and 585.

My friend, H. L. Long, also a Tarasconian, acquiesces in
this fact of distance, saying,—" The absolute distance of
" 75 m.p. measured from the Isère downwards, must always
" terminate at Roquemaure."—P. 21.

Though no one has controverted the fact, that the distance
of our διάβασις, from the Island is 600 stadia, two seem to
doubt the importance of the fact ; one of whom thinks that
Hannibal moved much slower, and the other that he moved
much faster. M. le Comte de Fortia d' Urban does not allow
Hannibal to bend his steps towards the Island at all, and
thinks that, having crossed the Rhone, he proceeded very

slowly, from knowing that the Romans were trying to over-
take him. H. Long, on the contrary, thinks that Hannibal
marched, not 600 only, but 800 stadia in those four days;
and says, p. 52 :—" Twenty-five miles per day is in perfect
" accordance with the usual pace of Hannibal, who fell like a
" thunderbolt upon Italy."—P. 32.

Thus a Polybian measurement assented to by all, fixes the
διάβασις for which we contend, at 75 miles below the Isère,
being, as already shown, about 65 miles from the sea.   One
distance satisfies the notion of " nearly four days' journey : "
the other distance satisfies the notion of " four days' march : "
these are the indicia of distance expressed by the historian.
Tarascon, the other place proposed, is hardly ten miles above
Arles : too near to the sea for a short ten days' journey ; and
too far from the Isère for a four days' march.

The single Stream.

Another circumstance in favour of the passage between
Roquemaure and Montfaucon is that the stream is here suitable
to the transportation of an army.   M. De Luc says, p. 54 :—
" Entre ces deux villages (Montfaucon et l'Ardoise) et Roque-
" maure, il y a un espace de 1,800 toises, où le Rhône n'a point
" d'iles, et où il n'a que 250 à 300 toises de largeur."   General
Vaudoncourt's map, which is on a large scale, corresponds
with that assertion.   In the Oxford Dissertation it is said,
p. 42 :—" The Rhone flows uninterrupted by islands from
" Caderousse (the large island above Montfaucon) to Roque-
" maure, a distance of nearly a league ; and, with the excep-
" tion of a similar stream immediately below the island at
" Roquemaure, though for a much shorter distance, this cir-
" cumstance does not occur for many miles up or down the
" river."

I do not know that all writers and map-makers are unanimous on the perfect absence of islands in this part of the Rhone. But the following corroborating statement is made by one who is likely to have ascertained safely what he relates. M. Baudé de Lavalette, p. 41 :—" L'inspection des " lieux entre Avignon et le Pont St. Esprit donne à ce " résultant un nouveau degré de précision. Le cours du " Rhône se montre, dans cet intervalle, embarrassé par une " foule d'iles qui le forcent à se deviser en plusieurs bras " tortueux, entrelacés de la manière la plus bizarre. On y " remarque huit iles principales indiquées dans les anciennes " cartes par les noms de l'Oiselet, le Chateau de Lers, le " Queironette, Piboulette, la Berre, Cadanet, l'Agace et " Crompa. Le fleuve egaré dans ce labyrinthe d'iles ne put " être traversé ni au-dessus du territoire de Montfaucon, ni " au-dessous de Roquemaure : on ne le trouve *réuni en un* " *seul courant* d'une étendue suffisante, qu'entre ces deux " villages. Là, il coule tout entier dans un lit de 245 à 250 " toises de largeur sur un longueur de 1800 toises. C'est donc " aux environs de Montfaucon que furent lancés les bateaux " et les radeaux dont Annibal fit usage : entrainés par le " courant, ils durent aborder 800 ou 900 toises plus bas sur " la rive opposée."

CHAPTER III.

Theory of Tarascon. Argument of Dr. Ukert. Distance from the Sea. Distance from the Island. Roman measurements in Gaul and Spain. Roads in Gaul. Policy of Hannibal. Vessels used in the Crossing. March of Scipio.

As Tarascon on the left bank still bears its ancient name, while Ugernum on the right bank has become Beaucaire, let the former place entitle this theory. I know only of three who subscribe to it: the anonymous of Cambridge, 1830; Dr. Ukert; and Mr. Henry Long. The first draws the red line of march in his map through Tarascon; and gives a reason, which he probably thinks to be enough. In p. 35, he says, "From Nîmes the Roman road branched off in two "directions, one to Arles, the other to Tarascon: and by one "of these, according to Polybius, the Carthaginian continued "his march to the Rhone." Again, p. 45, "Polybius describes "Hannibal as arriving by a Roman road at the banks of the "Rhone." Many, besides this critic, have written to the same effect: but they have writen in error: Polybius never said so: he had no more experience of Roman roads in Languedoc than Hannibal himself: there were none in his day. The learned Ukert is exempt from that delusion: but, as he has laboured much in favour of Tarascon, he claims our serious attention.

On the distance of Tarascon from the Sea.

This much commended geographer pronounces the place of crossing thus:—"When Polybius says that Hannibal crossed "κατὰ τὴν ἀπλὴν ῥύσιν, this was certainly north of the island, "which lies opposite to Beaucaire: and Hanno might choose "a place north of Aramon." He then takes great pains, but in a mysterious manner, to induce his readers to the notion, that this part just above Beaucaire and Tarascon was, in Hannibal's time, at such a distance from the sea, as to amount to "nearly four days' journey," which he represents as importing a distance of 600 stadia for an army, and more for a traveller.

Avoiding all direct assertion of the distance of Tarascon from any other point, Dr. Ukert first contrives a proof that the distance from the Durance to the mouth of the Rhone is from 700 to 800 stadia: and then he pronounces that Tarascon, being lower down, might be about four days' journey from the mouth. His proof of the 700 or 800 is by taking the length of the Rhone from Lyons to the mouth, and deducting the distance from Lyons to the Durance.

He exhibits the difficulty, and prepares us for the process thus :—"We must not think here of exact measurements. A " map drawn by Polybius would no doubt give us quite a " different picture of the country from that which our own " maps give ; especially as the whole nature of the country " shows us, that south of the Druentia there was formerly " much more water than at present : and, as thè mouths of " the Rhone have experienced many changes, we cannot " declare with certainty where the Roman Consul landed, " nor what road it was necessary to take at that time, which " was counted equal to a four days' journey. Our maps alone " cannot enable us to arrive at any conclusion.

" Let us therefore seek for information among the ancients. " Strabo says, lib. iv. p. 193 :—" ἀπὸ Λουγδούνου μέχρι τοῦ " Σηκουάνα χιλίων σταδίων ἐστίν· ἔλαττον δὲ ἢ διπλάσιον τού- " του, τὸ ἀπὸ τῶν εἰσβολῶν τοῦ Ῥοδάνου μέχρι Λουγδούνου.*

" If we attend to this, and at the same time compare with " it some other notices from Strabo, lib. iv. p. 185-6 : from " the Druentia to the Isère, 700 stadia—to Vienne 320—to " Lugdunum 200 = 1220 stadia, we find that the distance " from the mouths of the Rhone to the Druentia, is from 700 " to 800 stadia ; and the place accepted by us, as that where " the Rhone was crossed, Polybius might justly call about " four days' journey from the sea."—Ukert's Geogr. ii. 2d part, 581, 2, 3.

---

* *Translated.* It is 1000 stadia from Lyons to the Seine : and less than the double of that from the mouths of the Rhone to Lyons. N.B. Strabo is speaking of the carriage of goods from the Mediterranean to the British Channel up the Saone and across to the πλεόμενον of the Seine.

The calculation is this:—From Lyons to the Rhone's mouth is less than 2,000 stadia; from Lyons to the Durance is 1,220 stadia. Take 1,220 from less than 2,000: and less than 780 remains for the length of the Rhone from the Durance to the mouth.

Now the subject which Dr. Ukert takes in hand is a certain distance down the Rhone to the mouth; *i.e.* from the confluence of the Durance. He quotes Strabo for the total length of the Rhone from a higher point of the river, Lyons. Then, by way of showing the length below the confluence, he professes to deduct the length above the confluence from the total. But he does not do this: the length which he deducts is not a part of the total from which he deducts it: it is for the most part not along the Rhone. The 1,220 stadia which figure in his demonstration are borrowed from a line of distances drawn across country from Marseille through Cavaillon; and in which line the subject of his proof, Tarascon, would be looked for in vain.

This much-commended geographer has not looked attentively at his materials. He might have applied them for showing what he aims at. In the very passages from which he derives three distances of Strabo, there is something more to the purpose than "less than the double of a thousand."

When Dr. Ukert's argument seems to be carrying the reader along the Rhone to the sea, he is in fact travelling in a cross-country road to Marseille; and, as he did stray into that line, he might have profited by it. Strabo, besides reporting the three distances which Dr. Ukert has extracted as making 1,220 from Lyons to the Durance (which they do to Cavaillon on the Durance), completes that line to the sea at Marseille; making the whole 1,720 from Lyons.

Before Strabo gives that 1,220 stadia, which he reckons from Cavaillon to Lyons, he gives 500 stadia from Marseille to Cavaillon. The whole matter upon these distances is as

follows :—" If you start from Marseille, and proceed to the
" country between the Alps and the Rhone, the Salyes inhabit
" it as far as the river Durance, for . . . . . 500 stadia

" And if you cross the ferry to Cavaillon, all
" belongs to the Cavari, as far as the junction of
" the Isère with the Rhone :—

"To that point from the Durance is a dis-
" tance of 700   „

Afterwards we read—

" From the Isère to Vienne 320   „
" From Vienne to Lyons by land 200   „
By water a little more.   ————
                                       1,720 stadia.

Perhaps Dr. Ukert may apprehend the confluence of the
Rhone and the Durance to be here spoken of. But it is not
so : that confluence is never spoken of; and the idea of it is
excluded by the traveller being instructed to cross by the
ferry at Cavaillon. Whatever may be the excuse, this matter
of Strabo throws more light on the distance from Lyons to
the Rhone's mouth than "less than the double of a thousand."
He reports 1,720 stadia from Lyons to Marseille, and therefore
must have apprehended less than 1,720 to the mouth of the
Rhone; for we know that he attributed to Marseille a more
southern latitude. He calls the Galatic gulph, into which
the Rhone is discharged (p. 122), κόλπος μεταξὺ Μασσαλίας
καὶ Νάρβωνος : and he states as a fact, (p. 115), that Marseille
lies more south, νοσιωτέρα, than the recess of the gulph.
Thus, when Dr. Ukert was studying the length of the Rhone
from Lyons to the sea, he had before him something better
worth attending to than the uncertain numeral in p. 193 : he
would see not only that Strabo considered the line of Rhone
below Lyons to be "less than 2,000 stadia," but that he
onsidered it less than 1,720 stadia.

Let us then apply this in aid of Dr. Ukert's estimate of
Rhone below Durance.   Let us allow the total below Lyons
to be the full 1,720, though it is not so much.   How shall we
divide this into two parts, above and below the Durance?
Strabo does not help us to do this : and, as Dr. Ukert wishes
information to be sought from the ancients, let us refer to the
Roman Itineraries.   And first the length above the Durance :
the nearest point to the confluence which the Itineraries give
is Avignon ; and we make a further concession, if we divide
the two parts at that point, instead of the confluence which is
below it.   These registers exhibit from Lyons to Avignon,
162 m. = 1,296 stadia.   Take this 1,296 from 1,720, and there
remains 424 for the residue to the mouth.   The only remaining question is,—where in this length of 424 do we find
Tarascon ?   The place is mentioned in no Itinerary ; and we
must be content with the modern *Livre de Poste*, which gives
from Avignon to Tarascon, 23,000 mètres = 124 stadia.   When
this is taken from the 424, 300 stadia, or $37\frac{1}{2}$ miles, remain as
the distance of Tarascon from the mouth of the Rhone : such
is, in truth, the maximum distance of Dr. Ukert's διάβασις
from the sea, if he will interpret Strabo justly : rather a short
distance to represent the σχεδὸν ἡμερῶν τεττάρων ὁδὸν of
Polybius.

It is to be observed that Dr. Ukert, in recommending his
longer distance for four days' work, suggests the embarrassment
of water ; and that we know not Scipio's landing-place ; nor
the changes since made in the mouths of the Rhone.   Now
we may suppose, that the Roman general would not have
passed on from the friendly city of Marseille, and disembarked
his army nearer to the river's mouth, if he had been thereby
involved in greater difficulty of proceeding.   He did not land
as an adventurer in an unreported region : his native ally
added a force to his force, and would aid in fixing the spot
for a first encampment, having in view the obstruction of the

Carthaginian expedition. If it is meant to be insinuated that the sea has gained on the land, and so to favour the supposition that Tarascon was of old farther from the Rhone's mouth than now, I apprehend the contrary to be the fact. De Luc cites the testimony of M. Darluc from his Histoire naturelle de la Provence, 1782, p. 262. " La Camargue est " un grand terrain qui forme, par sa position, un triangle " équilatéral, ayant sept lieues de longueur de chaque côté. " Cette île sépare les deux bras du Rhône qui se divisent au- " dessous d'Arles. Son enceinte était moins considérable " autrefois. Les atterrissemens successifs que le Rhône a " formés à son embouchure, l'ont aggrandie. La tour de St. " Louis, qui fut élevée près des bords de la mer en 1630, en " est éloignée aujourd'hui d'une lieue." On these facts we may believe that, if the Tarascon of 218 B. c. differed from the Tarascon of to-day, it was in being nearer to, not further from, the sea than now. In other parts of the Mediterranean the land has advanced near the mouths of rivers. I believe this is the case, at the mouths of the Po, at the mouth of the Tiber, at the mouth of the Arno. In Languedoc, not far from the scenes we are speaking of, there is the little town of Aigues-mortes (equæ mortuæ) now some miles from the sea, formerly close upon the shore.

To his ill-advised commentary Dr. Ukert adds this. " Hanno may have crossed above Aramon." This would not be well said, even if the notion on Tarascon had been a wise one. Polybius relates that the crossing of Hanno was 25 miles above that of Hannibal. Aramon is not ten above Tarascon.

On the distance of Tarascon from the Island.

Dr. Ukert acquiesces in the text so far as to say this, p. 585 :—" After four days' march in succession from the

place of crossing, Hannibal arrives at the Island." Presently,
however, he appears dissentient, by starting a doubt on the
Island itself. He says, " Let us look back and ask where the
" Island is situated. Polybius tells us to look for it at a
" distance of 600 stadia from the place of crossing the
" river."

So far the writer seems to agree with all other critics, that
Polybius intends the length of the Rhone between the Island
and the διάβασις as 600 stadia. But he proceeds to
ascertain whether this is a correct measurement. There are
two modes of reckoning the space :—1. From the Island
down to the διάβασις. 2. From the διάβασις up to the
Island. Now the first mode is the safest; for the angle of
the rivers is a permanent point fixed by nature : the part
where Hannibal thought proper to cross the Rhone is not :
it is the thing sought. If Dr. Ukert had measured down
from the Island, 600 stadia would have brought him to
Roquemaure. But he treats Tarascon as the safe point to be
measured from. To try this in earnest would be dangerous :
but again he puts himself into the Marseille road, saying, " We
" learn from Strabo, that from the Durance to the Isère
" is 700 stadia."

The Durance at Cavaillon can prove nothing, being in a
very different latitude from the confluence with the Rhone. As
it has no application to the subject, it would have been better
to try to make out by some means the real distance of
Tarascon from the Island. Perhaps Dr. Ukert thought that
he had done so : for he does to a certain extent bring forward
the very road given by the Itinerary along the Rhone ; but,
unhappily, he just omits those parts which would have saved
him from a dangerous conclusion.

His object being to shew that Polybius might intend
Tarascon, as on the Rhone 600 stadia below the Island, he

refs to Itinerary (p. 553, Wesseling), and sets forth from
it a length of 600 up the Rhone thus (p. 590). *

Bellintum	
Avenio	V.
Cypresseta . . .	V.
Aransio	XV.
Ad Lectore . . .	XIII.
Novem Craris . .	X.
Aeunum	XV.
Batiana	XII.

75 m. p. = 600 Stadien.

Now Dr. Ukert knew Tarascon to be lower down than
Bellintum : and he knew the Island to be higher up than
Batiana.   His own map which follows his Dissertation places
Tarascon below Bellintum ; and the Jerusalem Itinerary,
which he is transcribing, has, above Batiana, XII. to Umben-
num ; and VIIII. to Valentia. He omits these 21 m. p. = 168
stadia, and 40 more which are from Valentia to the Isère :
also having first omitted the length, whatever it is, from
Tarascon to Bellintum.   The enumeration of these 600 stadia
is delusive, quite unmeaning.   Dr. Ukert would see that the
true distance from Tarascon to the Island was not the
distance which he was trying to insinuate, but rather about
860 stadia.   He might as well have reminded us of some
length of 600 along the Rhine or the Danube.

Not feeling that he succeeds in bringing the Island and
Tarascon nearer to one another than as nature and art have
placed them, Dr. Ukert resorts to the opinion, that the four
days' march did not bring the Carthaginian army to the
Island at all : and that, though Hannibal got there, the army

---

* This is an exact copy of the Jerus. Itin. except that Wesseling
writes Vancianis for Batiana : the figures are the same.

did not. This is his argument, p. 590 :—" The historian does
" not assert that Hannibal came to the Island with his army;
" this might remain more south : somewhere in the country
" of the Drome. And perhaps he settled the contest of the
" brothers, either by his appearance and the effect which the
" vicinity of his experienced bands gave to his words ; or a
" detached division supported the elder one."

The doubts here suggested must be solved by the context
of the history. Things are sometimes to be understood as
said of the general alone ; as, that he listened to the proposals
of one of the contending parties. But see what things are
alleged here. Having put the whole armament in motion,
the historian relates that Hannibal, by a four days' march,
came to the Island : he tells of operations carried on by him
in the Island; that he found in it two brothers at open war
for the sovereignty ; that he supported one, and attacked and
defeated the other : and, further, that after receiving supplies
from the chief whom he had befriended, his whole force being
refitted with necessaries, he advanced to the Alps attended
by his ally. The movements so told must be applied to
Hannibal with the force under his command. The words ἧκε
and ἀφικόμενος, as well as συνεπιθέμενος and συνεκβαλὼν,
must be understood of Hannibal with his army, not of
Hannibal without his army; and, whatever road he afterwards took to the Alps, the four days' march had been a
march to the Island.

I hope it has been shown that the διάβασις of Dr. Ukert
is too near to the sea, and too far from the Island. In both
instances Polybius gives the idea of space through the mention of four days ; one is "nearly four days," and must be
taken as less than the average for that time : the advance to
the Isère was, by obvious motive, a rapid march, and would
cover the full space.

I have expended many words upon that which is but a

small part of our entire subject. My apology is this : adverse arguments are not to be neglected because ourselves think them feeble : the character of the adversary is to be considered : and Dr. Ukert is placed before me on so high an eminence by the eulogies of Dr. Thirlwall, that, whatever I may think of his reasonings, no pains can be superfluous that are applied to resist them. There are further arguments of Dr. Ukert, which have as yet met with no resistance.

On Roman Measurements in Gaul and Spain.

Polybius, in c. 39, enumerates six distances, beginning from the Pillars of Hercules. To Carthagena : to the Ebro : to Emporium : to the passage of the Rhone : to the beginning of Alps : to the plain of Italy. And after the statement of distance to the Rhone, we read these words—"for these " distances have now been carefully stepped, and marked at " every eight stadia, by the Romans."

Every commentator, with the exception of Dr. Ukert, seems satisfied with those words as they appear in the text; thereby assenting to the notion, that the Romans had, in the days of Polybius, placed mile-stones, or other marks of distance, both along the Spanish and French coasts, as far as the Rhone. Dr. Ukert, with due regard to history, disowns Polybius as a witness to Roman roads in Languedoc : but he solves the difficulty by rejecting the words as spurious. I believe them to be genuine, but to have got out of their place.*

Dr. Ukert finds several reasons for rejecting the proposition altogether ; having quoted the words, ταῦτα γὰρ νῦν, &c. ; he writes thus—" What! Polybius, having the distances mea-" sured and given by the Romans, and himself giving a ratio

---

* Henry Long applies ταῦτα to the French line of coast only ! —P. 16.

" between the stadium and the Roman mile, could he satisfy
" himself with employing about—περὶ 1600 st. — ? Our doubt
" is increased, when we see that the ratio stated is not that
" which Polybius follows : for he reckons a mile equivalent to
" 8⅓ stadia.   When Polybius travelled through the south of
" Gaul, no Roman roads had been made then : it was in the
" year 118 B.C. that the Romans first entered these countries
" as conquerors, and in the same year founded the colony of
" Narbo : they could hardly have constructed regular roads
" before this period.   Moreover, Polybius wrote his work
" earlier than that : he was writing it in the year 145
" B.C., and he died in the year 124 B.C.—the words in
" question are probably a note of some later writer,
" which has fallen into the text. The accounts confirm
" this view, in stating that Caius Gracchus was the first
" who had roads properly measured and marked out by mile-
" stones.   Probably the merit of constructing a road into
" Spain through Narbonese Gaul belongs to Fonteius, who,
" in Cicero's time, occupied it with an army.   Polybius too,
" in this passage, speaks of the measured road as reaching to
" Cadiz : an inscription, by Gruter, ascribes this addition to
" Augustus."

One fact here stated is incontrovertible.   Polybius died
before the Romans had begun the conquest of Gaul.   He
cannot, therefore, have spoken of Roman roads in that country.
This objection of Dr. Ukert claims, and will receive, an
answer. The rest of his comment I consider to be of no value.

The notion that Polybius estimated a mile at one-third of a
stadium more than other persons, has already been dealt with
in Part II. of this work.   Dr. Ukert adopted that opinion in
1832, when he engaged in the controversy on Hannibal's
march : he had declined to acquiesce in it, when he was
writing on Roman measurements in 1816.   And I hope to
show that, while his correction of chronology is accepted, he

is still at liberty to reject the notion of 8⅓ stadia to a Roman mile.

As to what Plutarch says upon Gracchus bringing the business of roads and mile-stones into a system, this does not help us to the date when military measuring and marking of distances was first practised by the Romans : and the suggestion that Fonteius first constructed a road through Narbonese Gaul, though quite unimportant, is a mistake. Dr. Ukert himself helps to disprove it, by referring to Cicero's defence of him against the charge of extortion. Fonteius was prosecuted, among other things, for conniving at the neglect of the roads : in fact, for taking bribes from the natives, from whom he ought to have exacted the repair of them. Cicero thus notices the charge—" Objectum est etiam, quæstum M. Fonteium ex viarum munitione fecisse : ut aut ne cogeret munire, aut id, quod munitum esset, ne improbaret." In urging the injustice of making Fonteius criminally responsible for the roads, he represents that the immediate duty devolved upon his legates, themselves eminent men, " cùm majoribus reipublica negotiis M. Fonteius impediretur." Cicero names the Via Domitia, which was made in that country fifty years before the delinquencies of Fonteius. The charge against that officer concerned the repair of roads, not the first construction of them.

Dr. Ukert at last deems the passage spurious, on the improbability that Polybius should speak of a road measured to Cadiz. He might have spoken of a road to that place : for it existed. But he does not mention it : he only states the distance from the Pillars to Carthagena : and from that city his measurements of the march begin.

On the main historical fact, concerning roads in Gaul, Dr. Ukert's position is unimpeachable. The chronology of Roman dominion shows conclusively that Polybius can never have spoken of their indications of distance between the Rhone

and the Pyrenees. Such things did not take place in time
for him to notice them, even in his latest days. It was not
till 122 B.C., two years after his death, that the Romans
founded their first colony without the Alps, but within the
Rhone, Aquæ Sextiæ. In the next year they had their
successes on the banks of the Rhone and Isère: and not till
118 B.C., as stated by Ukert, being six years after the death of
Polybius, was founded the first colony beyond the Rhone.
Even then it is probable that for some time their armaments
continued to proceed from Italy to Spain by sea.

But, while history contradicts the existence of a stepped
and marked road along the Celtic coast at the period in
question, it does not contradict the existence of such a road
along the Iberian coast. And it seems to me, that the proposition in parenthesis, ταῦτα γὰρ, &c., which is quite Polybian, is not spurious, but has been shifted from its proper
place in the catalogue of distances. It should be read after
the 1,600 stadia to Emporium, not after the 1,600 to the
Rhone. When Polybius made his journey, the Romans were
in military possession of the Iberian coast, and had been so
from the time of his birth. During that period their entrance
to Spain was by sea: Emporium, the terminus of the measurement we are speaking of, was their place of landing ; and
here began their military line along the Iberian coast. We
may well believe that this ὁδὸς was stepped, and its division
into miles indicated σεσημενωμένη, if not κατεστηλωμένη.
Their military way, when afterwards made through the
Pyrenees into Spain, did not go through Emporium : it went
direct from Juncaria to Gerunda. Emporium is not in the
Itinerary.

If my suggestion is accepted, the historical error is relieved :
it vanishes as completely on transposing the words as on
erasing them. The minor objection, also, of περὶ being
applied to an ascertained distance, is removed at the same

time. The Iberian distances are alleged without περί.   Περὶ
is only applied to the scope of march which includes the
Pyrenees, and to that which includes the Alps.   Let us then
read Polybius thus :—

From the Pillars to the New City, whence
    Hannibal commenced his expedition into
    Italy, it is . . . .   3,000 stadia.
And from this city to the river Ebro, it is . .   2,600   „
And from this river, again, to Emporium . .   1,600   „
    (For these distances have now been care-
    fully stepped, and marked at every 8
    stadia by the Romans.)
And on from thence to the passage of the
    Rhone, *about*   1,600   „
And from the passage of the Rhone, for those
    who travel along that river as if to the
    source as far as the ascent of Alps, which
    leads to Italy   1,400   „
And the rest of the way over the heights of
    Alps, *about*   1,200   „
    Surmounting which, he would arrive in
    the Padan Plain of Italy.

On the Roads of Gaul in Hannibal's time.

Although Dr. Ukert has rightly rejected the notion that
Polybius lived to see Roman roads in Languedoc, he seeks
the aid of Roman roads to support his interpretation of the
δίαβασις—he says this :—" Supposing the passage (ταῦτα
" γὰρ, &c.) to be an interpolation, still we may, with good
" reason, assume that the early roads in these countries had
" been in the same lines that were afterwards used by the
" Romans when they formed their roads.   The nature of the
" country itself would require them to pursue nearly the same
" track along the plain region between the coast and the line

" of mountains: we find that here in later times there were
" Roman roads, and these in all probability led to the Rhone
" at that part where, according to the means then in use, a
" passage would be most easily effected. Polybius speaks of
" such a place ; but not of any town in the neighbourhood—
" which Strabo does in his description of this road.
" Nemausus (he says) lies on the road from Iberia to Italy,
" being 100 stadia from the Rhone and Tarasco."

It is true that the confined nature of the country between
the coast and the lines of mountains prescribed the route
from the Pyrenees as far as Nîmes. But from thence to the
Rhone there is no confinement : a north-east course, a straight
onward course, and a south-east course were equally open to
the invaders ; nature offers no obstruction to a march for
Avignon or Montfaucon, which lies over undulating plains.

Strabo tells us that the country near the Rhone is usefully
practicable. While he commends the depth of the river for
navigation, he says that the difficulty of ascending it is so
great, from the rapidity of the current, that merchants avoid
it, and transport their goods in waggons, the country being
level, towards the Arverni and the Loire, notwithstanding the
vicinity of the Rhone. iv. 189.

We know not that, so early as the time of Hannibal, a
route from Nîmes was established in any direction for crossing
the Rhone. He would make his election according to the
further parts to which he was tending. The state of things
two centuries later gives no criterion. When after the death
of Polybius, the two sides of the river, instead of belonging
to smaller separate states, came under one dominion, intercourse was promoted for Italian objects, and new tracks over
the Rhone would be established for travellers. But if Roman
usage could have borne upon our question, Arles would claim
the preference ; for it was in the great military way to Spain,
whether from the north or south of Italy : that way crossed

the Rhone at Arles, not at Tarascon. Strabo speaks of
Arles as πόλις καὶ ἐμπόριον οὐ μικρόν. The virtues of the
Tarascon road from Nîmes are also alluded to: passable in
summer, but deep in mud and flooded in spring and winter:
θέρους μὲν εὔβατον οὖσαν, χειμῶνος δὲ καὶ ἔαρος πηλώδη
καὶ ποταμόκλυστον. ii. 187. At a later period it came to be
improved. M. Astruc relates (Hist. Nat. de Languedoc,
p. 225) that milliary columns, of the age of Tiberius, have
been found between Nîmes and Beaucaire: a fact which
D'Anville tells with much satisfaction; adding that the space
between two of them, as they were found, was just 754
toises. "Notice de Gaule." Nemausus.

But all this has no bearing on the particulars or induce-
ments of Hannibal. If you imagine, for the period of the
Carthaginian march, the improvement in a Tarascon road
which the Romans gave it two or three centuries later,
Hannibal would not have availed himself of it for effecting
his march to the Island. The notion of crossing the Rhone
below the influx of the Durance, is only suitable to a theory
of going on direct to the Mont Genèvre. But Dr. Ukert does
not so construe Polybius. Why then does he struggle for a
passage at Tarascon? Because he intends his four days'
march to halt short of the Isère. Therefore it suits him to
find arguments for crossing the Rhone below the junction of
the Durance: a scheme favoured by no intrinsic probability,
but in favour of which he has provided other arguments
equally untenable.

On the Policy of Hannibal.   The Durance.

Dr. Ukert says, p. 583 :—" If it is objected to our doctrine,
" that Hannibal would have crossed too near to the coast and
" thereby to the Romans, this objection will be removed, if
" we consider that he did not expect the enemy here, as little
" indeed as the latter expected him. The difficulty which

" attended the passage of the Durance would also be as little
" thought of then as in later times, when the principal Roman
" Road was carried over the Rhone south of that river. People
" from Nemausus came either to Ugernum, or more south to
" Arelate : the road to the latter place then branched into two ;
" one went south-east to Aquæ Sextiæ, the other north-east
" over the Druentia. Hannibal came upon the dry season,
" before the river had been swollen with rain." I certainly
do make the anticipated objections, and I consider that Dr.
Ukert is mistaken in all the points which he here makes : the
expectation of resistance, the Durance, and the security against
floods.

Hannibal must have calculated upon opposition by the
Roman force : and that alone was a strong reason for him to
seek a passage above the influx of the Durance : his plan was
framed upon a study of all things necessary to be observed,
and was executed according to the purpose in which it was
framed. The risk of opposition by a Roman army must
always have dissuaded from crossing the Rhone too near the
sea. What pretence is there for saying, that the arrival of
the Roman army was unexpected ? A wise commander will
deem his enemy capable of wisdom. The question of Scipio's
approach must have been a subject of intense anxiety on the
part of Hannibal ; and he had far less reason to be surprised
by his arrival, than by his not having arrived sooner. In the
history of this war, there is nothing more remarkable than
the casualties which required Scipio's army to be retained in
Italy, and new levies to be made for his expedition to oppose
Hannibal. When the invaders were making their way from
the Pyrenees to the Rhone, Hannibal was not so well aware
of these favouring circumstances as we are now. The Rhone
was a great line of advantage for withstanding the effort of
invasion, and the Romans were just too late to avail themselves of it. If we believe that Hannibal might have been

repulsed in attempting the passage of the Rhone in face of a
Roman army, we must see the highest wisdom in his evading
so dangerous a contingency.

The avoiding of the additional passage of the Durance was
incident to Hannibal's decision on the place of crossing. Dr.
Ukert despises that difficulty : and, because in after-times the
Romans, masters of the country, carried one of their great
Ways across the Durance, he does not perceive that Hannibal,
in a strange country, and an enemy at hand to resist him,
could see any additional obstacle in that great river. But
presently this critic contradicts himself with a different argument : he proves the importance of the Durance, by contending that, if the Romans had to cross it, which they must if
Hannibal did not, the fact would have found place in the
history.   He says, p. 584 :—" If we do not allow Hannibal to
" have crossed it, the Roman consul with his army must have
" crossed it, and the detachment of cavalry twice : which
" would certainly have been mentioned by the historians."
It would be fitter to say that if, as Dr. Ukert imputes, Hanno
in his march down, and Hannibal in his march up, had been
required to pass the Durance, these are things which would
have been mentioned by the historian. Such impediments
are left by Polybius without description, when no incident of
interest has belonged to the surmounting of them. The
country was unfriendly to the Carthaginians, and they would
have had to force the Durance against resistance. This would
have called for the notice of history far more than the un-
opposed passage of that river by the Romans, when Hannibal
was in full retreat.

Dr. Ukert further requires us to believe that, at the end of
September or beginning of October, the Durance is so dry that
it could offer no impediment to military movements   It may
be that this season is not commonly considered as the season
of floods. But that Alpine river may be swollen by rains and

melted snow any day in the year. To shun it at any season was
prudence, even in September and October. In October, 1841,
when bridges were seriously damaged at Vienne and Grenoble,
the inundations at Tarascon were such that the communications were in danger of being cut off, and a regiment of
chasseurs were obliged to move to Nîmes. About the same
time the passengers by diligence between Avignon and Sorgues
were with difficulty rescued by boats, some having mounted
the roof, others clinging to the backs of the horses who were
swimming for their lives. The valley of the lower Rhone was
probably not better drained in 218 B.C. than it is now : and I
know, from a friend travelling in 1840, that the water standing in the road from Marseilles to Lyons was very inconvenient
to his boots as he sat in the diligence.

In October, 1842, the Courier de Grenoble reported that
houses had fallen at Vienne ; that the bridge of the Gabatières
had been again carried away by the floods ; that the Route de
Beaurepaire and the Route Royale had been rendered impassable, and the bridge of chains carried away : that an inn
near the bridge had fallen, burying an ostler in the ruins.
The report from Tarascon was that the Rhone had so inun-
dated the country that all communication was cut off. Who
knows but that the Alpine Durance, tum forte imbribus auctus,
had its share in these casualties, notwithstanding the eulogies
on its dry season pronounced by Mr. H. Long and Dr. Ukert ?
In the inundations of 1846, when the overflowings of the
Loire and the Var were so calamitous, the sudden rise of the
Durance arrested the construction of a railway viaduct ; and
the same cause might in 218 B.C. have disturbed the progress
of an army. On the 12th September, 1860, the *Times* corre-
spondent at Paris reported a letter from Remusat, in the
Drôme, saying that a waterspout, accompanied with terrific
thunder and torrents of rain, so suddenly increased the waters
in the rivers, that a new bridge over the Aigues was swept

away. Another at Vaucluse suffered the same fate, and a
vast amount of property was destroyed.

Dr. Ukert having given his argument on the motives of
Hannibal, founds another on the motives of Scipio. He
says, p. 584 :—" The Romans, from the known unfriendly
" feeling of the people of Gaul, would hardly have ventured
" so far into the country : whereas on the other hand the
" more southerly of these might be friendly through the
" mediation of the people of Marseille." Surely our question
is, not whether the Romans would desire to venture so far as
the Carthaginian entrenchments ; but whether they did venture so far under a necessity to do so. We have to discuss
the probable motives of Hannibal, not those by which Scipio
would have determined the place of his enemy's crossing, if
he could have prescribed it. He no doubt would have
preferred a point nearer to his ships and to Marseille : the
Massiliots were warm allies, and had some Celtic horse in
their pay. But these very things bring us again to a conclusion which is not that of Dr. Ukert ; namely, that the alliance
between Rome and those who dwelt nearer to the mouth of
the Rhone, would from the first disincline Hannibal from that
neighbourhood and the region south of Durance, and add one
to his many motives to seek a higher crossing.

On the Vessels used in the Passage.

Dr. Ukert offers us this further argument against Montfaucon and Roquemaure. " We ought to remember that
" Hannibal, in order to transport his troops, depended upon
" ships which could also serve upon the sea, like those which
" Cæsar at a later time caused to be built at Arles ; and the
" question is, whether these could be used higher up the
" stream. On the other hand, the spot where we suppose
" Hannibal to have crossed, is even now one of the most
" frequented ; two bridges of boats lead over the Rhone there,
" and it is a place of considerable traffic." (p. 582.)

I know not how Dr. Ukert has discovered that the λέμβος
of Hannibal, and the navis longa of Cæsar, were built on the
same model.   Is the resemblance in bulk, or outline, or construction?   And why should either one or the other have
been capable of swimming at Tarascon and not capable at
Montfaucon?   Cæsar's ships were never put to either of those
tests : they were built at Arles, and went at once to the sea—
" Naves longas Arelate numero XII. facere instituit.   Quibus
" effectis armatisque diebus XXX. à qua die materia cæsa est,
" adductisque Massiliam, his D. Brutum præfecit."*   These
ships had no occasion and no opportunity to explore the river
above the dockyard in which they were built.   They were
very soon engaged against the Massilian fleet, and, though
successful, were less efficient, from being built in a hurry and
of unseasoned timber (factæ subito ex humidâ materiâ).   They
certainly never found themselves in the reach above Roquemaure, but neither were they ever off Tarascon.

The vessels which took over the cavalry soldiers of Hannibal,
are called by Polybius λεμβοι : a term applicable to any kind
of transport vessel, and to river barges ; as, when Latinized,
—qui adverso vix flumine lembum Remigio subigit.   The
facts alleged of them are, that they were in great numbers ;
that they were much larger and heavier than the single-timber
barks used by the light infantry ; that the horses swam after
them, one man holding three or four from either side of the
poop ; and that they were employed for towing the rafts which
bore the elephants across the river.   All these purposes seem
appropriate to a river barge or small coasting vessel, more
than to the Roman war-ship.

The difficulties of the Rhone that affect the sufficiency of
water for navigation, are not at the towns here mentioned ;
they offer themselves near the mouth ; there it is that shallows
and shifting mud-banks are recorded as a nuisance.   Marius

* Comment. de Bello Civili, i. c. 34.

made the canal to avoid these impediments of entrance; and
the Massilians, to whom he presented this work, derived a
considerable revenue from the duties which they levied on
vessels thus entering and quitting the river. Str. iv. 183.
Cæsar's ships probably found their way to the sea by this
canal, which was cut from the eastern channel of the Rhone,
a little below Arles. M. Gosselin, in opposition to D'Anville,
and professing to interpret Ptolemy on the site of Fossæ
Marianæ, places the canal west of Aigues-mortes —Géog. de
Strabon. ii. p. 21, n. 1. This notion is contradicted by all
probability, and by the Itinerary, in which Fossæ Marianæ
occurs between Marseille and Arles. The military object,
when the canal was made in the Cimbrian war, was communication with Marseille, whence supplies would come to the
army on the Rhone. If the canal had come into the sea west
of the river's channels, the exit, besides being less convenient
for Roman purposes, would have been exposed to the *atterrissemens* from the river which the currents carried westward.

The climax of the merits of Tarascon pourtrayed by Dr.
Ukert is, that there are now two bridges of boats which, I presume, means one from Beaucaire and one from Tarascon into the
island which is between them. He does not explain in what
way this fact affects the probabilities of the subject. It may
be that the river there has a deeper current than elsewhere,
but he does not reason upon it, or assert it.

Dr. Ukert on Scipio's March.

Scipio advanced up the country from near the mouth of the
Rhone to the place where Hannibal had crossed that river.
Accordingly, an estimate of the time in which he could reach
that place may help to an opinion on its distance from the
sea.

Dr. Ukert (p. 583) invites that question in words which, I
believe, are fairly translated thus—" That the distance of the

" point of crossing was not so high up the river as Mandajors
" and others have supposed, is evident from the account, that
" Scipio, who had his camp near the coast on the eastern arm
" of the Rhone, came to the camp which the Carthaginians
" had left, on the third day after their decampment. One
" may, according to Polybius and Livy, reckon the time
" double : but, even if calculated the longest, the return of the
" cavalry, the preparations of the consul, his decampment and
" march to the position, cannot have occupied more than five
" or five and a half days at the most."

The expression so translated, 'reckon the time double,'
appearing obscure, I sought an explanation of it in the
Philological Museum, where (ii. 679) Dr. Ukert's views are
thus exhibited by Dr. Thirlwall—" That the distance of the
" place, where Hannibal crossed, from the sea was not so
" great as has been supposed by De Luc, seems to follow
" from Scipio's march to the Carthaginian camp from the
" mouth of the river.   He reached it in three days, if,
" indeed, this is not the time spent both in going and re-
" turning to his ships, as the language both of Polybius and
" Livy might be construed."   I cannot find that either history
suggests such a meaning for three days.   Polybius only says
that Publius was at the place of crossing ἡμέραις ὕστερον
τρισὶ τῆς ἀναζυγῆς τῶν Καρχηδονίων.   Livy says that he came
to the encampment triduo fere post quam Hannibal ab ripâ
Rhodani movit.   Neither historian assigns a duration to
Scipio's march.

I had recourse to competent persons, and received different
constructions of the words Man kann die Zeit doppelt
berechnen.   None were satisfactory in terms : but the words
certainly seem to contain the idea of measuring the time from
Hannibal's camp, down to Scipio's camp, and back again : for
it was near to the former that the conflict of the cavalry took
place.   The drift of the criticism appears from the words that

follow : those words suggest a calculation of the time which
would intervene between the conflict of cavalry and the
arrival of Scipio at the deserted entrenchments : Dr. Ukert
asserts that the things done in that time, namely, the return
of the cavalry, the consul's preparations, his decampment and
march to the position, would at the most have occupied five
days, or five and a half; and, by this, he seems to insinuate
that, if the encampment had been as high up as Roquemaure,
those things must have occupied a longer time.

I cannot admit that they would. Scipio came to the position " in three days after the decampment of the Carthaginians :" those three days are exclusive of the day of that
decampment : and it seems to me that all the things which
Dr. Ukert enumerates as only requiring five days and a half,
which he thinks not enough for our theory, could not only be
done in that time he names, but in less time. Three or four
days after the ἀναζυγή, would have been ample for our
theory, and decidedly too much for the theory of Tarascon.

Let us suppose that the engagement of cavalry took place
on a Monday morning, and that Hannibal and his army were
en route the following day, Tuesday : Scipio might reach their
encampment in three days after they were en route, namely,
on the Friday. The news of the engagement, which took
place in the morning and was soon over, would reach the
consul in the course of the following day, Tuesday : and we
may believe that he marched the next morning, and, by three
days' march reached the position which the enemy had
abandoned. It is to be observed that the day of Hannibal's
departure was before those three days of Scipio, who arrived
ἡμέραις ὕστερον τρισὶ τῆς ἀναζυγῆς. Where was the difficulty ? Was not a day and a half ample for the intelligence
to travel ? In the morning, before Hannibal assembled his
troops to the conference with the Cisalpine chiefs, he had sent
out the five hundred Numidian horse to reconnoitre : they fell

in with the Roman detachment almost immediately; " not
" far from their own encampment." After a sharp encounter
the survivors came in again pursued by the enemy, and
arrived just as the assembly was broken up. They were in
their own quarters again early in the day. The residue of
this day, together with the next day, sufficed for the report of
these proceedings to be carried to the consul. The speed of
this intelligence is not to be measured by the speed of an
army's march : and, though the history says that the Roman
horse returned to their camp and reported to Scipio, we need
not suppose them all moving together, the best horses keeping
back for the worst. News travels according to the speed of
the swiftest, not the slowest; and the native horse, familiar
with the country, were acting in this detachment. Even if
Scipio, neglecting ordinary foresight, had not provided for the
transmission of intelligence, sixty miles was no impossible
distance, in a day and a half with the intervening night, for
the best horses to carry news to head-quarters on so momentous an occasion.

The intelligence found Scipio in a full state of readiness.
He had known Hannibal to be on the Rhone before ever
he sent the cavalry forward, and had consulted with the
tribunes where he might best bring the enemy to action ; he
could not tell which he might see first, his own cavalry
returning or the enemy. We cannot doubt that he was in
march the next morning ; and three days' march would
easily bring him to the site of the encampment, opposite to
Roquemaure.

If any should doubt that a Roman army could be moved
sixty or sixty-five miles in three days, I say that my argument does not require it. I am not bound to contend that
Scipio's army did march that whole distance. In the first
place, sixty-five miles is our distance from the sea, and
the camp may have been some miles above high water-mark.

Then it is not improbable that the force was beginning to move to the interior, while this detachment was away; and certainly it is not to be assumed that the entire force ever completed that march, and actually reached the scene of the deserted entrenchments. Polybius says, " The Roman general coming to the place and finding the enemy gone, was exceedingly astonished." At this time, the mass of his army may have halted short of that place. But the consul would desire to satisfy himself on the enemy's proceedings : intelligence of what happened would meet him on his advance; and he would hasten forward with a sufficient escort. We are told that, when he found the Carthaginians to have abandoned the position, and to be three days in advance of him, he determined at once to retrace his steps to his ships. In all probability the order to that effect was received and obeyed by the mass of the army, without their ever reaching the site of the encampment.

Now consider the events as applied to the Tarascon theory. If the passage and the encampment were near to that place, the Roman cavalry must have gained their success at a distance of about thirty-six, certainly not forty, miles from the sea, and less from their own camp. Suppose this to be on a Monday morning—is it to be believed that Scipio, all ready and eager for action, σπεύδων συμμίξαι τοῖς ὑπεναντίοις, with no Durance intervening, with a more unqualified favour from the natives for expediting his communications, could not find his way to the place so as to know that the enemy was gone, until the Friday ? He would have been there on the Wednesday.

My friends of the Oxford Dissertation relate, p. 45, that Hannibal put his infantry in march on the day after the conflict, and himself followed with the cavalry and elephants two days after the infantry marched up the river; and that the consul arrived three days after the departure of Han-

nibal. Polybius says, " after the decampment of the Car-
"thaginians," τῆς ἀναζυγῆς τῶν Καρχηδονίων : and, if Hannibal had stayed two days behind, which he did not, ἀναζυγή
was the breaking up of the force when the infantry marched :
τὴν τῶν πεζῶν ἐκίνει δύναμιν ἐκ τοῦ χάρακος εἰς πορείαν :
this was the ἀναζυγή of the Carthaginians : and Scipio,
coming to the place in three days after this, came four days
after the fight.

But Hannibal did not stay two days behind: Polybius says
nothing to authorise that notion. H. Long says justly, that
" there is no reason for assigning different days to the departure
" of one force and of the other." The narrative imports
unambiguously, that Hannibal moved forward with the cavalry
and elephants in the course of the same day on which he
had sent forward the infantry. And why not? He had
been engaged in providing for the transport of the elephants
(c. 42) during the absence of Hanno. He had selected men
for the execution of the work (c. 44) before the conference
with the Cisalpine chiefs. The preparations being complete,
why should he not bring them over the river the next
morning, and proceed with them the same day? There are
no words which import the contrary; none that indicate
a continued separation of the forces, or that he passed a
night near the place of passage after the infantry had moved.
The historian says, that Hannibal at daybreak drew out all
his cavalry towards the sea (*i. e.*, below the scene of operations), and put the infantry in motion, &c., and that he
waited himself for the elephants : he describes the process
of their transportation; and then tells us that, when they
had been brought over the river, Hannibal went forward,
bringing up the rear with them and the cavalry. A march
of four consecutive days brought them to the island.

CHAPTER IV.

Tarascon Theory. Arguments of H. L. Long. Distance from
the Sea. Distance from Emporium. The single Stream.
Strabo and the Theodosian Table.

MR. HENRY LONG, as well as Dr. Ukert, has endeavoured to
prove that Hannibal crossed the Rhone at Tarascon. But
they have hardly a point of agreement in common. Ukert,
assenting to the obvious construction, by which the 1,400
stadia, from the passage of the Rhone to the first Alps,
are divided into 600 and 800, struggles against the most
palpable facts, to reconcile his route with these proportions.
Long, by a new mode of construing the text, makes the
division to be 800 for the march to the Isère, and 600 for the
progress to the Alps. This novelty, with the general merits of
his scheme, will be most conveniently examined under our
second head of inquiry : at present I notice those arguments
which are applied directly to the place of crossing the Rhone.

On the distance from the Sea.

The question of measurement along the Rhone is dispensed
with in Long's commentary, pp. 22, 23, by an intimation that
the four days' journey or march from the sea, which Polybius
speaks of, does not import a distance from the sea at the
mouth of the Rhone, but from the sea which Hannibal had
left behind him at Narbo. The idea is new. Suppose that
my friend, having just come up from Southampton, was
dealing with white bait at Blackwall, and some one should
inquire the distance to the sea. Would he in his answer
compute a measurement to Southampton, or to the mouth of
the Thames ? I think he would reckon to the mouth of the
Thames, though he would be much farther from the sea there,
than if he were at Tarascon. In the matter now before us,

context as well as proximity, bespeaks the mouth of the
Rhone : in the same sentence where Hannibal is said to be
nearly four days from the sea, he is said to be employed in
effecting a passage of the Rhone ; and the historian speaks
of vessels used for descending that river to the sea. The
reason for notifying the distance from the sea, is to define the
latitude of Hannibal's position on the Rhone. Very different
words would have been used, if he had desired to give the
distance traversed from a past point of the march. Reading
forward, we find that, while the elephants are passing over
the Rhone, the cavalry is drawn out ὡς πρὸς θάλατταν. Is
this too the sea at Narbo ?

It is fair to say that Long announces this notion with great
diffidence. I quote it, because it is useful to show the arguments to which the ingenuity of a theorist can be driven.
If ever he shall renounce Narbo, a terminus which requires
110 miles to be accomplished by hardly four days' work,
I hope he will lean to our construction, which performs 65 in
that time, rather than to Dr. Ukert's, which reduces it to 35.
Bnt alas ! if my friend gives up Tarascon, what will become
of Grenoble!

On the distance from Emporium to the passage of the Rhone.

Polybius states this distance to be about 1,600 stadia = 200
miles : an amount which, upon fair examination, is found to
accord so nearly with both the rival crossings that it furnishes
no preference to either. From Emporium to Nîmes, a space
which is common to both these lines, it is agreed to reckon
177 miles : the Oxford Dissertation adds 30 for their continuation to Roquemaure ; making 207 m. = 1,656 stadia.
H. Long adds 15 for his continuation to Beaucaire, making
192 m. = 1,552 stadia. Need we discuss whether 1,552 or
1,656 best represents "about 1,600 ?"

Long relies on this, that his distance is below the amount named, not above it: and he insists, p. 20, that, when Polybius employs the word περί, adding it to a round number, he commonly exceeds the real distance. Now if a man intends to exceed the real distance, he must have means of apprehending what the real distance is. Polybius in expressing the distances of this march, has used περί twice ; and he does so because he could not know the real distances : once, when he includes the passage of the Pyrenees ; once, when he includes the passage of the Alps. He could not have ascertained or heard of any measured distance in these two instances. Where was he to find an estimate to aid him ? There was none ; and therefore he used περί. My friend is in the common error of supposing that Polybius spoke with knowledge of Roman measurements between Emporium and the Rhone. When they did establish a Way through France into Spain, it did not touch Emporium. It is true that Polybius applies περί for qualifying an exaggerated total; when he has enumerated many amounts, which added together would be 960, he will probably say, ὥστε εἶναι περὶ 1,000 : but where, as in the instance before us, περί is merely prefixed to an amount not alleged as the addition of others, it need only imply doubt, and the number expressed need not be excessive. It is vain to strive here for a few stadia more or less than 1,600. We cannot plant a flag-staff on the shore of the Rhone as the very terminus of that section of the march : and, if any man should propose Arles in preference to Roquemaure or Tarascon, we would controvert it on better grounds than the distance from Emporium.

The single Stream.

Though diffident of one discovery, Long rests confidently on another which he has made, for indicating the place of

passage, and which has escaped all other critics : it concerns
the words κατὰ τὴν ἁπλῆν ῥύσιν, " at *the* single stream." His
views are expressed thus :—"These words have been thought
" to mean a part of the stream uninterrupted by any of those
" islands with which the Rhone abounds: an explanation in
" which I cannot at all concur; for the words are most cer-
" tainly applied by Polybius to the passage at Beaucaire, in
" contradistinction to the passage at Arles: for at Arles the
" bifurcation of the Rhone begins : at Arles there are two
" streams, and the passage would have been κατὰ τὴν διπλὴν
" ῥύσιν. Polybius, speaking of the Po, employs the same
" expression—τὴν μὲν γὰρ πρώτην ἐκ τῶν πηγῶν ἔχει ῥύσιν
" ἁπλῆν, σχίζεται δ' εἰς δύο μέρη κατὰ τοὺς προσαγορευο-
" μένους τριγαβόλους, the river flows from its source in a
" single stream at first, but is divided into two branches in
" the country of the Trigaboli."—P. 18.

The illustration is expected to help us in assuming, that the
term ἁπλῆ ῥύσις not only negatived the double crossing at
Arles, but that it affirmed another place of crossing : so that
we may learn from it, both where Hannibal did not cross, and
where he did cross. A hasty inference under any state of
facts ! Here it is connected with the old blunder of supposing
that Polybius testifies to Roman roads in France. Long
stamps them as Roman ways, saying, p. 17 :—" The words of
" Polybius are decisive : he distinctly points out a road
" between Emporium and the Rhone, measured and marked
" by the Romans. No other Roman way leading from Nîmes
" to the Rhone exists, even in tradition : it follows therefore,
" that, either at Beaucaire or Arles, Hannibal must have
" effected his passage ; and we are at once relieved from all
" doubt as to which of the two places we are to choose, by
" the words of Polybius himself, κατὰ τὴν ἁπλῆν ῥύσιν."
The best excuse for Long's error on Roman ways is, that our
common friends of the Oxford Dissertation had themselves

been similarly oblivious: they tell us, p. 39 :—" Polybius
" observes that he is correct in his reckoning, because the
" Romans have carefully measured and marked it at every
" eight stadia. It is evident from this, that he wishes us to
" understand that the army marched along that track which
" was afterwards the great Roman road to Nîmes." It has
been shown that Polybius never heard of it himself.

This argument, however, on the single stream is intrinsically
void of effect. If Roman ways had been established while
Polybius lived, and at the very points desired, he would not
have sought to be understood through so blind a reference.
If he had trusted that his Greek countrymen whom he
addressed, or anybody else, would identify "single stream"
with one town, and "double stream" with another, while he
mentioned neither, he would ill deserve the character which
he enjoys, of imparting ideas through intelligible symbols.
No student, Greek, Roman, or Gaul, would have been wiser
by such instruction. Moreover, the instruction would not
have been true. It is true that about 600 years after the
invasion, Arles was celebrated for the duplicity of its river.
The double bridge is among the praises sung by the poet
Ausonius: and this renown of Arles perhaps excited the
argument, and seduced a lover of poetry into his contrast of
ἁπλῆ and διπλῆ. But the contrast is imagined against fact:
in this river of islands, other places, more or less favoured by
fame than Arles, can boast a duplicity of stream. Not only
the greater towns on the Lower Rhone, but Long's own emblem
of simplicity, Beaucaire itself, enjoys a double crossing, having
the same advantage by means of a small island, which Arles
has by the apex of a large one : and, when he proclaims " at
Arles there are two streams," he may add with equal truth,
" at Avignon there are two streams," and " at Tarascon there
are two streams :" κατὰ τὴν ἁπλῆν ῥύσιν, without more, dis-
proves a crossing at Tarascon.

On ancient Registers of Distance.

As Dr. Ukert declines to antedate the commencement of
the conquest of Gaul, there is not much comment in which he
and H. Long run together.   Indeed Strabo's fact, that in the
time of Augustus there was a way of getting over the Rhone
at Tarascon, supplies the only item in which there is sympathy
between them.   From this result of Roman conquest, both are
encouraged to conceive, that, two centuries earlier, a Carthaginian invader of Italy had taken that crossing : one critic
making it incident to the route of the Mont Cenis, the other
to the passage of the Little St. Bernard ; each with a view to
his own ulterior constructions.   But neither backs his case
with practical authority.   They bring forward no instances of
that crossing being used by armies : it is not suggested that
the colonisers of Narbo crossed at Tarascon; nor the troops
of Fabius, or of Marius, or Pompey, or Cæsar.   Illustration is
wanting.

The Itineraries have been searched in vain ; both that
which bears the name of Antoninus, and the later one of
Jerusalem : unhappily, neither furnishes the wished-for track.
The Via Aurelia proceeds by the Maritime Alps to the Rhone
at Arles : the Iter in Hispanias proceeds by the Cottian Alps
to the Rhone at Arles : nor Ugernum nor Tarasco exist in
these registers.   Long at last brings forth a witness not
adverted to by the other patron of this passage : he appeals
to the Theodosian Table, a geographical portrait of unknown
manufacture, but considered to represent a state of things 600
years after Hannibal.   The artist certainly might have known
that there was some crossing at Tarascon : and, if he had
exhibited it, we should take the fact for what it is worth : he
may have known more than he draws : but we are asked to
reason from what he does draw.

In page 17 of Long's march of Hannibal, he rejoices in

two roads leading from Nismes to the Rhone. He says, " they are really Roman, as well as being still in use as " important thoroughfares. Of these, one runs in a direction " due east from Nismes to Beaucaire, the ancient Ugernum ; " the other takes a south-easterly course to the celebrated " city of Arles, formerly the more celebrated Arelate. The " road to Arles seems to have been the most frequented " of the two, and appears in all the Itineraries ; that to " Beaucaire is given in the Theodosian Table, and is noticed " by Strabo." Unhappily, in this Theodosian Table we look in vain for " two roads leading from Nismes to the Rhone." We know that Beaucaire is on the Rhone : but perhaps the Theodosian artist did not : his Ugernum is not on the Rhone : the portrait which is appealed to, gives only one road, which seems to reach the Rhone at Arles ; and Ugernum is exhibited as a half-way house between that place and Nîmes. Whatever be the pretensions of Beaucaire and Tarascon to have given passage to Hannibal, my friend must not rest them on the delineations of the Pentingerian Chart—animum picturâ pascit inani.

Tabula Peutingeriana.

Carte de Peutinger, or, Table Theodosienne.

This old document, just referred to, will be mentioned again, so I take the opportunity of giving some account of it.

These tables are supposed to have been made A.D. 393, at Constantinople, by order of the Emperor Theodosius, and to have accompanied him when he crossed the Alps to oppose Eugenius, and when he came after his successes to Milan. On the decay of the Empire, they fell with other spoils into the hands of barbarians, and were carried into Germany : they are supposed to be alluded to by Jornandes, Bishop of Ravenna, who flourished about A.D. 552.

Their known history is this,—In 1459 Conrad Celtes was employed by the Emperor Maximilian to travel in search of ancient manuscripts and curiosities ; he found this document in a library at Spiers : instead of carrying it to his patron, he gave it to his friend Conrad Peutinger of Augsburg, and confirmed the gift by his will. Peutinger always intended to have these tables engraved and published ; but he died in 1547, not having carried his intention into effect. He had a small portion of them copied ; and the copy was discovered in 1587 by Marc Velser, a friend of the Peutinger family, who published it at Venice in 1591 : in about seven years after that, Velser succeeded in finding the original parchments ; and he had them engraved in copper-plate on a reduced scale, and published at Antwerp. Towards the end of the seventeenth century and the early part of the eighteenth, there were fresh editions by different persons ; but all derived from that of Velser, without any fresh inspection of the original document; the last being that of Nicholas Bergier in 1736.

In the meantime the Tables themselves were beginning to move from their obscurity ; about 1714 Wolfgang Sulzer, probing into the dusty recesses of the Peutinger library, discovered them, and suggested to one Küz, a bookseller of Augsburg, that he might endeavour to purchase them. The Peutinger who then owned them, allowed Küz to have them at no extravagant price ; and, on the death of Küz, his family were willing to sell this curious relic, which many persons of distinction were desirous to possess. Prince Eugene became the purchaser in 1720 ; and in 1738 it went, with other literary treasures that had belonged to that celebrated man, into the imperial library of Charles the Sixth, and it is at Vienna at this day. In 1741 it underwent a scientific reparation : accurate engravings were made by Solomon Kleiner, of the size of the original Tables, and published in 1753 by Francis Christopher de Scheyb.

THE ALPS OF HANNIBAL.

PART IV.

POLYBIUS INTERPRETED. THE BEGINNING OF ALPS.

CHAPTER I.

The march of 1,400 stadia may be taken in two parts: 1. to the Isère, 2. to the beginning of Alps. Hannibal, crossing the Isère, went forward. Most critics make him recross the Isère, and then seek the Alps. Five incidents mark the progress to the Alps: ten days; 800 stadia; along the river; country for cavalry; country of the Allobroges.

In discussing the first litigated terminus, the place of crossing the Rhone, we have gained a knowledge of the march, for 600 stadia beyond that point; namely, to the Isère: we now have to delineate the remaining 800, for completing the 1,400 of Polybius.

Here the combatant critics are of two sorts: those who continue the march north of Isère, and those who turn to pursue it south of Isère. None leave that river quite untouched, save the accola of the Eygues, who finally parts from the Rhone soon after he has crossed it. We propose to cross the Isère with the whole armament, and to proceed on our march to the Alps. Some carry the whole force over, but bring it back again: and our most laborious opponents, the Cenisians, make a reluctant admission, that some operations may have been at first conducted on the other side of the river.

Little need be said for identifying the Island. Some indeed have invented islands for their particular theories. Mr. Whitaker's Island is the town of Lyons, enclosed by its hills and two rivers. Others have insulated a space with the Rhone, the Isère, the Drac, and the Drome: and M. Fortia d'Urban found the Island near his own farm on the Eygues. Those, however, whose speculations deserve serious notice, commonly accept the region enclosed by the Rhone, the Isère, and their connecting chain of mountains, as the Island of the Polybian history.

Some who have pretended that the army did not cross the Isère, have relied on this—that Polybius does not relate the operation. That argument favours no theory. Every scheme of march requires river-crossings not mentioned in the narrative. The more recent commentators make Hannibal to recross the Isère, bringing the auxiliary force with them: and then send the whole expedition over the Drac, which they paint as most formidable. As they cannot pretend that Polybius has told them these things, it is idle to rest on his silence about rivers. From the Ebro to the Po the only river whose passage is described or asserted is the Rhone.

Hannibal's passage of the Isère, however, is not left to conjecture. It is necessarily implied in the operations told: it appears in the words καταλαβὼν ἐν αὐτῇ· συνεκβαλών. If a man has kicked another out of a house, we are apt to believe, that for the operation both were in the house. And, if it were suggested that he only kicked him out by persuasion, such a word as συνεπιθέμενος would give the idea of personal conflict, requiring the presence of the agent as well as the patient. The details prove movements beyond the Isère: and the crossing of it is a known fact, without being separately alleged.

It is because that river was crossed, and because the region beyond it became important as the scene of events, that this region, the Island, is the object of particular description by the historian, as to its character, size, and boundaries: while not a word is bestowed upon the country on the left bank, which so many writers hold up as the course of the march. M. De Luc rightly commends the judgment of Polybius in his designation of the boundaries of the Island, and the assimilation of it to the Delta, a place which his public employments had brought him acquainted with. He says :—
" Je ne crois pas que l'on puisse trouver nulle autre part en
" Europe, un pays dans une situation semblable à celle de
" cette contrée qu'on appeloit l'Isle. Il y a bien des rivières
" qui se rencontrent ; mais où sera la chaine des montagnes
" qui, en s'étendant d' une rivière à l'autre comme une
" haute muraille, enfermera un pays de manière à l'isoler
" complètement." Dr. Ukert, indeed, refers to the same expressions ὄρη δυσπρόσοδα, καὶ δυσέμβολα, καὶ σχεδὸν, ὡς εἰπεῖν, ἀπρόσιτα, for a proof that Polybius did not conceive Hannibal to have marched through the mountains which bound the Island: and Dr. Thirlwall has inadvertently called that remark sagacious. Sagacity, if any there were, would belong to M. Larauza, who had ventured upon it before. I see far better sense in the Oxford Dissertation, where the description is spoken of as agreeing admirably with the lofty barrier that extends from Grenoble to the Rhone, and where the term σχεδὸν, ὡς εἰπεῖν, ἀπρόσιτα, is said to point evidently to a passage through it. That which is really ἀπρόσιτον would not be called σχεδὸν, ὡς εἰπεῖν, ἀπρόσιτον. Niebuhr, recording the irruption of the Gauls, calls the Alps, "the seemingly impassable mountain barrier of Italy." *

* Translation by Hare and Thirlwall.   3d edit. ii. p. 511.

Seeing that Hannibal crossed the Isère and entered the
island, we pursue our subject by inquiring how he got out of
it. We read that he aided a prince of that country in re-
pressing a revolt of his subjects, and that he received from
him substantial proofs of gratitude. The progress to the first
Alps is told as follows (c. 49, 50) :—" But the chief thing was
" this: as they were in a state of much apprehension about
" their progress through the country of the Gauls called Allo-
" broges, he covered their rear with his own forces, and so
" gave security to their march until they got near to the
" passage of the Alps. Hannibal, having in ten days per-
" formed a march of 800 stadia along the river, began the
" ascent to the Alps ; and it came to pass that he fell into the
" greatest dangers. As long as they were in the plain country,
" all the detached chieftains of the Allobroges held off from
" them, partly in fear of the cavalry, partly of the barbarians
" who escorted them. But, when the latter had turned back
" homewards, and Hannibal's troops were beginning to ad-
" vance into the difficult places, then the leaders of the
" Allobroges, collecting themselves together in sufficient force,
" pre-occupied the advantageous posts, by which it was neces-
" sary that Hannibal's forces should make their ascent."

These few words exhibit five things as necessary incidents
to this very interesting part of the controverted track—1. The
progress was performed in ten days. 2. It was a progress of
800 stadia. 3. It was along the river. 4. It was, so far as
the ally accompanied the army, over a country where cavalry
could act. 5. It was through the country of the Allobroges.
By these five tests I propose to try all the routes which have
been offered to us from near the confluence of the rivers to the
beginning of Alps. Any which does not fairly embrace these
incidents cannot pretend to be that which Polybius has
described.

There are three routes by which the march has been supposed to proceed onward from the Isère ; that is to say, to quit the island without recrossing that river. One of these is our own way by the Mont du Chat. Another is that which, following the Rhone to Geneva, and along and beyond the lake, finds the first Alps at Martigny.* Another is that which keeps the right bank of Isère, through Grenoble to La Buissière, under the heights of Fort Barraux. The routes which are traced to the Alps by proceeding southwards from the Isère are numerous.

CHAPTER II.

The Mont du Chat fulfils all the requisites of Polybius.

In our march to that which we deem the ἀναβολή of the history, we satisfy the text in all respects. The line of progress which we maintain attends the Rhone to Vienne. There, leaving the river, it finds it again at St. Genix, and, having attended its course for a time, encounters the first Alps in the Mont du Chat, at the northern part of the mountain barrier which ranges from the Isère to the Rhone, commonly called the chain of the Grand Chartreuse. There, we say, begin the Alps of the history.

While I support my own views, it will be convenient sometimes to contrast them with the doctrines by which the pretensions of other tracks are exposed. But I shall give, in addition, some separate notice of each adverse track ; two of which proceed north of Isère, and the rest south of Isère, till they severally reach the Alps.

* A further progress up the Rhone has been suggested : but I do not propose any separate discussion of it.

1. *The Ten Days.*

The time and space belonging to the progress now spoken of, are to be reckoned from the expiration of the time and space which belonged to ·the previous progress, from the passage of the Rhone to the Island. That progress was accomplished by four days' marching : and our ten days will run from the end of those four days, as our 800 stadia will be in continuation of the 600 which must have been covered in those four days. There is little dissent on this point. Our weightier opponents date their further time and space from near the confluence of the rivers.

No part of these ten days can have been employed in free and easy progress. The march was in some degree embarrassed by an enemy hovering in front, instead of being urged by the apprehension of one in pursuit. But had all been in so practicable a country as the plain of Dauphiné, a continuous march of 100 miles would not occupy ten days. But it had been retarded by the operations in the Island : not only by interference with the hostilities, but by the collecting and distributing of the supplies ; for which purpose we must suppose a halt at Vienne, the probable head-quarters of the ally. There was also the crossing of the Isère by the Carthaginian armament : and, although this must have been facilitated by friends instead of being obstructed by enemies, we may take it into the account of time. Accordingly, though a given progress was made in the ten days, it is unlikely that each could be a day of progression. We shall find hereafter, that of the fifteen days in which the Alps were traversed, some were not days of progress. In this march to the beginning of Alps, there is one who must be displeased with the slowness of our advance, Mr. H. L. Long, who, in his own allotment of ten days, reckons six of them as halting days.

2. *The 800 stadia.*

The ten days were in continuation of the four days to the Island. In those four days an advance was made of 600 stadia to the Isère : and to reach the ἀναβολὴ Ἄλπεων is now the object of the remaining 800, being the terminus of the 1,400 announced by the history.

General Melville, like Mr. Hampton, had made the track to quit the Rhone at St. Rambert, a place below Vienne, and to cross the country to les Echelles, not touching the Rhone again.* M. De Luc made the important correction here, in showing that the line of march, though it would avoid the great elbows made by the Rhone to Lyons and St. Sorlin, would come upon the river again at St. Genix d'Aoste, and proceed near it towards the foot of the Mont du Chat. This beginning of Alps is near to Chevelu, a village which is in front of the Chat, and which corresponds in site with the Lavisco of the Itinerary, a place appearing as being half way from Augustum, St. Genix d'Aoste, to Lemincum, Chambéry ; 14 miles from each.

The length of this scope of march from the Isère to the foot of the Chat, is such as fairly to satisfy the 800 stadia = 100 miles of Polybius. The Itinerary of Antoninus, Wesseling, pp. 346, 358, gives the distances from Valentia to Ursolis, Vienna, Bergusia, Augustum, Labiscone, 98 miles : but this includes the 5 miles from Valencia to the Isère, which, being deducted, we have 93 miles. M. De Luc, however, measuring from Port de L'Isère to Yeune exhibited the actual distance, showing it to amount to 73,550 toises = $97\frac{1}{4}$ Roman miles. But Yenne should be avoided in moving to Chevelu : to get to Yenne, you put yourself without any necessity within a range of hills, only to come out again, and go forward to Chevelu ; a point on which

* De Luc. 2d edit. p. 84.

De Luc was corrected by the Oxford Dissertation. As to distance, Yenne appears to be but twelve miles beyond Augustum, which is two less than to Chevelu : and I have seen myself, in an excursion from Aix, that the ἀναβολή may fairly be taken as nearer to the Col, than where the village of Chevelu stands. It is quite just to say, that the ascent to Col du Chat well fulfils the 800 stadia of Polybius.

This route, from its superior facility, became afterwards a regularly constructed road of the Roman empire, the only one through this chain of‑mountains. Its perfection as a posting road at this day, of course proves nothing for our subject : indeed, there has been of late another equally good, by Les Echelles through the tunnel to Chambéry. Between the Chat and that route there are two mountain passes used by the natives : but they are mere mule tracks ; and neither of them has the Col so depressed as that of the Chat : one goes over that part of the range which is called the Mont de l'Épine : the other more south by the village of Aiguebellette.

D'Anville has conjectured that Novalèse is the Labisco of the Itinerary : a place by which one, who has come from the west across the Guiers, may proceed over the Mont de l'Épine to Chambéry. This is not said by him in relation to Hannibal's track : nor is he contesting the pretensions of any other place to represent Lavisco : he had probably never heard that any part of the range of the Grande Chartreuse affected to have given passage to Hannibal. He is dealing with the word Labisco in his " Notice de l'ancienne Gaule : " and the ground of his conjecture is, that he perceives a similarity between that word and the word Laisse : so he points out the village of Novalèse, which is a few miles from St. Genix d'Aoste in the direction of the Mont de l'Épine ; and says that a small stream, called, La petite Laisse, runs from

thence into the Guiers. I see in Raymond's map the river
Laisse, on the other side of the mountains, running from
Chambéry into the lac de Bourget. But, supposing that
there is a petite Laisse, such as D'Anville speaks of, the
resemblance of words will not identify it with Lavisco, in the
Roman road ; especially when, for supporting his notion, he
has to alter the figures of the Itinerary. He admits that
a road from Aoste to Chambéry by Novalèse and the Mont
de l'Épine would not exceed 17 or 18 Roman miles, en droite
ligne : the Itinerary gives 28 : so he reduces it by altering
the XIIII of the first half into VIIII. He does not notice
the possibility of any other track through those mountains,
but says " il faut franchir le Mont de l'Épine," and does his
best to manage the word Lavisco. His thoughts never strayed
to that region in the view of understanding Polybius. We
are now so employed, and in considering the most probable
track through the Grande Chartreuse chain, are brought to
the opinion, that the Polybian incident, distance, accords best
with Chevelu and the Mont du Chat.

3. *Along the River*—παρὰ τὸν ποταμόν.

All who have written on this portion of the march, excepting De Luc and the authors of the Oxford Dissertation, have
declined to acknowledge, in the words of Polybius, c. 50,
παρὰ τὸν ποταμόν, the meaning which I assert as plainly
belonging to them—' along the Rhone.'

We contend that, by grammatical reference and the ordinary use of language, the river Rhone, and no other, must be
intended : and that for the ten days, as for the prior four days,
the same words must have the same meaning. This also is
necessary, for accordance with the primary description of the
march in c. 39, where the section of ' 1,400 stadia from the
passage of the Rhone to the Alps' is said to be παρ' αὐτὸν

τὸν ποταμόν. Nevertheless the advocates of rival theories
rely on the word παρὰ, as excluding our march to the Mont
du Chat from all claim to favour; they say that our course is
not along the river Rhone, because it bears away from it at
Vienne, and rejoins it at St. Genix; and that therefore some
other river must have been intended.

I admit that, if the historian was studying to pourtray a
march keeping always 'at the river-side' or 'along the very
'banks,' as our adversaries express it, he cannot have conceived
the line of march which we attribute to him. But, if he meant
a march proceeding up the valley of a river to a mountain
pass which rises in the vicinity of the river, then the march
which we give from the passage of it to the Alps, is along
the river : and those who will note the distinction between a
towing path on the shore of a river and the valley of the river,
and will bring plain grammar and common sense to aid the
comprehension of a simple expression, will find that the requisite conveyed in παρὰ τὸν ποταμόν is rightly fulfilled by
this route only, and is the conclusive test which should remove
every scruple of criticism on the first Alps of Polybius.

The importance which belongs to these words can hardly
be overrated. No incident in the narrative so much deserves
to be received as a key to the Alps of Hannibal, as the fact of
his seeking them along the Rhone. This fact has been denied
or held dubious, by all who either know not the narrative of
Polybius, or depreciate it, or evade it, from Chevalier Folard
to Mr. Ellis. It is, however, to my mind, as clear a fact as
ever was told by words. I proceed then to encounter the
formidable array of critics, who have declined to recognise in
those words the sense which I impute to them.

At the head of the list I must put the Chevalier Folard, as
he has the honour to be cited, and to have been almost followed
by Professor Schweighæuser. The Chevalier is the author of
voluminous notes appended to a translation of Polybius by

Dom Vincent Thuillier, published at Paris in 1728, in six quarto volumes. The work would, perhaps, have been as useful if it had not been ' enrichi de notes.' The translation by Dom Thuillier of the words which express that section of the march with which we are now engaged, is unobjectionable. " Depuis " le passage du Rhone en allant vers ses sources jusqu'à ce " commencement des Alpes d'ou l'on va en Italie, on compte " quatorze cent stades." But his commentator rejects the 800 of Polybius, an important part of the 1,400, as " une faute des copistes," which Polybius would laugh at. Folard, I believe, is the founder of this error, in which he has some distinguished disciples ; a march up the Isère from that river's mouth. His course is, that Hannibal left Grenoble on his left hand, and proceeded by Vizille and Bourg d'Oysans up the Romanche, crossing the Mont de Lens and the Lautaret, and so by Briançon to the Genèvre. This he calls " la route la plus ordinaire et la plus pratiquée des Gaulois en Italie."— Tom. iv. 89.

Those opinions of Chevalier Folard were published in 1728 ; and I am not aware of any further criticism that may be adverted to concerning the ποταμόν of Polybius until the discussion of them by Schweighæuser in 1792.* During that period D'Anville was flourishing, but was silent on such a subject. That eminent man published his "carte pour l'expédition d'Annibal" in 1739. If he had then heeded Polybius, or afterwards when he published his "Notice de l'Ancienne Gaule" in 1860, he might have questioned or assented to the construction of Folard, and roused the attention of others to the river. But he did not heed Polybius, nor canvass his story of Hannibal's march : he attached himself to Livy ; and never invited the learned to Polybius, as the historian of Hannibal. I am aware of his citing Polybius once : that was to help Livy ; and he got himself into a scrape by doing

---

* In the German edition 9 volumes. 5th vol. Adnotationes.

so.   But D'Anville deserves his great name, notwithstanding
some obliquities.

The criticism of Schweighæuser on Folard is somewhat
elaborate ; but at last he rightly hesitates to abide by what
he laid down at first.   In 1792, commenting on the words ἧκε
πρὸς τὴν καλουμένην νῆσον, he wrote thus :—"*Ad insulam*
" dicit, non *in insulam*.   Nec enim dicit Polybius, trajecisse
" fluvium Hannibalem cum toto agmine, sed *juxta fluvium*
" *progressum* ait cap. 50. 1, quod cum Folardo de Isarâ intelligi
" potest, ita quidem, ut Isaram à lævâ habuerit.   Substitit
" quidem per aliquod tempus cum exercitu ad illam insulam,
" alteri ex fratribus, qui in illâ de regno dissidebant, sup-
" petias ferens ; sed id facere potuit parte copiarum fluvium
" trajectâ, reliquo exercitu interim in stativis agente.   Quod
" si etiam totum exercitum Isaram trajecit Hannibal (quod
" credi potest eo consilio fecisse, ut fluvium hunc à tergo
" haberet, si sequerentur Romani), non multum tamen deinde
" versus Septentrionem in Insulâ progressum videtur agmen,
" sed prope Isaram substitisse, ac deinde adversâ hujus fluvii
" ripâ iter continuasse."—*Adnotationes ad Polyb.* iii. 49.

In a subsequent note on πορευθεὶς παρὰ τὸν ποταμόν,
commenting on the Latin version of Casaubon, which is
" propter Rhodanum," Schweighæuser says :—"At non *propter*
" *Rhodanum*, sed *propter fluvium* Polybius dicit : neque Rho-
" danum, sed *Isaram* fluvium nunc dici a Polybio putem.
" Nec enim immanem illum anfractum, quem facit Rhodanus
" ad Lugdunum, emensum esse agmen, probabile est ; et, si
" hâc viâ iter fecisset, multo longius sane, quam centum
" millium passuum, iter fuisset ab Isarâ, Rhodani ripam se-
" quendo, usque ad eum adscensum Alpium, à quo deinde
" quinto decimo die in Italiam pervenire agmen potuit.
" Omninoque hoc dicere Polybius videtur, adversâ Isaræ ripâ
" versus fontem ejus fluvii, decem diebus per C. millium pass.
" spatium progressum esse agmen ; eamque viam postquam

" per convalles emensum est, deinde ipsa montium juga con-
" scendere cœpisse. Sed jam video, eodem loco, quem modo
" citavi, (cap. 39, 9) ipsum Polybium diserte dicere videri, non
" discessisse à Rhodano Hannibalem, donec ad conscensum
" Alpium pervenit. Quod si ita est, intelligo, corruere ea,
" quæ de itinere, adversâ Isaræ ripâ instituto, dicta sunt.
" At dubitare fortasse licebit, an adeo stricte in hanc senten-
" tiam accipienda sint prædicto loco Polybii verba."

These are the words of a candid man, not the partisan of a
theory ; and his Latin version is " propter Rhodanum."

Mr. Whitaker does not adopt the Isère ; he ascends the
Rhone, but forgets the limit of 800 stadia : he says, p. 96,—
" Hannibal kept close to the Rhone, and thus advanced up to
" Lyon. He still kept close to the Rhone, and thus advanced
" up to the Alps." Mr. Whitaker finds Alps for him at last ;
not at Lyon, nor Geneva, but at Martigny.

M. Letronne is strict upon παρά, which he applies to the
Rhone for the four days, but afterwards to the Isère and the
Drac, saying,—" Annibal, dit Polybe, marcha dix jours, le
" long du fleuve, l'espace de huit cent stades, et atteignit la
" montée des Alpes. Les mots, le long du fleuve, ne s'accord-
" ent pas avec la route qu'a choisi M. De Luc; car, dans son
" idée, Annibal a quitté le Rhone à Vienne, et a traversé la
" plaine du Dauphiné, &c. tandis que Polybe dit formellement
" qu'Annibal a suivi la fleuve—il le suivit jusqu'au dixième
" jour ; cette mesure équivaut à 100 milles romains ; prise le
" long de l'Isère et du Drac, elle porte à Saint-Bonnet."
(*Journal des Savans*, Janv. 1819, p. 31.) M. Letronne uses
bits of three rivers to make " le fleuve," rather than omit an
angle made by one.

General St. Cyr Nugues pursues boldly the same principle
(pp. 49, 50) :—" Les mots παρὰ τὸν ποταμόν désignant le
" Rhône, ne permettent pas la moindre aberration. Sur les
" 54 milles de chemin que l'armée d'Annibal, au sortir de

" Vienne, doit parcourir le long du Rhône pour arriver à la
" montée des Alpes, M. De Luc commence par lui faire
" faire 42 milles loin du Rhône."

M. Bandé de Lavalette sings the same song, pp. 54, 55 :—
" Il résulterait de là qu'au lieu de faire les 800 stades en
" entier le long du fleuve, Annibal en aurait parcouru 400
" LOIN DU FLEUVE !"

H. L. Long says, " There is no possibility, with any rational
" result, to produce a march of 100 m. p. along the river, after
" Hannibal's arrival at the Isère (p. 45)."

M. Larauza considers that the words παρὰ τὸν ποταμόν
condemn our system below Vienne as well as beyond it. He
was ready, no doubt, to limit 50,000 men and thirty-seven
elephants to a towing-path. He says, p. 39 :—" Quand on
" connait cette partie du fleuve, qui se trouve entre l'Isère
" et Lyon, on ne peut douter que de ce côté il lui eût été im-
" possible de continuer à marcher le long du fleuve παρὰ τὸν
" ποταμόν : dans toute cette partie de son lit, surtout depuis
" les environs de Gisors, jusque vers St. Vallier, il se trouve
" encaissé entre des rochers escarpés qui, sur plusieurs points
" de sa rive gauche, soit baignés par les eaux, et ne laissent
" nul passage aux piétous." The extent of error is exhibited
thus, p. 41 :—" De Vienne à St. Genix d'Aouste M. De Luc
" compte 32,300 toises, c'est à dire 16 lieues de poste environ
" sur 37, pendante lesquelles M. De Luc nous tient éloignés
" du Rhône, à une distance de 6, 5, et 4 lieues à vol d'oiseau.
" Or, peut-on dire sérieusement que ce soit là marcher le long
" du fleuve."

Dr. Ukert chimes in with a liberal translation of the leagues
of M. Larauza, saying, " Those who lead Hannibal through
" the Island, are obliged to make him march some hundred
" stadia away from the river : which is contrary to Polybius."

Dr. Arnold did not doubt the fact of the march up the
Rhone to the Mont du Chat, but he does not acknowledge

that he learned it from Polybius. He rather justifies the
dissent of other critics, saying, " It does not appear whether
" the Carthaginians ascended the left bank of the Isère or the
" right bank ; or whether they continued to ascend the Rhone,
" &c." Without helping to explain either παρά or ποταμόν, he
arraigns the historian as the cause of confusion, saying,
" These uncertainties cannot now be removed, because Poly-
" bius neither possessed sufficient knowledge of the bearings
" of the country, nor sufficient liveliness as a painter, to
" describe the line of march so as to be clearly recognised."
(iii. 83.)

Mr. Ellis reverses that method : he does not learn from
Polybius without confessing his guidance : on the contrary,
he confesses that he understands the author well ; but he
renounces him in favour of the fancy which he has resolved
to cultivate ; his motto is, " video meliora proboque : de-
" teriora sequor." He favours us with notions which would
have come with useful weight from Dr. Arnold : he states,
p. 22, in reference to c. 39 : " From this account it is certainly
" most natural to conclude, that it was the same river which
" was followed ·up all the way to the beginning of the
" Alpine ascent ; and not, in the first part of the march the
" Rhone, and in the second the Isère." Again, p. 27, " The
" most obvious interpretation of the words παρὰ τὸν ποταμόν
" in chap. 32 would lead us to think, that Hannibal followed
" up the Rhone from the place where he crossed that river,
" up to the first ascent of the Alps." These words are the
bright spot in Mr. Ellis's work. It is effaced, and the good
sense of it abandoned, without any reasonable apology.

M. Replat (Chambéry, 1851) writes, in subservience to
prior authorities, " Il est remarquable, que depuis le chap.
" 49, où il a nommé le Scaras, soit l'Isaras, Polybe cesse
" de désigner nominativement le Rhône, dont il avait jusque-
" là fait mention plusieurs fois."

Dr. Liddell in his history does not deal with παρά or ποταμόν : he believes in the L. St. Bernard; but as he makes the grateful chief take leave of Hannibal on the Isère, and near Grenoble, I cannot claim him for an ally on behalf of the Rhone.

There is still another author, and an able one, Mr. George Long, who rather sides with our opponents. In his article "Insula Allobrogum," in Dr. Smith's Dictionary of Geography, he says this :—" Hannibal, after staying a short time " in the country about the junction of the Rhone and the " Isère, commenced his march over the Alps. It is not " material to decide whether his whole army crossed over " into the Insula or not, or whether he did himself, though " the words of Polybius imply that he did. It is certain " that he marched up the valley of the Isère towards the " Alps ; and the way to find out where he crossed the Alps " is by following the valley of the Isère." Whether the writer of this inclines to the right bank or the left bank, he does not say, nor does he quite say, that the invaders went no farther up the Rhone.

Such is the accumulation of wisdom, which refuses to confess that Polybius in the words παρὰ τὸν ποταμόν spoke of the Rhone. Now I doubt exceedingly that any man ever rose from a perusal of the history itself, having received from it the impression that the author meant the Isère ; or that he intended a succession of rivers, together representing ποταμόν. Fact is, however, that critics innumerable have on this point come to be infested with the fancy of substituting the Isère for the Rhone of Polybius : and the error, if such it be, ought to receive correction.

It is quite true, that our line of march up the Rhone does at a particular point strike away from the river, and, avoiding Lyons, is for a time quite away from the stream. Accordingly, you may think, if you will, that Polybius makes too liberal use of the word παρά, and may employ it as an argument against us. But the thing to be debated is this: What river flowed between the passage of the Rhone, which is one terminus of the progress here spoken of by Polybius, and the beginning of Alps, which is the other terminus? If it is clear from the author himself that this river was the Rhone, the first Alps can be no other than the Mont du Chat.

From the time of Hannibal's reaching the Rhone, that river is the main geographical feature in the narrative, till the expedition reaches the Alps: the valley of the Rhone is the scene of the events that are told. M. De Luc observed that, before the sentence in question, the Rhone has been designated fourteen times as "the river." This is strictly true. He is mentioned by name only in the following instances: when the historian describes the course of the Rhone: when he speaks of invasions of Italy made by the dwellers on the Rhone; and when the Rhone is named as a boundary of the Island: these are all the instances of Ῥοδανός. When he is mentioned in the military movements, he is spoken of as "the river." Hanno marches παρὰ τὸν ποταμόν. Scipio marches παρὰ τὸν ποταμόν. Hannibal, after crossing, marches παρὰ τὸν ποταμόν: and in the sentence before us, having been refitted by the prince of the Island, he continues his march to the Alps παρὰ τὸν ποταμόν. They who allow ποταμόν to be the Rhone in every other instance, ought to show good reason when they say that it is not the Rhone in this instance.

In the host of writers to whom I have referred, many do no more than grumble on the word παρά. Neither Dr. Arnold, nor Dr. Liddell, nor Mr. G. Long help the question with any reasons for doubt on παρά or on ποταμόν. M. Letronne alone ventures to argue the question, and deals with the words of the historian, giving reasons that ποταμόν

should mean the Isère. He admits the other instances when
De Luc has shown it to mean the Rhone ; and says on them,
—"Dans ces passages, les mots παρὰ τὸν ποταμόν suivent
" immédiatement le nom du Rhône, en sorte qu'il n'y a point
" de doute à cet égard; au lieu qu'ici le nom du fleuve qui
" précéde immédiatement est celui d'Isaras; le nom du
" Rhône n'est point répété dans l'intervalle ; il est donc
" naturel d'appliquer à l'Isère les mots παρὰ τὸν ποταμόν."
—*Journ. des Savans*, Janv. 1819.

In all the criticism that has been heaped upon the subject
of the march, there is nothing more futile than this grammatical dogma. Dr. Ukert cannot subscribe to it : he is quite
ready to get rid of the Rhone : but, as will be seen, he invents
facts, instead of perverting language. Others, in their emer-
gency, have been tempted to accede to the logic of M. Letronne.
Larauza tells us, " C'est de l'Isère qu'il a parlé en dernier
" lieu, et depuis cet endroit τῇ μὲν γὰρ ὁ 'Ροδανὸς, τῇ δ' ὁ
" 'Ισάρας,* il ne nom plus le Rhone une seule fois." So De
Lavalette :—" L'intention de Polybe a du être en effet de
" désigner l'Isère, puisqu' il venoit d'en écrire le nom."

If there were truth in the supposed rule of construction,
which there is not, this application of " en dernier lieu "
would be ludicrous. When Polybius describes the shape of
the Island, c. 49, 'Ροδανός and 'Ισάρας are bracketed together,
as the nominative to ἀποκορυφοῦσι. Then we have the narrative of Hannibal's interference with the contending parties,
and the refitting of his army. We then read that, having in
ten days marched 800 stadia παρὰ τὸν ποταμόν, he began the
ascent. Here it is that M. Letronne interprets ποταμόν the
Isère, because it was " the river last named." C'est de l'Isère
qu'il a parlé en dernier lieu !

---

* iii. 49, 6. This is the only place where Polybius names the
Isère.

To know what river is intended, we have to regard that
which is the subject of the story that we are reading,* not that
whose name has last occurred in the text. The historian, in
describing country, might pause to enumerate all tributary
streams which flow into the Rhone below Geneva: when his
narrative is resumed, "the river" will not intend the last of
that catalogue.

This is but common sense; and we need not go far for a
confirmation of it. Let us try M. Letronne by his own test
of "the river last-named." Polybius says, c. 49, that in three
days after Hannibal had marched forward, Scipio came in
search of him to the passage of the river—ἐπὶ τὴν τοῦ
ποταμοῦ διάβασιν; and probably, when M. Letronne read
the history, he believed this ποταμοῦ to be the Rhone: but,
if he had looked back for the river last named, and applied
his own rule, he would have found that Scipio was looking
for Hannibal on the Po. Indeed that principle would transfer
much of these operations to the other side of the Alps: for
again, if you will read Hannibal's address to his army after
crossing the river, and interpret the word ποταμοῦ by "le nom
" qui précède immédiatement," you will perceive that he con-
gratulated them on their successful passage of the Po. As for
the Isère in the instance before us, M. Letronne does not even
fulfil the philosophy of his own precept: for when, to understand ποταμόν, he retreats through the text in search of a
river, the first he stumbles upon is in truth neither Rhodanus
nor Isaras: he first encounters τὰς τῶν ποταμῶν ῥύσεις, the
streams which confine the Egyptian delta. Thus it would
better accord with the spirit of his doctrine, to maintain that
Hannibal marched to the Alps up the Nile.

There is another test, to which the discovery of M.
Letronne must be subjected; the illustration of an author
by himself. This also he encountered boldly. Polybius in

* See note in Appendix.

c. 39, dividing the whole march into five sections, mentioned this section, " from the passage of the Rhone to the beginning or ascent of Alps," as being 1,400 stadia παρ' αὐτὸν τὸν ποταμόν: and one would say, that the term παρὰ τὸν ποταμόν, as used in the narrative of this same progress, must import the same river which was described in that section. See how the expression is used.

Statement of this section of the march in c. 39.

Ἀπὸ δὲ τῆς διαβάσεως τοῦ Ῥοδανοῦ πορευομένοις παρ' αὐτὸν τὸν ποταμὸν ὡς ἐπὶ τὰς πηγὰς ἕως πρὸς τὴν ἀναβολὴν τῶν Ἄλπεων, τὴν εἰς Ἰταλίαν, χίλιοι τετρακόσιοι : and from the passage of the Rhone, for those who proceed along this very river, as if to the source, as far as the ascent to the Alps, which leads to Italy, 1,400 stadia.

The same progress in the narrative.

c. 47. 1. Περαιωθέντων δὲ τῶν θηρίων, Ἀννίβας προῆγε παρὰ τὸν ποταμόν. The elephants having been brought over, Hannibal led forward along the river.

c. 49. 5. Ἀννίβας δὲ ποιησάμενος ἑξῆς ἐπὶ τέτταρας ἡμέρας τὴν πορείαν ἀπὸ τῆς διαβάσεως ἧκε πρὸς τὴν καλουμένην Νῆσον. Hannibal, having marched from the passage of the river for four consecutive days, came to the Island, as it is called.

c. 50. 1. Ἀννίβας δ'ἐν ἡμέραις δέκα πορευθεὶς παρὰ τὸν ποταμὸν εἰς ὀκτακοσίους σταδίους, ἤρξατο τῆς πρὸς τὰς Ἄλπεις ἀναβολῆς. Hannibal, having in ten days marched along the river eight hundred stadia, began the ascent to the Alps.

Now, supposing a man to have doubted whether the narrative represents the four days' march to the Island, and the ten days' further march to the ἀναβολή, to have been along one and the same river, one might expect his doubts to be removed on reference to c. 39, which states the entire march of 1,400 stadia as being παρ' αὐτὸν τὸν ποταμόν. M. Letronne is not so influenced. He assents to the division of the 1,400 stadia into 600 and 800 : but does not allow that the river of the 800 is the river of the 600; nor that the words of c. 39 give the whole 1,400 to those who do the journey along the river from the passage of it to the beginning of Alps. He admits 1,400 stadia to be the distance between those termini; but not that the words πορευομένοις παρ' αὐτὸν τὸν ποταμὸν ὡς ἐπὶ τὰς πηγάς are applicable to that scope of march : he limits their effect to this—that the progress was begun up the stream : and contends that πορεύομαι means only "to set out."

These are his words—" Si M. De Luc avoit fait attention " lui-même à la phrase de Polybe à laquelle il renvoie, il y " auroit vu que les 1,400 stades n'y sont pas comptés le long " du fleuve, et que son opinion à est égard tient à ce qu'il ne " saisit pas le sens de l'original, qui du reste a été fort mal " entendu. Par les mots παρ' αὐτὸν τὸν ποταμὸν ὡς ἐπὶ τὰς " πηγάς, Annibal ne fait qu'indiquer en général le direction " de le route à partir du passage du Rhône : il veut dire " simplement qu'au lieu de se diriger droit à l'est, vers les " Alpes, on commence par remonter le fleuve ; sans prétendre " appliquer a la longueur de la route le long du fleuve, la " mesure de 1,400 stades jusqu'a la montée des Alpes." (*Journ. des Savans,* Dec. 1819.)

It seems to me that, if this idea of " movement along the river, as if seeking the source," is connected only with the terminus à quo, and disconnected from the terminus ad quem, you take from those words all their value. Their value is, that they help us through ἕως πρός to find the Alps. There is a peculiarity of expression in telling this section of the march, not used for the other four sections of it. The others

are told in c. 39, by naming the termini and the distance
between them. But in this instance, the march is further
explained, as performed by those who travel a certain distance
of a river to a certain point. What distance? Not a fraction
of 1,400 stadia, but the whole, from one terminus to the other.
If πορευομένοις is applied only to the διάβασις of the Rhone,
as the terminus "à quo," the sentence will not connect the other
terminus, and the latter part of the march to it, with any
river: and yet the words employed bespeak such connexion:
you are to march ὡς ἐπὶ τὰς πηγάς, and you are to do this
ἕως πρὸς τὴν ἀναβολήν. The idea "along the river as if
tending to the source," attaches itself to the whole scope of
1,400 stadia: and those who deny the Rhone are driven to
maintain, that διαβάσεως intends the passage of one river, and
πηγάς the source of another. If Polybius had only wished to
express that the inchoate movement from the place of crossing
was up the stream, he would have abstained from all those
expressions, and been content with ἀντιοῖς τῷ ῥεύματι.

In each section of the march, the whole length of the
section is to be regarded, the terminus "ad quem" being the
terminus "à quo" in the next section. The peculiar terms of
this fourth section give the most useful instruction. They show
where Hannibal was to reach the Alps, and quit the Rhone.
They are in conformity with the statement on the three boundaries of the island—Rhone was one side, Alps were another:
and the effect of those words is, that you are not to desert
the former till you are brought to the latter. I say, then, that
there is a plain and sufficient meaning in the author, more than
M. Letronne, or Dr. Ukert, or Dr. Arnold give him credit for.
A man in the nineteenth century can say, " Go to the Mont
du Chat." Polybius had no equivocal term: but he would say,
and to my apprehension he does say, " Go up the valley of
" the Rhone as if seeking his source; do this for 1,400 stadia,
" and you will find the ascent or beginning of Alps." We

march from the διάβασις by this instruction; we abstain
from wanderings in the plain that would be frivolous for those
who are striving towards the source; we find the Alps at the
given distance; we find them in the Mont du Chat.

These comments I have thought due to the efforts of an
adversary such as M. Letronne. When Schweighæuser saw
that the great river crossed by the Carthaginian army lasted
to the Alps, he withdrew his opposition to the Rhone. Not
so Mr. Ellis; he still maintains the Isère, persevering in a
bad cause, and after a bad fashion. In my criticism of his
"Treatise," I quoted his confessions as they appear above.
Either by accident or design, Mr. Ellis had omitted αὐτόν both
from his quotation of and his comment on c. 39. I exhibited
him in his own words. When he comes to defend himself in
the *Journal of Philology,* ii. 315, he most disingenuously
charges me with the omission, saying, "Mr. Law carefully
"ignores the word αὐτόν." It was himself who had omitted
the word in that place, and I quoted him accurately.

He is still shy of the word. In this second effort he makes
no comment upon it, but leaves us to speculate on the drift of
an empty insinuation. This is not difficult: though αὐτόν is not
to be found in his "Treatise" (for his translation of Polybius
does not begin till Scipio has re-embarked for Italy), we know
how Mr. Ellis construes αὐτόν. In his own exposition of
the history, he says ("Treatise," p. 22), "Hannibal went along
the very river bank." Now, if the word *bank* is thrown away,
not being in Polybius, the remaining words which are in
Polybius, give the actual meaning—"along the very river;"
which is literal and true. I say myself, that the river of the
narrative, c. 50, is necessarily the Rhone, without aid from
c. 39; but the words of chapter 39 leave no excuse for a
pretence to doubt. What river can be meant, but "the very
river" which is named in the same clause of the same sentence? See the immediate context of the words πορευομένοις

παρ αὐτὸν τὸν ποταμὸν ὡς ἐπὶ τὰς πηγάς.　The words which immediately precede those words are ἀπὸ τῆς διαβάσεως τοῦ 'Ροδανοῦ: and the words which immediately follow them are ἕως πρὸς τὴν ἀναβολὴν τῶν "Αλπεων.　This amount of progress is one of the five sections into which the whole march of invasion is divided by Polybius.　You do not walk up one river to find the source of another.

Some critics have not known that this particular length of march is so expressly alleged to have been up one and the same river. Mr. Ellis did know it ; he does not, like Letronne, proceed under a delusion upon the force of πορευομένοις : he rightly apprehends " the obvious interpretation," and tells us so.　Though he only begins his translation of the history in the forty-ninth chapter, he read the thirty-ninth, and tells us so.　Why then persist in pretending that it was one river at the initial terminus, and another at the final terminus of this section of the march ? or, if believing it, why shrink from asserting it in plain English, and insinuate that his adversary avoids a topic, which he himself dares not grapple with ?

All honest and rational interpretation is set at nought, when it is urged that the author contemplated that progress of 1,400 stadia as made, not along one river, but along many in succession.　If one, it is the Rhone : if more, there is much to choose from.　A long list of critics, ending with Replat and Ellis, make up their ποταμόν 1,400 stadia, with a length of Rhone and a length of Isère : Letronne and de Lavalette add to this a length of Drac.　The Cambridge anonymous of 1830 does not reach his ἀναβολή, till he has performed fractions of Rhone, Isère, Drac, Luie, Durance, and Ubaye. Against these and other pluralists, I stand for one : the 1,400 stadia were along one and the same river, and that river was the Rhone.

If Ποταμόν is the Rhone, the protest founded on the word παρά becomes an idle scruple, which has unworthily haunted

the minds of learned men. They have reproached us with
the distance à vol d'oiseau between Bourgoin and the Rhone.
An object may be alongside to the right or left, without being
near to you. Hannibal was twice as far from the coast when
he reached the Rhone, as ever he was from the river in his
march to the Alps: yet he reached the Rhone, "having the
" Sardinian sea on his right hand." Polybius tells of irruptions
into Italy with large armies before the time of Hannibal,
made by Celts whom he describes as dwelling along the
Rhone, οἰκοῦντες παρὰ τὸν 'Ροδανὸν ποταμόν: that they
crossed the Alps, and joined force against the Romans with
the Gauls of the Po. I should like to hear from our opponents, what were the limits of this military constituency:
how near to the river's bed or banks were the huts of those
who were admitted to the ranks of the invaders. Let critics
take further example when they come to the great Italian
river, and speak of "plaines qu'arrose ce fleuve"—"plaines
"que le Po arrose de ses ondes." Let them remember that the
chain of Alps divides τὰ πεδία παρὰ τὸν παδόν from the
valley of the Rhone (Polyb. iii. 47, 4); and that those πεδία
comprehend a space bounded by the Alps, the Appennine,
and the Adriatic. (iii. 14, 18).

An apology for the historian is made by the Oxford
Dissertation, which I think is not needed for him. It is
said, "We must remember that Polybius was ignorant of the
" angle made by the Rhone at Lyons." Why assume this?
It is possible certainly, that he never explored above the
latitudes of the Carthaginian march, and did not appreciate
the amount of zigzag. But let him have known the river's
course as by the best modern survey; he would write as he
has written: he would estimate a measurement of the march;
not a measurement of the river. Even if he had been reporting the length of the river, he need not have traced
it in its wanderings. Strabo, the oracle of our strongest

adversaries, imputes this shorter method to Polybius, and commends it : reporting the length, which Polybius had ascribed to the Tagus from the source to the mouth, he adds, οὐ δήπου τὸ σὺν τοῖς σκολιώμασιν (οὐ γὰρ γεωγραφικὸν τοῦτο) ἀλλ᾽ ἐπ᾽ εὐθείας λέγων.—ii. 107. Again, reporting Polybius's estimate of the circumference of the Peloponnesus, he says, viii. 335, that he reckoned it μὴ κατακολπίζοντι, for one not coasting the gulphs or inlets.

These words amply vindicate the Polybian distance from the Isère to the Alps, as avoiding the σκολιώμα to Lyons. Our adversaries measure the zigzag line of the river, and say that 800 stadia is too short : we measure the line of march, and are satisfied. Hannibal's guides had the sense to save time and distance by not adhering to the banks of that devious stream : he kept away from it till it offered itself again : and the history rightly shows his course παρὰ τὸν ποταμόν, prescribing it μὴ κατακολπίζοντι.

4. *Through a country where Cavalry could act.*

The correspondence of Northern Dauphiné with the country here described by Polybius cannot be disputed : it is an open country of undulating plain ; and this character is essentially interwoven with the historical explanation of events. To a certain point the hostile bodies, which were apprehended by the Carthaginians as threatening their advance, were deterred from attack by two things ; the native auxiliary force, and the Carthaginian cavalry, that arm of war in which Hannibal was always superior to his enemies. When is this terror said to operate ? so long as they were in the plain country—ἕως ἐν τοῖς ἐπιπέδοις ἦσαν. When did this terror cease ? when the ally turned homewards, and the army moved into the difficult ground for the assault of the Alps : cavalry, the object of fear in an open country, loses all advantage in a mountain pass.

In Polybius's account of this part of the route, every term has its value and effect: and in this requisite of a country fit for the operations of cavalry in protecting the advance of the army, there is great value and effect; it is fulfilled by the march which I am now delineating: whether it belongs to any of the routes south of Isère, we may hereafter inquire. Though I consider our adversaries to fail in providing this requisite, they acknowledge its importance: and we find the most distinguished man among them, Letronne, on reaching a point deep in the mountains, which, in distance, suits the track that he adopts, rashly to exclaim, " jusque-là l'armée " s'étoit trouvée en plaine !" M. Larauza imputes to our route the want of the required plain, because of the rocks which occur on the shore of the Rhone in a part below Vienne, " depuis les environs de Gisors jusque vers St. Vallier." But, if the country just there is not quite plain, of which I know nothing, our cavalry has less occasion for it short of Vienne. That place was probably the head-quarters of the ally, when he refitted the Carthaginian force after the success which Hannibal procured for him: from that place to the Alps the apprehension of Allobrogian assault operated, and the services of the cavalry became most important. In all theories of a progress south of Isère, the favouring incident of plain should be expected, from the point at which any critic may require Hannibal to recross that river attended by his ally.

5. *Through the country of the Allobroges.*

It is important to inquire into the position of this people; and the importance of it is shown by the efforts which our antagonists make to get rid of them, by the confusion, the perversion, and the invention of history. All are ready to give the Allobroges wrong boundaries, or no boundaries : anxious only to erase them as an item in the argument. It seems to me that, as they are the only people named, from the

Pyrenees to the plain of the Po, they claim particular notice
when we seek to identify the line of march. Now the passages of the history, where this people is expressly named,
are these :—

The friendly prince lent the aid of his force till Hannibal
drew near to the Alps, because of the apprehensions which
the Carthaginians entertained of the march through the Gauls
called Allobroges.

While the march was in the plain country, the several
leaders of the Allobroges abstained from attacking them.

When the Carthaginians were getting into the difficult
places, the leaders of the Allobroges pre-occupied the pass.

In forcing the pass, Hannibal destroyed, or put to flight,
the greater part of the Allobroges ; and afterwards occupied
the town whence they had come forth in the morning to the
attack.

It is thus an essential part of the history, that the progress
from the confluence of the rivers to the first Alps was made
through the people called Allobroges, and that the pass was
forced, and the town beyond it occupied, against the resistance
of many separate leaders of that nation. At whatever point
began the Alps of Polybius, there was the struggle with the
Allobroges : and those who say with Dr. Arnold, that " it
" does not appear whether the Carthaginians ascended the
" left or the right bank of the Isère, or continued to ascend
" the Rhone, and that these uncertainties cannot be removed,"
must embrace in this uncertainty whether the Allobroges of
Polybius were on one side of the Isère or the other. Dr.
Arnold does not mention them at all: but Mr. G. Long, who
has two articles in Dr. Smith's Dictionary, Allobroges and
Insula Allobrogum, speaks of them as north of Isère, and
gives no hint of their being to the south of it.

Where then in the time of Hannibal, or in the time of his
historian, dwelt the Allobroges? Was the district, which is

so clearly and minutely described as the Island, the Island of
the Allobroges? And was the southern boundary of the
Island, the Isère, also a boundary of their possessions? One
of our strongest opponents, M. Letronne, conceded the former
point, when he said, " Cette île est donc l'insula Allobrogum."
—*Journ. des Savans,* Janv. 1819, p. 27. The concession is
complained of by M. Larauza, who says of M. De Luc's argument, that it is "forte, et très forte, mais surtout contre
" M. Letronne, qui, plaçant dans l'île les Allobroges, fait à
" ses adversaires, et bien gratuitement, une concession tout
" à son désavantage." M. Letronne himself regretted the
concession : for, in a subsequent number of that work, he
retracted it, saying he was without information on the
subject.

But we can afford to lose M. Letronne as a believer in the
Allobrogian Island. We have the ancient authorities that
this people spread beyond the Island to the north and east.
Geneva belonged to them : and their north-eastern boundary
may perhaps be drawn from that town by the lake of Annecy
to Conflans, where they bordered on the Centrones. The
Isère was a boundary of their island to the south: Polybius
plainly places them on the right bank. What we know
of the left bank opposite to them, places there in succession
the Segalauni, the Vocontii, and the Iconii, otherwise called
Uceni.

The most diligent mystifier of the Allobroges, M. Larauza,
says ("Hist. Critique," p. 35): "Nous convenons que du tems
" de Cicéron, de César, et même avant, les Allobroges occu-
" paient tout ce pays qui se trouve entre le Saône et l'Isère :
" c'est encore là que, plus tard, les placent Strabon et
" Ptolemée, en leur donnant Vienne pour capitale. Mais
" étaient-ils là à l'époque dont il est ici question? Les seuls
" auteurs qui puissent fournir quelques lumières sur ce sujet
" sont Polybe et Tite-Live." It is true that these lights are

enough for those who will construe them. But there are other sufficient authorities to the same purpose.

Cæsar, relating his march from the interior to the ulterior Province, says, i. 10, that he arrived " in fines Vocontiorum, " inde in Allobrogum fines : ab Allobrogibus in Segusianos : hi " sunt extra Provinciam trans Rhodanum primi." Now, to enter the Allobroges from the Vocontii, he must have crossed the Isère : and to get on to Lyons, the chief city of the Segusiani, he must have marched through Allobroges and crossed the Rhone.

In the year which followed the murder of Cæsar, Plancus, proconsul in the ulterior province, who had been coming to the relief of Modena, wrote to Cicero—" ipse in Allobrogibus constiti," x. 11. In his next letter, when starting to oppose Anthony, who was flying into Gaul by the maritime Alps, he says—" itaque in Isarâ, flumine maximo, quod in finibus est Allobrogum, ponte uno die facto, exercitum traduxi," x. 15. In another letter, he reports that he is advancing, having secured the bridge on the Isère, for D. Brutus's force to follow on arriving from the Graian Alp : and in another, x. 23, that he has been obliged to retreat through the Vocontii, crossing the Isère and destroying the bridges. This letter is dated " Cularone,* ex finibus Allobrogum." I think there is another letter, in which the Isère is mentioned as separating the Allobroges and the Segalauni.

Strabo, after placing the Vocontii along the Durance, iv. 179, says that they reach northward through mountain valleys μέχρι ᾿Αλλοβρίγων—203. And of the Allobroges he says, that they are the occupiers from the Isère to Lyons ; and of Vienne he says, that it is now raised to the rank of a city, where those of high distinction live ; but that, in the earlier

---

* The ancient name was Cularo ; in a later day Gratianopolis, whence Grenoble. Civarone and Cujarone are also found in manuscripts.

days of their power, it had been their metropolis, when only a village.

Pliny recognises a similar division of peoples by the Isère : he says, iii. 5, " In agro Cavarum Valentia: Vienna, Allobrogum."

Ptolemy, in his catalogue of States and Towns of Keltoga-latia Narbonensis, ii. 10, says :—" Of those who occupy the " country east of the Rhone, the most northerly are the " Allobroges, whose city is Vienne, in the middle of them : " and next to them are the Segalauni, whose city is Valentia : " below them the Cavari."

These testimonies are calculated to satisfy most persons on the position of the Allobroges. But the partisans of the Hannibalian controversy are not persuadable like the rest of mankind. Larauza is prominent among a host of critics who, interpreting the Allobroges of Polybius, deny to them all local habitation. He designates them as "une population essentielle-ment vagabonde : " whereupon Letronne, repenting in December of what he had laid down in January, that the Insula was Insula Allobrogum, consents to be ranked among the ignorant—" On " peut assurer que nous ignorons tout-à-fait l'état des choses " au tems d'Annibal. Comment se faire une objection de ce " qu'il est impossible de connoître."—*Journ. des Savans*, Dec. 1819. An anonymous Englishman of bolder chronology declares, " Nor is there any account of the Allobroges that will " assist in the present question till about two centuries after " Hannibal's entrance into their territory." Cambridge, 1830.

Such conception of ubiquity in this people enables the advocates of the Cenis, the Genèvre, or the Viso, to place the overthrow of the Allobroges by Hannibal in any part of Gaul south of Isère, which may suit a theory : one slaughters them near St. Bonnet—another on the Ubaye—another in the valley of the Arc—one catches them, after he has got over the Cottian Alps, in the valley of Césanne. The curious thing is, that these writers limit the privilege of being Allobrogian to the regions south of Isère: regions throughout which innumerable peoples are acknowledged with their own well-authorized names. It is denied only to the island, a country for whose inhabitants no ingenuity has ever suggested any name other than Allobroges.

I cannot help thinking that, for knowing who lived in the Island, the narrative of Polybius is much to the purpose. But M. Larauza says, p. 37, that the vagabond life of the population of that period makes topographical distinction impossible. He is content with the etymology of Bochart. " Ce mot Allobroges est composé de deux mots, *all* qui veut " dire *haut,* et *bro* qui signifie *terre,* dont on tire aisément le " nom de montagne, et celui de montagnard, qu'on rend par " celui d'Allobroge."* Each expression of Polybius is twisted to favour the ubiquity of the Allobroges ; that they were not a nation, but many "peuplades distinctes," as Larauza would explain κατὰ μέρος ἡγεμονες : and he apologizes for Livy not having understood the word Allobroges. It seems to me that these separate leaders were influential members of one state. The commonalty in an old Celtic people were subject to the control of an aristocracy, while they owed allegiance to the government of the nation. In a civil war for the chiefdom, each leader of a clan would exercise his separate influence— it was to be expected that some of these, "quorum auctoritas apud plebem valebat," should be in movement with their immediate dependants.

Larauza thinks his view to be confirmed by the expression Ἀλλοβρίγων καλουμένων Γαλατῶν, as if it was meant for a name not national but descriptive; and so applicable to many peoples. He might have seen that the term καλουμένον is common with Polybius, on mentioning a thing which his hearers may not already be acquainted with. Larauza's

* Or see the Gallobriges of Mr. Whitaker, and Briges and Brogue, i. p. 136.

fancy suggests a most unfortunate illustration; namely, that Allobroges may then have comprehended the Tricastini, Vocontii, and Tricorii, also mentioned by Livy. This is a bold denial of nationality. Just before the death of Polybius, the Vocontii suffered a great defeat by the Romans, and there was a consular triumph over them; two or three years later, the Allobroges were defeated, and there was a consular triumph over them. You might as well include the Allobroges under a common denomination of Vocontii, as the Vocontii under a common denomination of Allobroges.

Besides the skirmishing efforts, which have been noticed, for placing the Allobroges everywhere or nowhere, the adversaries profess to have ascertained that that nation was not on the right, but on the left bank of the Isère. And one argument is, that Polybius must have viewed them as a distinct people from those who inhabited the Island; inasmuch as he calls that enemy Allobroges, but calls the inhabitants of the Island Barbarians. There is no such distinction, though the suggestion was first made by one of high authority.

Polybius tells of the two brothers in the Island contending for the sovereignty: one expects therefore that the combatants in a civil war, if they were Allobroges on one side, would be Allobroges also on the other. Professor Schweighæuser, in a note on this passage, says, " Duos illos fratres " de regno contendentes, Allobroges fecit Livius, xxi. 31. " Polybius vero hoc cap. vers. 13, et cap. 50, 2. satis disertè " ab Allobrogibus eos distinguit. Credi tamen potest, varias " fuisse Allobrogum gentes."

Larauza, p. 35, adopts the distinction. " Polybe ne nomme " nulle part le peuple qui habitat l'Ile: il dit que le chef de " cette nation escorta les Carthaginois qui s'effrayaient d'avoir " à traverser le territoire des Gaulois nommés Allobroges." Dr. Ukert, p. 190, develops the same idea:—" The inhabit- " ants of the Island are not mentioned by name, but are only

" spoken of in general terms as barbarians. Polybius names
" the Allobroges as being inhabitants of the country through
" which Hannibal pursued his march when he set out again :
" they are Gauls : they dwell in the plains, and are under
" many chiefs. According to the account of Polybius, we
" must look for them in our maps south of the Isère."

Mr. Ellis in his Treatise, p. 133, asserts that it is clear from
Polybius, that the Allobroges were not inhabitants of the
Island in Hannibal's time. In my criticism, p. 17, I pointed
out the causes which had led to that error. Mr. Ellis, in his
Defence (*Journal of Philol.* ii. 316), without replying to my
comments, adopts the substantive error himself, and is as
proud of it as if he were the inventor. He proclaims that
the Allobroges were south of Isère, and denounces the contrary notion as absurd. He neither defends the view of
Schweighæuser and Ukert, nor combats my remarks, but
brings out a new idea of his own. He gives in translation
sentences from the 49th and 50th chapters, and where
Polybius speaks of the allied force he adds the words, " The
men of the Island ;" and then pronounces judgment thus :
" Now if for ' the men of the Island ' the expression Allo-
" broges be substituted, these two passages become absolute
" nonsense. That the men of the Island were the Allobroges
" of Polybius, is thus a proposition at once susceptible of a
" *reductio ad absurdum.*"

Mr. Ellis seems to defy us to meddle with Polybius ; but
in fact he is only defying us to meddle with himself : he is
the inventor of the expression " men of the Island." I
subscribe to the doctrine which he calls absolute nonsense,
and am quite prepared to add the idea " Allobrogian " in
both places of the text ; but I should not thereby substitute
it for a term which never was in the text.

Schweighæuser, Larauza, and Ukert had been misled by
this. They saw that Hannibal's friends were called βάρβαροι,

and they saw that his enemies were Allobroges. Hence they hastily concluded that the two must be distinct nations, and were emboldened to place them on different sides of the river. But they were not distinct nations. Polybius has first mentioned the country which he so fully describes, not by the name of the nation or inhabitants, but by another name, the Island. He announces the arrival of Hannibal, not at the country of the Allobroges, but at a region called the Island; and, having explained why it was so called, he continues to speak of the country under that name; mentioning, among other things, the contention for the sovereignty of it, and all this without occasion to express the name of people or inhabitants. But on the first occasion, when people or inhabitants are to be named, which is when he states the apprehension entertained about marching through them, he speaks of them by their name Allobroges, and any doubt which may have been is relieved.

The error of supposing that the inhabitants are called Barbarians in contrast with the Allobroges, rests on this: that, when the narrative is bringing us to the Alps, the leaders of Allobrogian detachments are said to abstain from attacking the Carthaginians in the plain country, being deterred partly by their cavalry, partly by the barbarian escort. This was supposed to show a contrast between Allobrogian and barbarian. But it is not so. It is true that this barbarian escort belonged to the Island, but so also did the Allobrogian enemy. If you read forward, you will find that the term "barbarian" tends to identify Hannibal's ally with Allobroges, not to distinguish them from Allobroges: it is applied to both. In the next sentence but one, we read what was done by the general of the Carthaginians, when he learned that the barbarians had taken possession of the advantageous posts. He occupied those posts, when the barbarians, according to their practice, had withdrawn for the night; and we read of the attacks made

by the barbarians, when in the morning these things were perceived by them. The barbarians are the Allobroges themselves.

Both in the one instance where the friends are called barbarian, and in these instances where the enemy is called
barbarian, the word means, in effect, "native," and is used in
contrast with Carthaginian, as it is used elsewhere by Polybius
in contrast with civilised nations. This contrast is particularly marked in the instance on which the adverse argument
is built; the troops of the ally are called barbarian, being
mentioned together with the Carthaginian cavalry, and would
have been called so, if their proper name, Allobroges, had
occurred twenty times before. The distinction is in frequent
use. In the third book, where Polybius describes the operations of Hannibal, against the Carpetani and Olcades, these
peoples are called by their proper names in one sentence, and
the barbarians in the next. So in the thirty-third Book, c. 8,
where the contrast is with Roman, the Oxybii are named in one
sentence, and called the barbarians in the next. In fact, there
is no more contrast here between Barbarian and Allobrogian,
than there is, in c. 47, between θηρία and ἐλέφαντες, words
employed in one sentence to signify the same thing.

Our adversaries, flattering themselves that they have swept
the Allobroges of Polybius out of the Island to the other side
of the Isère, grow bolder, and seek to push them still further
south, and near to the shore of the Mediterranean. Dr. Ukert,
iii. 591, says of the Allobroges : "When in earlier times men-
" tion is made of wars which they undertook, they appear
" (*stehend*—stand) quite in the most southern part of Gaul."
These references are given :—Polybius, iii. 50; Strabo, iv. 186;
Livy, xxi. 31 ; Dion Cassius, xxxvii. 47 ; Florus, iii. 2 ; Livy,
Epitome, lvi.—ciii.

I do not find a word in these passages referred to that
warrants the assertion that the Allobroges are spoken of by
these authors as inhabitants of the south. They are exhibited

fighting for a short time south of Isère, but not inhabiting. In the year when the Romans, invading Gaul, pushed their course up the Rhone, Allobroges are seen fighting a few miles above Avignon, " ad oppidum Vindalium ; " and again near the confluence of the Isère and the Rhone. What then? If in the previous year they had sent a brigade across the Durance in aid of the Salluvii, would this locate them south of Durance? Does the field of battle enable you to fix the national boundaries of the combatants? A military nation threatened with aggression need not stay at home to receive the enemy. When many peoples are breathing the same hostility to the sweeping ambition of one domineering state, some will come to fight on the soil of their neighbours. Many tribes left their own villages and joined force on mountains not their own to oppose the progress of Cæsar through the Alps : and some of these had shortly before descended into the plain of the Rhone to aid a rebellion against the supremacy of the great republic. Her conquests would have been more easy, if each people had fought only on its own ground.

In the same view of giving a late date to their position north of Isère, Larauza had imagined and laid down a history for the Allobroges, with an outline of historical fact asserted positively and without obscurity. He says, pp. 37, 38 : " C'est " en deça de l'Isère, et surtout dans la partie la plus mé- " ridionale de la Gaule, que l'on voit se passer la plupart des " guerres qu'ils eurent à soutenir contre les Romains depuis " la première, l'an 630 de Rome, jusqu'à celle qui mit fin " à leur indépendance, l'an 692. Nous serions même assez " fondés à croire que ce dut être vers cette époque que, " subjugués par les Romains, ils furent repoussés au-delà de " l'Isère, et forcés de se renfermer dans le pays borné par se " fleuve, la Saône, et le Rhône."

This statement has the one merit of perspicuity : it asserts, that a course of warfare was sustained by the Allobroges for a

period of 62 years—from 630 to 692 U.C. : that is, from 124
to 62 B.C. : that their independence was then at last crushed,
these wars having been carried on by them in the most
southern parts of Gaul : that, though when Strabo wrote
they were restricted to the north of Isère, yet, in the time of
Cæsar, they had only just been driven within that boundary.

Now, though M. Larauza was a laborious, zealous, and
amiable man, and Dr. Ukert enjoys a very high reputation
for the knowledge of ancient geography, I conceive this
continuous warfare of the Allobroges with Rome to be an
unauthorized notion ; a mistake of a few simple facts, which
are these. At the beginning of the period spoken of, the
Allobroges in one campaign lost their independence and
became subject to Rome : at the end of that period they
broke into an insurrection, which was presently quelled by
the Prætor of the Province ; and in the intermediate time
there were no hostilities at all.

The first entrance of the Romans into Gaul by land was
in the year 154 B.C., when they came to protect the Massilians
against the Oxybii and Deciatæ. Polyb. xxxiii. 4. By this
interference, which occupied little time, their friends were
established in the possession of an increased territory. The
Romans did not cross the Maritime Alp again for 29 years.
They then went again in aid of the Massilians : this was in
125. In 123 they defeated certain transalpine Ligurians,
who were supported by the Vocontii.* In the next year,
122, they founded their first colony beyond the Alps, Aquæ
Sextiæ, Aix en Provence ; subduing the Salluvii, who seem
to have had some assistance from the Allobroges.† In the

---

* It appears from the Fasti Capitolini, quoted by Mr. Clinton,
vol. iii. 130, that the Vocontii had fought against Fulvius Flaccus :
for he is recorded as having a triumph over them.

† Velleius Paterculus states that the Allobroges joined the
Sallyes in resisting the Romans under Sextius, i. 15.

following year, 121, the proconsul Domitius Ænobarbus defeated the army of the Allobroges; and the consul Fabius also routed them with prodigious slaughter, together with the Arverni and Ruteni, a great force having been brought into the field on the part of the Gauls. Thus speedily was effected the subjugation of the Allobroges. These three campaigns led to the erection of the Province: and never did the Allobroges regain their independence. The accounts of their subjugation are consistently told by Strabo, Livy, Pliny, and others; and there is no reason to think that, when they became subject to Rome, there was any change in their boundaries.

From the earliest to the last of the extant historians, all give in effect the same representation of this Gallic war of five years, and the consequence of it to the nation of Allobroges, who in the last year bore a prominent part. Ammianus Marcellinus, writing 500 years after the transactions, says this: " Hæ regiones, præcipuè quæ confines " Italicis paulatim levi sudore sub imperium venêre Ro- " manum : primò tentatæ per Fulvium, deinde præliis parvis " quassatæ per Sextium, ad ultimum per Fabium Maximum " domitæ: cui negotii plenus effectus, asperiore Allobrogum " gente devictâ, hoc indidit cognomen." Lib. xv.

Such was the first Allobrogian war of M. Larauza. Where is the next? Having assigned to a particular district " la " plupart des guerres depuis la première, l'an 630, jusqu'à la " dernière, l'an 692," he might be expected to bring to our attention something that happened between those two extremes. But he furnishes nothing. Neither in his work, nor elsewhere, is there an act of discord between the Allobroges and the Romans after that first short war of conquest, until the very end of the stated period, " l'an 692." In that year things are recorded, which M. Larauza treats as the climax of a continuous contest : and, because this people is seen for

a month or two in arms at the end of that period, he pre-
sumes that they had been fighting against Rome throughout
the interval. But in truth even that one fact is misrepre-
sented : it was but an effort of insurrection speedily quelled.
The only authorities on the subject seem to be Livy and
Dion Cassius. There is an interesting question on the
identity of places : but it does not affect our inquiry.

There cannot well be a stronger specimen of exaggeration
than the sixty-two years' struggle proclaimed by this critic,
founded only on a few conflicts, which cannot have occupied
many weeks, at the close of that period. If this rebellion
had been serious enough to require a Roman reinforcement to
cross the boundary of Italy, which it did not, how stands the
assumption, that these hostilities concluded a long contest ;
and that up to that moment the Allobroges maintained their
independence ? Two years before this affair of Ventia, we
find them to be clearly in a state of subjection. In 691 U.C.
was the conspiracy of Catiline : and the accounts of that
event show that the Allobroges were at that time subjects
of Rome. Their envoys were at Rome, preferring charges
against their rulers or magistrates. P. Umbrenus, an agent
of the prætor Lentulus, who was a chief performer in Catiline's plot, sounds them by entering into a discussion of their
grievances. " Postquam illos videt queri de avaritiâ magistra-
" tuum, accusare senatum quòd eo auxilii nihil esset ; miseriis
" suis remedium mortem expectare : At ego, inquit, vobis, si
" modò viri esse voltis, rationem ostendam quâ tanta ista mala
" effugiatis."* They pledge themselves to the conspiracy ; and
afterwards repent of it. " Quinto Fabio Sangæ, cujus patrocinio
" civitas plurimum utebatur, rem omnem, uti cognoverant, ape-
" riunt." Fabius reports these disclosures to Cicero, who frames
the scheme that ensures the public safety : and the senatorial

* Sallust. Bell. Catilin. c. 40, 41 ; and see Appian. de Bello Civ.
ii. 430.

traitors forfeit their lives through the evidence of the Allobroges. The charge against their magistrates, the grumbling at the non-protection of the Senate, the patronage of the Fabii, the very act of assenting to the conspiracy, all show the Allobroges to have been at this period in a state of political dependence.

Thus the alleged probability of the Allobroges having been first driven beyond the Isère in the year 692, vanishes, with all the statements on which it is built. They lost their independence in 630 : and, while there is no evidence that they ever regained it, there are ample circumstances tending to satisfy us that they did not. See the progress of events in the south of Gaul during that very period, the sixty years of which we speak. What is it but the continuous progress of Roman power ? The foundations of it were laid gradually but strongly. We may look back to the eighty years that preceded those sixty years, the time of the Ligurian wars, wars with those who shut up the avenue to Spain with their mountains on the sea—ἀποκεκλεικόσι τὰς εἰς τὴν Ἰβηρίαν παρόδους, τὰς διὰ τῆς παραλίας. Strab. iv. 203. While that struggle lasted, Rome was becoming acquainted with the politics of Gaul through their maritime communications with Marseille and the Rhone. Under pretence of defending the interests of her allies, as Livy calls the Œdui, she attacks the nearer of the transalpine states. The first colony is founded, Aquæ Sextiæ. Then is the downfall of the great states, the Vocontii, the Arverni, the Allobroges. The colony of Narbo is established. Outer Gaul is now their battle-field against the barbarians who had overrun Spain, and carried their hopes of plunder to the plain of Italy. The famous canal is constructed by Marius for avoiding the shallows at the Rhone's mouth, offensive to navigation. Not restricted to maritime communication, the Romans now marched to the Pyrenees and Spain through countries that owned their mastery. Toulouse is garrisoned, and a Roman general can withdraw his troops into France for winter quarters. Finally, before the end of the sixty years' imaginary war, the higher central Alps are laid open to the rush of Roman armies into their Gaulish and Spanish provinces.

This is the period in which it is assumed that, during such progressive movement of Roman power, the Allobroges were stemming the torrent and defying a pressure to which their neighbours had to yield. The notion put forth by Larauza, and assented to by Ukert, as a basis for the migration of Allobroges northwards beyond the Isère in the latter days of the Roman republic, is nothing less than this—that this humbled nation, who had flourished in the south towards the Mediterranean, bordering on states treated with less severity than themselves, rallied from their defeat in 633, and maintained a series of unrecorded wars, which, after sixty years, were concluded only by the surrender of Ventia and the burning of Solonium, told by Dion Cassius. I believe both those places to have been in their northern and original territory : and I hope it has appeared that a march through the Allobroges, the fifth and last requisite for our accordance with the Polybian narrative, is, with the rest, truly fulfilled by a march from the confluence of the rivers to the Mont du Chat.

CHAPTER III.

Adverse Theories on the beginning of Alps. Two by which Hannibal marches forward in the Island. Mr. Whitaker, going through Geneva, finds the Alps of Martigny. Mr. H. L. Long, going through Grenoble, finds them at Fort Barraux.

I HAVE now to deal with this terminus, the first Alps, as it has been variously fixed in the several theories hostile to my

own. In explaining my own views on the subject, I have
contrasted them to some extent with others. Nevertheless
I will advert to the ἀναβολή of each other theory *seriatim*,
only not repeating matters already discussed.

First, let us take the two schemes of march which, as well
as our own, proceed from the Island without turning back to
recross the Isère. I encounter Mr. Whitaker as the champion
of the Great St. Bernard, seeking his first Alps at Martigny ;
and Mr. Henry Lawes Long, who, on entering the Island,
proceeds through Grenoble to his first Alps at Fort Barraux,
and then joins us at Montmélian.

March by Lyons and Geneva to Martigny. Mr. Whitaker.

Among the English commentators, Mr. Whitaker stands
forth as the laborious, and 1 believe the most recent, advocate
of the Great St. Bernard. And he may be considered to have
contributed greatly to the discussion of the matter. General
Melville, whose effort to explain Polybius was made in 1775,
communicated his notes of what he saw and thought to
Mr. Whitaker and M. De Luc. In 1794 Mr. Whitaker published a long work in support of the Great St. Bernard, and
against the views of General Melville. In 1818 M. De Luc
was induced to publish his excellent work, having become
acquainted with the General in 1795, and finding his own
views to correspond with what he learned from him. He
has not failed to speak his opinion of Mr. Whitaker's
merits—" Animé du diabolique esprit de contradiction, en-
" traîné par une imagination desordonnée, et privé du sens
" commun quoiqu'avec une prodigieuse érudition, il voulut
" se frayer une route différente de toutes celles qu'on avoit
" imaginées jusqu'à lui, sans s'embarrasser des absurdités
" sans nombre dans lesquelles il devait nécessairement
" tomber."

I will deal with Mr. Whitaker as I find him. I do not dwell upon his mode of reaching the Rhone, as none are following him. He asserted, that Hannibal, after crossing the Pyrenees, quitted the coast, and made his march through Carcassone, Lodève, Le Vigan, and Anduse, and so came upon the Rhone at a part opposite to the influx of the Drome, and crossed to a place called Loriol. Mr. Whitaker selected this place as being half-way between Lyons and the sea; knowing it by means of another circumstance which he reports, namely, that Arles is at the mouth of the Rhone. This fact, which also is exclusively his own, removes in favour of his hypothesis the length of Rhone usually recognised below Arles; and brings his place of crossing so much nearer to the sea. In conformity with these views, Mr. Whitaker makes Hanno's division to cross the Rhone three miles above the influx of the Isère; so as to have crossed the latter river before he comes down to take the enemy in flank. Being satisfied that a διάβασις at Loriol fulfils all the requisites of the Greek narrative, Mr. Whitaker conducts the march up the Rhone, and in four days brings the Carthaginians to Lyons; where his Island is the ground now occupied by the city and enclosed by the two rivers and the hills which over-hang the place. After settling the affairs of the Segusiani, he replaces Hannibal on the left bank of the Rhone, and continues the march undeviatingly along the windings of the river, by Seyssel, Geneva, and the Lake, to Martigny.

I am not aware that these tenets have received assent, saving in the applause of Mr. Tytler (Lord Woodhouslee), who promptly published a pamphlet in express commendation of Mr. Whitaker's discoveries. When we remember that Polybius represents the passage of the Rhone to be a short four days' march from the sea, that he attributes 1,400 stadia from that passage to the beginning of Alps; and prescribes 1,200 from the beginning of Alps to the plain of Italy, we might be satisfied, without more, to dismiss the Great St. Bernard from the list of candidates for representing the pass intended by Polybius. But, though it would be a waste of labour to scrutinize such a journey through all the tests of conformity with the Greek history, some notice is fitly bestowed on a known writer, whose zealous display of learning upon our subject is among the curiosities of literature : we add to the security of truth by encountering all that has pretended to illustrate her. I shall, however, endeavour to comprise in this chapter all that needs to be said on Mr. Whitaker's construction of Polybius, that I may not recur to it on further topics : also, as he vibrates in his feelings of respect, such as it is, between the two ancient authorities, I hope to be excused if, while I interpret one, I notice his treatment of the other, disregarding in this instance my own rule of criticism.

Mr. Whitaker expresses his satisfaction, that Polybius is confirmed by the authority of Livy in bringing the march to Lyons as the Insula of the history. From that place Hannibal marches along the Rhone, being attended as far as Geneva by the "friendly King of Lyons;" and keeping close to the banks of the river, with the stream on his left, Mr. Whitaker discovers a blot in the Roman historian, for turning at Lyons to his left hand instead of his right : but upon the whole applauds him for his improvements on the Polybian narrative, in the progress to Geneva.

Among other things, he considers Livy to have forwarded the knowledge of the truth by introducing the river Druentia. He represents that the Arve, which falls into the Rhone at Geneva, is not navigable, and that the Druentia of Livy is "non navium patiens :" that therefore the Arve is the Druentia of Livy. Dwelling on this discovery, as he says p. 145, with a parental fondness, he rejoices in the confirmation of it by Strabo. That writer has told us, iv. 203, of a river called

Druentius, which, rising in the highest summits, runs into the
Rhone.   This Mr. Whitaker declares to be the torrent which,
rising near the Col du Bonhomme, rushes down the Val de
Montjoye, and joins the Arve at Passi.   After quoting
Strabo on the Druentius rushing to the Rhone, and the Doria
on the other side of those mountains mixing with the Po,
he says, " This quadrates very accurately with all that I have
" said of the Arve; and forms a full demonstration of itself,
" that the Arve was actually denominated the Druentia or
" Druentius by the Romans." i. 141—150.

Having still further settled the identity of this river by
the aid of Silius Italicus, Mr. Whitaker forwards the expedition under the auspices of Livy, who reports Hannibal
to have reached the Alps " campestri maximè itinere," which
he thinks to have peculiar application to a route from
Geneva to Martigny.   i. 157—160.

Having travelled some way amicably enough with the two
ancient authorities, Mr. Whitaker begins to suspect a want
of harmony between them.   Not doubting that Hannibal
climbed the Great St. Bernard, and knowing, from the third
book of Cæsar's Commentaries, that, in order to get there,
it was expedient to pass through the Nantuates and the
Veragri, he is shocked to find these nations quite overlooked
by Polybius, who actually brings Hannibal to the ascent
of the Alps in 1,400 stadia from the passage of the Rhone.
Mr. Whitaker rebukes him in these words :— " All that march
" of Hannibal, though it was pursued through a couple of
" nations, is totally omitted by Polybius.   He considers the
" position of Geneva as the beginning of the Alps ; therefore
" carries Hannibal a hundred miles from Lyons, and instantly
" sets him to enter the Alps.   Hannibal, he tells us, having
" marched along the river about a hundred miles, began the
" ascent of the Alps.   This is certainly one of the many
" deficiencies, and of the very important too, that just criticism

" must for ever lament in the narrative of Polybius. A range
" of country about sixty miles in length is annihilated by the
" negligence of this writer ; and we find a great gulph yawn-
" ing wide before us, when we would pursue his march of
" Hannibal with geographical fidelity. Yet such has been
" the reverence shown to the pen of Polybius, such the
" idolatry paid to his name, that his very faults have been
" consecrated with his excellencies, and the erring mortal
" has been enshrined in the glory of the Divinity. Though
" Livy comes in very happily to supply his deficiency here,
" and exposes it very strongly by supplying it, yet little
" attention has been given him, and the historical world has
" generally preferred the falsehoods of this Plato to the truths
" of Livy. Livy, indeed, has hitherto been considered by
" all, not as he ought to have been, not as an equal planet
" with Polybius in the horizon of our history ; but as a kind
" of satellite only to him, attentive to his movements, re-
" flecting his brightness, and hardly noticeable in the lustre
" of his beams, and this false idea has contributed to give
" a false turn to many parts of the history of Hannibal."
i. 168—172.

Notwithstanding the contrast thus portrayed, it is difficult
to perceive that Livy has so happily supplied the defects of
his rival, yet from Martigny to the summit he appears still to
supplant him in the favour of Mr. Whitaker. At St. Branchier,
above Martigny, Mr. Whitaker brings Hannibal among the
Salassi—and says in a note, p. 232: "Livy is most luminously
" particular here, while Polybius wraps up all in a dull gene-
" rality of narration." At Orsières a conference is held with
natives, some coming from places higher up, Liddes and St.
Pierre : and Hannibal is over-reached by their cunning. The
Salassi offer to guide him by a better route ; so he casts off
his own guides, turns away with these new friends into the
Val de Bagnes, and ascends the eastern branch of the Drance.

This brings the army to the Rock of Luttier,* the destined
scene of the outbreak of the treachery; on which Mr. Whitaker, p. 274, note, says, " Livy alone informs us of this bold
movement in the Salassi, xxi. 34." In pp. 202–3, we find
that the assailants received so severe a chastisement that they
presently vanished; Hannibal is exhibited as returning to the
guidance of his Italian friends: he still struggles onward, the
line of glaciers edging close upon his left, among which Mr.
Whitaker names, from a map in De Saussure's second volume,
those of Chermotane and La Valpeline, and in another direction those of De Tzeudy or Valsoret, as north or west of Mont
Noir and Mont Velan, embarrassing his movements and compelling him to feel his way. It is said that " Livy is the only
" historian supplying this portion of the narrative, Polybius
" by an unpardonable negligence omitting all notice of it."
Again, p. 284, " Polybius smothers that history, which we see
" so lively and so active in Livy, concerning the dubious, the
" circuitous, the retrograde progression of Hannibal in his
" march from the hill of ambuscade to the crest of the Alps."
We learn from Mr. Whitaker, that, "moving in a line in
" which no army ever moved before or since, Hannibal reached
" the regular road at St. Pierre, which he had left five days
" before at Orzières, only about seven miles below." " The
" next day he found himself happily mounted, with all his
" army, upon the real ridge of the Alps."—P. 289.

It is right to mention, that, in spite of the apparent satisfaction with which Mr. Whitaker seems to accept the aid of
Livy, there comes a moment when he spurns it altogether. It
happens that that historian has declared in unequivocal terms
that Hannibal did not come over the Great St. Bernard: and

* I presume this to be the place mentioned as Lourtier in the
very interesting account of an excursion in 1856 by Mr. W. Mat-
thews. See 3d edition of " Peaks and Passes," published by the
Alpine Club, p. 23.

for this error, he falls, pp. 133-4, under the lash of that paramount authority which is relied on throughout the work. Mr. Whitaker remarks that " Livy's testimony is of no weight; " that it is opposed by the whole tenour of Polybius's history, " and encountered by the whole tenour of his own ;" and thus condemns him :—" The historian, who stands striding like a " giant across the plain and by the temple on Great St. " Bernard, brandishing his iron mace, and forbidding me all " passage with Hannibal along that avenue, I am compelled " to face, because he stops me ; to knock down because he " would dislodge me ; and to march over his prostrate body " (if I can) into Italy." As if this were not enough, Mr. Whitaker presently quotes the heretical opinion of Livy, and proceeds :—" This is all a mass of inaccuracy, forgetful- " ness, and error. I am sorry to use such language con- " cerning such a writer: but it is necessary to the assertion " of truth and the ascertainment of the history. There is a " false modesty hanging upon every mind that comes to " examine a writer of Livy's celebrity in the world of history, " which would chill the current of examination, and bind up " the critical powers of the judgment in a kind of frost, if we " were not on our guard against it ; if we do not prevent its " benumbing influence by continual exercise." i. 350.

This explosion coincides with a principle before disclosed, when Mr. Whitaker ridicules the writers " who feel their " weakness too sensibly to walk upon their own legs, and are " obliged to hobble on the crutches of authority." We look back to see how Mr. Whitaker walked himself without his crutches, and gave his clenching argument for the Penine Alps. It was this—that Hannibal came by a road ; a formed road: that there was in those days no formed road over the western Alps : that the tribes upon the Alps made no roads across their mountains, nor suffered them to be made by others : that they were in hostility with all mankind till the days of Augustus, who reduced many of these tribes, and carried along the mountains a train of formed roads.

These ideas are so laboured by Mr. Whitaker from p. 100 to p. 125, that one began to expect that Hannibal cannot have come over the Alps at all. But at last a circumstance is disclosed which relieved the author from that conclusion. It is this: that though even in the days of Cæsar those western Alps were in a wild and ferocious state, and furnished no good passage from Gaul into Italy, yet in the northern Alps there was such a passage. Mr. Whitaker appeals to Cæsar's account of Galba's exploits, where, speaking of the Great St. Bernard, he says that he desired to lay open the road through the Alps, by which the merchants had been used to travel. " This," says Mr. Whitaker, 123-4, " shows us the one only formed road of the times." And he adds, p. 124, " All this coincides in an extraordinary manner with " the movements of Hannibal. He goes not towards the " Alps of Mont Genèvre. He knows there is no formed road " over them. He knows that the only formed road is on the " northern side of the mountains, near the rise of the Rhone."

We certainly read that Cæsar was desirous of laying open a road over the northern Alps; but this does not lead to the inference that Hannibal had found a well-formed road there in earlier times: and, as to those northern Alps alone being practicable, we happen to know that Cæsar had in his previous campaign himself crossed the western Alps, carrying his army over the Genèvre in his expedition to stop the Helvetii. Mr. Whitaker anticipates this remark, and disarms it, by admitting that Cæsar did not in that instance carry his legions by a formed road, inasmuch as there was none. Accordingly he apologises for Cæsar having taken such a course of march, pleading the urgency of the occasion, p. 105. " He was too eagerly bent upon his plan of operations, at " this grand commencement of his Gallic warfare, to take the

" customary way from Italy to France. He wanted to push
" directly into the north of Dauphiny. He entered the Alps
" at Ocelum, that is, Exilles : he turned off short on his right
" at once : passed Mont Cenis close on his right, and Mont
" Genèvre remotely on his left : and he fell in probably with
" the line of the future road from Grenoble to Briançon at
" Villars d'Arenes."

On one point we shall agree here with Mr. Whitaker ;
namely, that in Cæsar's time there was no formed road from
Exilles or anywhere near it across country to Villars d'Arenes :
we would assent, if he had said that there never will be.
But, whatever was Cæsar's route from the inner to the outer
Province, if it was good enough for him, why not good enough
for Hannibal? Why was an African invading Italy to be
more fastidious concerning a formed road than a Roman
general hurrying to a Roman province? And was not
Hannibal eagerly bent upon his plan of operations? But let
us inquire what could be Mr. Whitaker's ground for supposing that Cæsar had the advantage of a formed road in his
northern Alps and not in his western Alps? Is it the word
" iter " that haunted his mind, so as to warrant the contrast?
I see nothing else in his quotations that could suggest this
idea of a formed road, as the peculiar incident of the northern
track. He quotes, p. 123, " Causa mittendi fuit, quòd iter
" per Alpes, quo magno cum periculo magnisque portoriis
" mercatores ire consueverant, patefieri volebat ;" and then
says, " These words show us the one only formed road of the
times through the Alpine mountains."

On this we have still to ask, " Why formed ? " and why
the only one ? The " iter" through the Penine is spoken of by
Cæsar as a track used for merchandise ; but which he wished
to improve into a route for armies : for this purpose it
required patefaction. It escaped Mr. Whitaker's observation,
that Cæsar also applies the word " iter " to his route over the

western Alps : the difference is, that he does not say that this
route required patefaction ; indeed, we have good reason to
believe that it had undergone patefaction by Pompey, about
sixteen years before Cæsar resolved to patefy the Penine. The
word " iter " was prominent in Cæsar's short account of his
march through western Alps : indeed, Mr. Whitaker quotes
every word of that account (pp. 103—106), excepting these :
" quà proximum iter in ulteriorem Galliam per Alpes erat,
" ire contendit."

Mr. Whitaker, however, could not be expected to acknowledge Pompey as an improver of the Genèvre pass : for he
informs us, that that general had himself taken advantage
of the Penine when he led his army into Spain; a fact
which is not disclosed by any authority prior to Mr. Whitaker.
It happens that Pompey, speaking in a dispatch[*] of having
crossed the Alps, says, " Per eas iter aliud atque Hannibal,
nobis opportunius, patefeci." Mr. Whitaker, p. 123, not
daunted by these words, and "in deference to common sense,"
corrects " aliud " into " idem ; " and so makes Hannibal and
Pompey go the same road. With equal facility he brings
Appian to confirm the fact. That writer, though his geography is rather queer, plainly states that Pompey went
a very different way from that of Hannibal : " de Bello Civ."
ii. 419. Mr. Whitaker, however, not only understands that
it was the same, but gives Pompey's reason for pursuing that
line ; a reason which must have been highly satisfactory to
the Roman Senate. " Pompey declined the more direct route
" over the western Alps, and took the circuitous road across
" the northern, because this was Hannibal's, and because he
" was proud to emulate Hannibal." i. 122.

In summing up the merits of the light which he has
thrown on this point of history, Mr. Whitaker acknowledges
his obligation to the ancient historians to a degree beyond

* Sallustii Fragmenta.

what might be expected. He professes to have conducted
Hannibal from the Rhine to the Po, "stage by stage, and
"step by step, as the concurring narratives of Polybius and
"Livy have held out the clue. Geography has united with
"history to confirm their narrative and my account." ii. p.
230. Notwithstanding this generous expression of gratitude,
I look upon Mr. Whitaker as exempt from the foible which
I impute to most modern commentators, a vain desire to
reconcile conflicting testimonies: he swears only by one
master.

Let all who have any misgivings in favour of the Great
St. Bernard, study Mr. Whitaker's volumes. They may rise
from the perusal cured of their error. They will find much
research of various matters drawn from all ages: much
excellent sentiment, moral and political, which, though not
bearing at all on the invasion of Italy, well becomes the
worthy man who delivers it. He abounds in historical
illustration, as in comparing the revolt of the Segusiani with
the revolutions of France and Poland; and establishing the
Alps of Hannibal by modern references. If the publication
had been delayed till after the battle of Marengo, we should
have had additional chapters, proving the route of Hannibal
by that of Napoleon. The events told excite throughout the
feelings of the writer; as in the chastisement which he inflicts
on the native obstructors of the Carthaginian progress. The
inhabitants of the valley of Aosta appear not to have molested
the Carthaginian march in their descent; a circumstance
which constitutes one of Dr. Arnold's doubts on the route.
Mr. Whitaker, on the contrary, imputes the great calamities
of the march to the treacherous conduct of that people: and
for that purpose locates them on the ascent, and thus rejoices
in the discomfiture of their machinations. "The well-fabri-
"cated balloon of Salassian villany had burst with its own
"gas within, and those who were mounting to the clouds

" in it were thrown to the ground, severely hurt ! " Many
are his reproofs of dissentient critics. Menetrier and Breval,
who in their dealings with Lyons rivalled Mr. Whitaker
himself, have this as their reward : " The sepulchral lamp
" of the antiquary goes out the moment we come up to day-
" light, and leaves only a smoke and a stench behind it."
Equally crushing is the solemnity with which, after demon-
strating Druentia to be the Arve, he condemns some who
would construe it the Durance. " The whole backbone of the
history is bent double by the violence of this folly." But abler
specimens than these will be found of the vituperative powers
of this writer. He has faithfully fulfilled his own injunctions
to the intellects of others : " To prevent the benumbing influence of false modesty by continual exercise."

There is an author, a man I believe of high reputation,
who, in his zeal to fulfil one of the conditions of Polybius,
violates all the rest, still further pursuing the valley of the
Rhone,—M. Arneth, Director of the Museum at Vienna. His
views on the subject were published in the " Wiener Jahr-
bücher" for 1823, and they are criticised, as well as those
of Dr. Ukert, by Dr. Thirlwall in the third volume of the
" Philological Museum." M. Arneth does not pause with
Mr. Whitaker at Martigny ; but, in order to make sure of a
descent into the Insubres, and to bring Hannibal to Milan,
carries the Carthaginian army over the Simplon. Perhaps in
an improved edition, Hannibal will explore the Rhone to his
glacier, ἐπὶ τὰς πηγάς, cross the Furca, and lead the invaders
into Italy over the St. Gothard.

Through Grenoble to Fort Barraux. Mr. Henry L. Long.

The notion of a march up the right bank of the Isère is likely
enough to suggest itself to an observer of the map of France.

But we have to try it by the text of Polybius : and if his history, rightly construed, shall be found to express that Hannibal, after entering the Island, still pursued the valley of the Rhone, the theory of Grenoble cannot stand. Other difficulties present themselves to the doctrines of Mr. Long.

The local features are known and admitted. The Oxford Dissertation says, p. 64 :—" The rocks on the northern bank " of the Isère came formerly so close to the river, that it " would have been impossible to have turned them." Mr. Long himself, who more than all has studied the environs of Grenoble, says, p. 57 :—" The precipices of the Sassenage and " the cliffs of the Grande Chartreuse lock so closely, that the " entrance of the valley leading to Grenoble is in some " lights absolutely undistinguishable ; and we are at a loss " to know whence the river can possibly come." So speaks the critic who is taking much pains to prove that Hannibal's march lay through the town of Grenoble. So sensible was he that the army could not have passed through that place without opposition from the Allobroges, that he asserts it as the scene of their conflict with Hannibal. To obviate the numerous objections, he has recourse to that peculiar inter-pretation of the text, which I will set forth and examine.

Mr. Long's work is entitled " The March of Hannibal from the Rhone to the Alps." Now, though he constantly quotes two or three lines at a time from the Greek text, he never quotes the few words of Polybius which describe that par-ticular section of the march on which he writes. He gives, in the historian's own words, the previous section of the march, from Emporium to the Rhone ; but not that which follows, from the Rhone to the Alps. Accordingly he never deals with those words of the 39th chapter which exhibit that march as " 1,400 stadia along the river." When he is upon the narrative of events in c. 49, and is beginning the march up

the Rhone, which, as we have seen, he crosses at Tarascon, he
notices the expression παρὰ τὸν ποταμόν, saying that it shows
the march from the passage to be up the Rhone; and he
observes that that expression occurs frequently in Polybius :
yet somehow he seems to have missed them in the earlier
chapter, where that expression is applied to the whole march
from the Rhone to the Alps. Not that he was unacquainted
with that chapter : for he fully acknowledges 1,400 stadia as
the distance from the passage to the Alps; but he only
connects a portion of it with the Rhone. He exhibits the
component parts of that distance in a way peculiar to himself : he does the 800 as soon as the Rhone is crossed ; and,
as he crosses it lower down than most other interpreters,
600 would not bring him to the Isère : so he takes the 800
to be from the crossing, and by that means professes to get
as far as Valence, saying, p. 50—"The distance of 800 stadia,
" 100 m.p. 'along the river,' having expired at Valence, we
" must at that town turn away from the Rhone, and con-
" sequently take the road leading towards Romans."

This innovation on Polybius is aided by another, also
original. It is commonly thought that four days brought
Hannibal along the river to the Island; and that ten days
then brought him 800 stadia further, the two being separate and
independent efforts of progression ; and that the last of the two
brings Hannibal to a point, where an interpreter of Polybius
is bound to find a beginning of Alps for him to contend with.

My friend's hypothesis is shortly this—Hannibal, crossing
the Rhone at Tarascon, at once made a march of 800 stadia
from thence to Valence, marching it in *four days:* he remained
there *six days*, communicating with certain friendly barbarians, the Segalauni : a body of whom joined their forces
with his, and assisted him in his progress to invade the land
of the Allobroges : with his allies, he entered the Island at
Romans, and pursued the present line of route to Grenoble :

the plain country, in which their aid was of service to him, came to an end at Moirans, at which place they left him, and returned home. Long speaks of "the contest between two " brothers for the sovereignty of some Celtic tribe, the name " of which is not given by Polybius ;" but, though Hannibal assisted one, and was recompensed with abundant supplies, it was not this party who attended and gave security to the march until they got near to the passage of the Alps. These are still the Segalauni.

Long had once thought with the Oxford Dissertation ; but is sincere in his new opinions. He says : "I had always, till " lately, believed that the distance of 800 stadia along the " Rhone ought to be measured north of its confluence with " the Isère. But, 1. The thing cannot be done. 2. If they are " measured after Hannibal's arrival at the Insula, wherever " they terminate, the Alps ought to begin."

I hope I have shown, in a past chapter on παρὰ τὸν ποταμόν, that the thing can be done : and that, at the termination of the 800 stadia, the Alps do begin, the Mont du Chat being the ἀναβολή.

I may give quotations of Long's own words to the contrary. In p. 44, having quoted in Greek the first sentence of the 50th chapter, he translates it thus :—" Hannibal, after ten " days, having marched along the Rhone to the distance of " 800 stadia, began the ascent towards the Alps." He pro- ceeds :—" The historian here sums up the time and distance " passed by Hannibal on the banks of the Rhone previous to " his striking away from that river towards the Alps. The " 800 stadia is exactly the distance between Tarascon and " Valence ; and the ten days seem to be composed of the " four days' march from Tarascon, *added to six, which we may* " *safely assign* as the period of his stay among the friendly " barbarians." Long had already said, p. 37 :—" In my own ' mind I have not the slightest doubt but that Valence was

" the scene of these operations." Now it was likely that a
reader would be startled at hearing of *an ascent* from Valence :
this is indicated in p. 47, where Long points out that the
ἀναβολή was πρὸς τὰς Ἄλπεις, " *towards* the Alps "—not
τῶν Ἄλπεων, " of the Alps." Now let us try to imagine some
practical difference between the expressions : my friend cannot
profit by it here : he plainly contradicts the history. Long
says that Hannibal began the ἀναβολὴ πρός from Valence,
when the ally joined him. Polybius says that Hannibal
began the ἀναβολὴ πρός from Valence, when the ally had left
him. As to the other difficulty, no conjecture is offered, to
account for four days meaning ten.

Such is the success with which this theory directs us to
Grenoble. When we have got through that place, we must
keep a look-out for making up the 1,400 stadia. The features
of the country are well and pleasantly described from p. 52 to
83 : and anecdotes are introduced for illustrating the history
of the district in modern times. As regards the subject of
the work, the march to the Alps, the effort is to make us
apprehend that the combat with the Allobroges, told by
Polybius, was quite unconnected with, and still distant from
Alps. The way under the cliff by the river being in those
days impracticable, Hannibal and his chosen band are supposed to scale the heights of Mont Rachais in the night,
gaining the advantageous posts which the enemy had in-
cautiously deserted on retiring to rest in Grenoble itself.
Long describes his battle of Grenoble with much spirit,
still insisting that no Alpine character belongs to the
Polybian scene of action, or to his own. He points out,
that our Mont du Chat, being at the other end of the same
chain of mountains, is far too Alpine to represent the scene of
the combat, and assumes that the narrative does not even
connect that combat with Alps. He exhibits his own apprehension of the history :—" Instead of Alps, we meet with a

" battle and the capture of a town. Nothing implies the
" difficulties attendant on any arduous ascent and descent.
" Now in the Mont du Chat they would have had to en-
" counter as severe a mountain for its elevation as any to be
" met with in the high Alps."—Pp. 46 and 77.

In furtherance of these views in favour of Grenoble, Long
translates ποιεῖσθαι τὴν ἀναβολήν to make a passage, and so
spares the invaders the labour of ascent: at the same time
he exaggerates the severity of our mountain the Mont du
Chat. Now, though the ascent to that col from the west
must always have been easy, the descent to the lake of
Bourget, then unimproved by art, was exceedingly steep and
hazardous. This character Long does not recognise as belonging to the description of Polybius: but, if that description is carefully studied, every expression for defiles and
precipices, every term for mountainous obstruction, that
occurs afterwards in the Polybian account of the dangers of
the higher range, snow only excepted, will be found in the
tale of the Allobrogian conflict. Such things indeed are not
wanting in Long's own history of the battle: when he grows
warm upon the beauties and the terrors of the Grenoble
scenery, a semblance of Alpine things betrays itself: " Arid
" walls of precipitous mountains — towering precipices —
" stupendous crags—cliffs and rocky heights—shaggy steeps
" —scuffling on the brink of a precipice:" and at last, p. 78,
" Hannibal, at height of at least a thousand feet above his
" own men, charging down the hill."

As one error leads to another, a marked variance appears
in the dates of progress between Polybius and his interpreter.
According to the history, the ten days along the river to the
Alps are followed by nine days of ascent to the summit.
According to Long, those ten days are between Tarascon and
Valence; viz. four of marching and six without marching:
and at Valence begins the ἀναβολὴ πρὸς τὰς Ἄλπεις: two

days later Hannibal crosses the Isère (p. 84), then in two
days more gets to Moirans ; and in two days more assaults
and captures Grenoble, and halts for a day : then in two days
more reaches Chapereillan : and, the ἀναβολὴ πρός being
finished, he begins the ἀναβολὴ τῶν Ἀλπεων, p. 89. The
progress is told thus :—" We roll along the post-road through
" the glorious vale of Grésivandan, and meet no obstacle
" in the shape of hills until we arrive at the village of La
" Buissière, lying at the foot of the heights of Fort Barraux—
" the Isère runs immediately under the heights of Fort
" Barraux, compelling the road to ascend at once the hills
" near the fort, and to approach Mont Meillan by the way of
" Chapereillan. This is the first ascent we have encountered :
" and, associated with the changes in the country above-
" mentioned, and its distance, which begins to be about two
" days' march from Grenoble, it is sufficient to induce us to
" conjecture that we must be at or near the ἀναβολή."
—P. 89, &c.

I have endeavoured fairly to set forth a very curious theory,
invented by one capable of doing justice to a better cause.
Like many others, he has allowed himself to indulge in a
fancy : all is subservient to Grenoble : we see in the lively
expressions of the author's feelings how, as he says himself,
his convictions have been aided by an examination of the
country. Examples abound of this influence :—" It is quite
" impossible to hesitate for a moment, in perceiving that this
" place of Hannibal's encampment πρὸς ταῖς ὑπερβολαῖς
" was at Moirans or in its immediate vicinity. It is so
" clearly just in front of the heights of the Grande Char-
" treuse, and so ostensible a situation for a halt, while the
" plans of the enemy in advance were investigated, that no
" doubt can be entertained on the subject." " Such is the
" country and such the objects we come upon at La Bui-
" serade : the first burst of it all upon the view is sufficient

" to show, that here, along these declivities and rocky
" heights, are the δυσχωρίαι, through which the Carthaginians
" had of necessity to pass. There, at the Bastile, are the
" εὔκαιροι τόποι, the advantageous positions, commanding the
" road across Mont Rachais, daily guarded by the Allobroges.
" And in Grenoble, the ancient Cularo, we find, beyond all
" doubt, the ' adjacent town,' to which they retired during
" the night." " Whatever security we may have experienced
" in fixing upon Moirans as the place of his last encamp-
" ment, is nothing compared with the certainty with which
" we now see him taking up a position at La Buiserade. No
" doubt then can exist as to the exact spot of this encamp-
" ment." Thus fascinated by the illusions of his own senses,
has a professed disciple of Polybius been enabled " to set
this long pending discussion at rest for ever."

We may sympathise with the fervour of such imaginations,
without accepting their aid to the decision of a critical
question. They were induced by the contemplation of
striking scenery, and they disturbed the author's earlier and
more sober apprehension of the Greek narrative. The result
was that through Grenoble the march must go : and the
1,400 stadia will reach farther up the Isère than the critic
would desire : therefore it begins at Tarascon. Still there
was this difficulty ; that the 600 stadia, commonly supposed
to bring you to the Island, would be exhausted short of the
Island. So the 800 are taken first, and the 600 afterwards :
the princely combatants become Segalauni instead of Allobroges : Valence savours of Alps, Grenoble disclaims them.
All for an hypothesis !

Long, though at last he goes over the right mountain, sadly
dislocates the chronology of the march in doing so. Polybius
represents Hannibal as fighting his way over the first Alps
before he reaches the Allobrogian town. Long finds the
Allobrogian town first, and his Alps two days afterwards.

Instead of reaching the summit with Polybius on the ninth day from the beginning of Alps, being the seventh day from the Allobrogian town, he gets there on the ninth day from the town, and the seventh from the beginning of Alps. Long wrote to correct our common friends the authors of the Dissertation; prescribing Tarascon for Roquemaure: 800 stadia as four days' march: Grenoble as the place assaulted. Unhappily for me, beyond the summit, he agrees with them in the only point on which I think them wrong; namely, where they make the historian to contradict himself, and impute eighteen days to his Alps instead of fifteen.

I cannot suppose that any remonstrance will cure my friend of his theory. The most likely prescriptions I can recommend are, 1. That he will read once more the 39th, 49th, and 50th chapters of Polybius. 2. That he will take into consideration these words of Dr. Thirlwall :— "Polybius contrasts the march " along the plain with the ascent of the mountains, in a " manner which clearly implies that the latter begins at the " end of the ten days' march." *Phil. Mus.* ii. 675.

Notice of Grenoble by Dr. Liddell.

It is fair to my friend, Mr. Long, to say that a distinguished scholar, the latest historian on the subject, has said that the track of Hannibal lay near Grenoble. These are the words of Dr. Liddell, in which he narrates the Carthaginian progress beyond the Isère to the ἀναβολή, i. 340 :—

" Hannibal continued his march up the Rhone, and crossing " the Isère, found himself in the plains of Dauphiné, then " inhabited by the Allobrogian Gauls. He marched thus far " in a northerly direction, about one hundred miles beyond " the place where he had crossed the river, at the invitation of " a chieftain who was contending for the dominion of the tribe " with his younger brother. Hannibal's veterans soon put

" the elder brother in possession; and the grateful chief
" furnished the army with a quantity of arms and clothing,
" and entertained them hospitably for some days. He then
" guided them to the verge of his own dominions, and
" took his leave. This must have brought him to the point,
" at which the Isère issues from the lower range of the Alps,
" somewhere near the present fortress of Grenoble. Up to
" this point there is little doubt as to the route taken by
" Hannibal: but after this all is doubtful."

Up to this point the words of this author seem rather to
conduct us to Les Echelles: the introduction of the Isère and
Grenoble negatives the Mont du Chat. The particulars of
the controversy on the Carthaginian march are not minutely
entered into: but in proceeding to Italy an opinion is occasionally expressed; and I will notice the following :—

Vol. i. p. 341.—" In seven days after Hannibal began the
" ascent, did he reach the summit Polybius says *nine :* but
" this must include the two days' halt at the top of the
" pass." I confess I think nine to be right; that is, that
Polybius is supported by his context.

P. 342.—" The last year's snow frozen into ice, lay thick at
" the top of the pass, and fresh snow began to fall, which
" covered the traces of the path." Here I would observe,
that we do not read about the last year's snow at the top of
the pass; but at a very much lower level; and there it is
quite accounted for.

I am pleased at least to know, that Dr. Liddell's pass is not
doubtful. He says, " Hannibal descended among the mountains of the Salassians." Though the Penine, as well as
the Graian, would have led him through the Salassians, he
was not likely to be there after being just behind Grenoble.

It is further said, in a note to 343, that General Melville
carried Hannibal into the Insubrian country, and so back to
Turin. I cannot know whether the General ever said " back

to Turin." I should not so express his opinions, so far as M. De Luc has reported them.

Also it is said that " others follow Livy in taking Hannibal " from Grenoble up the Romanche, and so over the Genèvre " down to Turin." I am not aware that any but Folard have so construed the route of Livy from the Isère. It is true that all our critics speak of Turin (*i.e.* Augusta Taurinorum) as existing in the time of Hannibal : but I am not aware that any authority is cited for it.

CHAPTER IV.

Theories of tracks south of Isère.

IF it has been satisfactorily shown, that the march issued from the Island by the Mont du Chat into the vale of Chambéry, the foundation of all theories of a progress south of Isère from the confluence of the rivers is shaken. Whether the expedition is supposed, on retreating from the Island, to move down the Rhone again, or to ascend the Isère, these suppositions can be indulged no longer, if the Mont du Chat is recognised as the ἀναβολή reached by the valley of the Rhone.

Each route invites notice on the five requisites of Polybius. To some extent this has been given, by contrasting the views of others, when explaining my own. When not done already, I will point out the errors, as they may occur to me. To this hour men of learning and renown have been driving against our hypothesis of the Graian Alp : and the charm of names is to be dispelled. Accordingly, each combatant, though he may have stumbled irrecoverably in an early part of his course, shall nevertheless be watched to the end of it, or so far as he may have developed his scheme. In the further progress after reaching the Alps, the Cenisians will claim the chief notice: for they labour their case to the end, and with a perseverance not shown by others.

Some method is to be observed in bringing to notice the rival plans, so that each may be made intelligible, and comments upon them be apprehended without confusion. It seems convenient to set them out in some geographical order, as from the confluence of the rivers; first taking the scheme by which Hannibal, after his concerns at the Island, is made to retrace his steps far down the Rhone: then those which go down the Rhone, but not so far: then that which, going along the Isère, bends from it to the Drac: then that which leaves the Drac for the Romanche: then that which parts from the Isère between Grenoble and Montmélian; and lastly, that which bends from La Chavane to Aiguebelle and the Arc. Thus they may be taken, as they radiate more and more eastward from the common beginning near the mouth of the Isère.

There will still remain two theories, not brought under this arrangement: one in which Hannibal never has bent towards the Isère at all: and one in which he moves still more north, and has Mont Blanc for his λευκόπετρον. The former will receive a short separate notice: as to the latter, I had an opportunity of challenging it, when sojourning in the district whence it sprang: and that small act of warfare shall tell its own tale, as I gave it from Chambéry in September, 1854.

1. *Down the Rhone again to St. Paul-trois-Châteaux: thence across country to the Alps of the Ubaye. The Marquis de St. Simon.*

This course is urged in a long preface to the author's history of the campaign in the Alps of 1744. Having carried Hannibal over the Isère into the Island near St.

Marcellin, 30 miles above the mouth, he proceeds to Vienne : from that place he supposes him to march down the Rhone again as far as St. Paul-trois-Châteaux, before he bends away in search of the ἀναβολή, which he finds at last in going up the Ubaye. (Quoted by Larauza, *Hist. Critique* 61, 215).

This curious march, which should be 800 stadia, and ten days from the mouth of Isère, does not well answer to that time or to that distance ; nor is much of it ὡς ἐπὶ τὰς πηγάς. As little does it suit the tenor of the history. The history prescribes a march of 1,400 stadia from the crossing of the Rhone to the Alps, along a river. The progression cannot be fulfilled by a lengthened doubling upon the track, unless matter of context should be found, warranting such construction. But there is not a word in the history which countenances the notion, that in this or in any respect Hannibal ever altered his course from that which he at first designed.

The latter part of the Marquis's line to the Alps is not more Polybian than the first. Having marched down the Rhone again nearly to where he crossed it, he performs some hundreds of stadia more, in search of mountains ; reaches the valley of the Durance above Tallard ; attends that river for a time ; and, turning from it up the Ubaye, finds the ἀναβολὴ Ἄλπεων in a defile on this river.

This critic has not explained the efficiency of Hannibal's cavalry in his cross cut from St. Paul to Tallard : and, though a plain country favourable to his cavalry ought to have given him advantages before he approached the Alps, the plain in which he rejoices is only in the angle made by the Durance and the Ubaye above La Breoule. His Allobroges, as might be expected, rest their claims on etymology.

This commentator will presently be joined by an Englishman, and by some means each will fancy himself at the Viso.

2. *From Valence by Die and Luc to Remollon on the Durance.*
General Vaudoncourt, and General St. Cyr Nugues.

These commentators march to their first Alps from Valence.
Proceeding by Chabreuil, Crest, Die, Luc, Mont Saleon and
Upaix, they find their object near Tallard on the Durance.
General Vaudoncourt marks his ἀναβολή thus, p. 45 :—" étant
" arrivé à Tallard, Annibal s'arrête au pied des montagnes : il
" s'approche jusqu' aux bords de la Vence, au pied d'un
" défilé qui s'étend jusqu' à près Remollon." His Allobrogian
town is Chorges.

In vindicating their march of 800 from Valence, these
generals exercise rather an arbitrary discipline over the
manuscripts. Not thinking the river a necessary accom-
paniment of the march of 800 stadia to the first Alps,
General Vaudoncourt dispenses with it thus :—" Le passage
" est évidemment altéré : le genitif à été changé en accusatif
" par erreur et caprice, des copistes : ainsi il faut lire à
" Rhodano et non pas propter Rhodanum." General St. Cyr
Nugues in accordance with this idea substitutes ἀπό for
παρά ; so as to express the idea, " en s'éloignant du fleuve."
Now I cannot think that this exchange of ideas would be
satisfactory : ἀπό would not instruct you on the direction
of the march so well as παρά. Also those who propose the
change ought to make it more largely : παρ' αὐτὸν τὸν
ποταμόν describes the march of 1,400 stadia in c. 39, of
which the 800 is a part ; the prior part (600) being from the
crossing to the Island. Polybius applies παρά to each part,
and to the whole. But these generals have not told us to
change παρά into ἀπό in the other two instances, which seems
necessary for their consistency. Indeed, if " s'éloignant du
fleuve " should become the amendment of the earlier part of
the 1,400, Hannibal should strike away across country to the
Alps as soon as he has crossed the Rhone : and the two
generals might as well have adopted the theory of M. Fortia

d'Urban, who, in order to march through his own estate,
makes Hannibal go direct from the Eygues to the Po.   But
in that General St. Cyr Nugues could not have joined him :
he had local attachments as well as the accola of the Eygues ;
he announces, p. 9, " Je suis habitant des bords de l'Isère."
We shall see soon, that this fact has some value : it makes
the general a sound witness on the banks of that stream,
though it does not make him an authority on manuscripts.

3. *Up the Isère and the Drac to St. Bonnet.   M. Letronne and M. Bandé de Lavalette.*

The inventor of this theory, which discloses the first Alps
at St. Bonnet on the Drac, is M. Letronne; "sanè haud
spernendus auctor :" a man of literary eminence, and the
first assailant of M. De Luc.   In two papers of the *Journal
des Savans,* 1819, he thus explains the Carthaginian progress
to the ἀναβολὴ τῶν Ἀλπεων, which he seems to identify with
" l'entrée du Département des Hautes Alpes"—" Annibal arrivé
" sur le bord de l'Isère, marcha dix jours le long de ce fleuve,
" jusqu'à la montée des Alpes.   Parvenu au confluent de
" l'Isère avec le Drac (qui dit-on, avoit alors lieu un peu au
" dessus de Grenoble, près de Gière,) il ne traversa ni l'Isère
" ni le Drac, torrent extrêmement large et impetueux à son
" embouchure : il remonta ce torrent, que sa largeur dut lui
" faire prendre pour la même rivière que l'Isère.   Il le suivit
" jusqu' au dixième jour, dans l'espace de huit cents stades, à
" compter du point ou il avoit trouvé l'île des Allobroges.
" Cette mesure prise le long de l'Isère et du Drac, porte a
" Saint Bonnet, à l'entrée du département des Hautes Alpes.
" Jusque-là dit Polybe, l'armée s'étoit trouvée en plaine : alors
" elle commença à gravir les Alpes."   It is the distinguished
writer of these words, who ventured to designate the theory
of M. De Luc as "une opinion insoutenable jusqu' au point
d'être absurde."

Time and Distance.—Time of travelling will depend not only on distance, but on character of country, on impediments, whether of nature or art. Much of M. Letronne's track, though he calls it all plain, is through a difficult country, both up the left bank of the Isère, and the left bank of the Drac; and, though, on arriving at St. Bonnet he says here is my ἀναβολὴ Ἄλπεων, and proclaims, "Jusque là l'armée s'étoit trouvée en plaine," some will consider that he plunges deep into Alps, to find the beginning of Alps; and that the conformity of his track requires to be considered under the next head.

Plain favourable to Cavalry.—We know, from Polybius, that the march of the army in company with the ally, after being refitted by him, was through plain country, ἐν ἐπιπέδοις, where the enemy, hovering about and threatening their progress, was deterred from attack by fear of the Carthaginian cavalry; and that this was the case till they were near to the first ascent. M. Letronne's course of plain is in two parts: that which borders the left bank of Isère, and that which borders the left bank of the Drac. I believe that his plain up the former river will, after the first few miles, be found to fail him. Perhaps he had no personal acquaintance with the country. Indeed, not one of those who follow that south bank of Isère and call it plain, profess that they have ever seen it: none have spoken in a way which directly offers their personal credit to the advantages of it for cavalry. While they follow the windings of the stream, there is a careful abstaining from responsible assertion of the character of the banks.

In questioning this river march of my adversaries, I do not bind them to "son lit;" I will allow their valleys the scope which belongs to them, though none is allowed to our valley of the Rhone; my doubt is whether any scope can be found in the adjacent country for their cavalry to take advantage of.

In the Oxford Dissertation it is said, p. 157, "Some of the
" highest of the secondary chains of the Alps take their rise
" immediately to the south of the Isère, and very much lower
" down the river than Grenoble. There never was any Roman
" road on the south bank of the Isère, between Valence and
" Grenoble, and the road which now exists there is barely
" passable, and nothing more than a mere communication
" from one village to another, and it is indeed only laid down
" in maps of a very large scale." I have referred to Cassini's
map, where it is not laid down at all : a route will probably
be given in the great map of France which is now in progress, General St. Cyr Nugues, repudiating this as the line
of Hannibal, says, "De hautes montagnes escarpées y bordent
" l'Isère, depuis les environs de Pont-en-Royaus jusque vers
" Sassenage ; la dominent et en resserrent le cours, parti-
" culièrement vis-à-vis Moirans, où le rocher fait une énorme
" saillie."

There is also an amusing and most honest confirmation of
the true character of the river bank that I speak of, in the
comment of M. Bandé de Lavalette, who adopts M. Letronne's
track, following him to St. Bonnet. M. Larauza's scheme of
progress had corresponded with theirs, as far as the Drac, and
he includes the whole line in his description, "riche plaine et
fertile ;" but, when he escapes from them into the plain of
Grésivaudan, he exposes the roughness of their further march
to St. Bonnet, saying, p. 53 :—"Lorsque de ce point (Grenoble)
" l'on prend à droite pour suivre le cours du Drac dans le
" direction de la montagne de Sassenage, on le voit traversant
" la plaine de Grenoble, à peine à deux ou trois lieues de la
" ville, s'enfoncer déjà dans les gorges que lui ouvrent les
" Alpes. Annibal, en se dirigeant de ce côté, serait donc
" entré dans ces montagnes, n'ayant fait au plus que 582 stades
" le long du fleuve."

M. de Lavalette protests against the unfairness of this, and says with much candour that, if M. Larauza can be satisfied with a march on the south shore of the Isère below Grenoble, he is not the man to object to the valley of the Drac:—" Si, " malgré les obstacles que parait offrir le pays situé entre " Valence et Grenoble, le savant professeur a cru qu'Annibal " avait franchi cette distance, il ne sauroit être admis à pré- " senter comme impossible le trajet de l'embouchure du Drac " à St. Bonnet "—p. 64. This piece of good sense might have induced its author to dissent from M. Letronne's doctrine, " jusque là en plaine ;" a proposition which is applied to the Isère below Grenoble, as well as to the Drac above it. We accept the comment as the evidence of a candid adversary, writing at Montpellier, whose summer excursions probably familiarised him with the romantic side of the Isère.

Along the River.—Having admired the usefulness of M. Letronne's cavalry from Pont-en-Royans to Sassenage, and seeing how their manœuvres still surprise us in approaching St. Bonnet, we may again notice his fulfilment of the requisite παρὰ τὸν ποταμόν. In addition to his ingenuity upon words, M. Letronne gives a moral explanation of the turn up the Drac. He has found the cause to be that, when Hannibal came to that river, he took it for the Isère, and so followed it. He has not told us where he picked up this anecdote: but, if it were true, it would show that Hannibal's intention had been to proceed along the Isère ; so that, instead of M. Letronne's route by St. Bonnet to the Mont Genèvre, he must have designed a march either to the Cenis or the Little St. Bernard. On this point M. Letronne leaves us quite in the dark : he does not go on to say, whether Hannibal ever discovered his mistake, or whether he cared for it.

March through Allobroges.—M. Letronne insisted on the position of the Allobroges as occupants of the Island, in the *Journal des Savans*, Janv. 1819 : but objected to the cir-

cuitous route attributed to Hannibal by De Luc, as " un
" détour bien étrange, quand il pouvoit arriver à Montméillan
" en suivant l'Isère. Rien ne l'empêchoit, puisque les Allo-
" broges, loin de contrarier alors sa marche, lui fournirent de
" vivres, &c.—Quand à ce que Polybe appelle l'île, habitée,
" dit il, par les Allobroges, on ne peut trouver un canton, &c.
" —Cette île est donc l'insula Allobrogum." He speaks
of "l'opinion incontestable qui place l'île entre le Rhone et
Isère: " and explaining his own views of the route, M.
Letronne says, "C'est à partir des Allobroges que com-
mencent les grand difficultés de la question."

Such and so rational were M. Letronne's own impressions.
When M. De Luc's reply made him aware that the truths
which he admitted were unfavourable to a march up the
Isère, he thus shuffles out of his opinions—" Cette difficulté
" repose uniquement sur l'opinion qu'on a de l'étendue du
" pays habité par les Allobroges à une époque fort postéri-
" eure au passage d'Annibal : mais on ignore absolument
" si les Allobroges, nation puissante, n'avoient point à cet
" époque étendu leur domination sur la plus grande partie
" du Dauphiné ; en sorte qu'il a pu avoir toujours à com-
" battre les armées Allobroges. La circonscription du
" territoire de la plupart de la Gaule, au temps de Cesar
" d'Auguste, est encore fort incertaine : mais on peut assurer
" que nous ignorons tout-à-fait l'état des choses au tems
" d'Annibal. Comment se faire une objection de ce qui
" n'est pas possible de connoître ! "

We may be satisfied, that such an antagonist has no better
consolation against the evidence of Cæsar, Cicero, and Strabo,
to which in his simplicity he lately subscribed, than that
these writers were not coeval with Hannibal. In January he
pronounced in a tone of some decision, that the island which
Polybius describes as the country of the Allobroges, was
on the north of the Isère. In December he reconciles himself

to a march up the Drac to St. Bonnet, as the πορεία διὰ τῶν Ἀλλοβρίγων καλουμένων Γαλατῶν, and proclaims a victory gained over that people in the mountains beyond.

4. *By Moirans and Grenoble—up the Drac—down the Luie to the Durance near Tallard—up to the plain of La Breoule and to the defile on the Ubaye. A member of the University of Cambridge. 1830.*

This critic takes his ἀναβολή from the Marquis de St. Simon : his mode of getting there is his own. Having said that "after a continued and rapid flight of four days, Hannibal arrived at the Island," he conducts the army through Moirans to Grenoble, without Allobrogian obstruction. He recrosses the Isère at Grenoble and proceeds along the Drac and by Gap to the Durance—then across the latter river near Tallard, and for some miles along it, to the valley of the Ubaye and the village of La Breoule ; and finds the ἀναβολὴ Ἄλπεων in a defile above that place.

Time and Distance.—As this author wrote a book to show that Polybius's distances are wholly without value, one could hardly expect him to give to time a respect which he denies to space. His march is singularly favoured by fortune. Unlike Mr. H. Long, he finds no enemy at Grenoble. Unlike M. Letronne, he finds no enemy near St. Bonnet—the hostile population do not avail themselves of local advantages to disturb him. He is aware that the 800 stadia are expended : but pushes on, calling M. Letronne an eminent scholar, and manages a few additional marches before he finds a portion of plain.

Along the River.—This author, p. 6, in challenging the march to the Mont du Chat, construes παρ' αὐτὸν τὸν ποταμόν " along the river by its very banks." When, in p. 61,

he applies the ποταμόν of the narrative to his own route, he
says that the river along which Hannibal marched about 800
stadia in ten days, must be the river Drac. Still his interpretation of ποταμόν is liberal : his text and his red line of
march disclose to us that the partiality to the Drac was not
exclusive : the ally seems to have attended the march along
the very banks not only of Rhone, Isère, and Drac, but of
Luie, Durance, and perhaps of Ubaye. He then turned
homeward. Hannibal vanquishes the defile of the Ubaye,
and captures the Allobrogian town.

Plain country for Cavalry.—Though the march of this
commentator is twice as long as that of Polybius, he does not
require the cavalry to act till he is near the end of it, and
just beginning the ascent. The Allobroges, an unsettled
tribe of barbarians, of whom he says that nothing is known
till 200 years after Hannibal, were enraged against him : he
fortunately had the clothing and stores furnished by the
sovereign of the island for assisting him in the battle of the
Allobroges, p. 60 : he crosses the Durance near Tallard, then
for some miles marches to the valley of the Ubaye, and
borrows from the Marquis de St. Simon these words of
comfort :—" On voit au-dessous de la Breoule, sur les bords
de la Durance, une espèce de plaine." The failure of plain,
and the scene of combat, are thus brought near together :—
" As long as the Carthaginians continue in the plains leading
" to La Breoule, ἕως ἐν τοῖς ἐπιπέδοις ἦσαν, and the escort
" from the island remains to protect them, they are un-
" molested ; but, on the departure of their guards, when they
" begin to push forward to the defiles, they find them pre-
" occupied and closed against them by the enemy. Hannibal,
" entering the pass by night, seizes on the heights. In the
" morning the barbarians attack as they move slowly out of
" the defile. Hannibal makes a descent on the enemy with
" entire success, and captures their town," &c.—Pp. 62, 63.

Through the Allobroges.—In this advanced region, according to the anonymous critic, was fought the battle of the Allobroges, " who, on the departure of the island guards, commenced hostilities against Hannibal as he began the ascent." One hardly expected that this people would be allowed so great a stretch of territory ; for the writer has recognised the Vocontii at the mouth of the Drac, and is now tending to Barcelonette. However, he sustains the current of Allobroges, like many other critics, till he has passed his chosen spot for fighting with them. We leave him now, proceeding by the Chemin Royal ; but shall hear of him again on the Col de Viso.

5. *Up the Isère and the Romanche by Bourg d'Oysans to the Mont de Lens and the Lauteret. Chevalier Folard.*

The Chevalier, writing in 1728, sought the Isère at Romans : proceeding up the river, and leaving Grenoble on his left hand, he faced the Drac vis-à-vis Vizelle. But, when he had got over it, and found himself in a practicable country, he did not profit by this advantage : he declined the "large et belle vallée," and encountered the arduous defiles of the Romanche. He says, iv. p. 89 : "Je suis persuadé que la route " la plus ordinaire et la plus pratiquée des Gaulois en Italie, " étoit celle qui conduit du Mont de Lens, du Lauteret, et de " Briançon au Mont Genèvre." One would infer from this that he apprehended the first Alps at the Mont de Lens : for after crossing it, he has the first combat with the natives " ceux du païs." One cannot reconcile the landmarks of this writer with those of Polybius : for the historian certainly places the Allobrogian conflict at the first Alps ; and it is not easy to deny the character of Alps to the mountains between Bourg D'Oysans and Briançon : but the Chevalier brings the Allobroges into action " entre Sezanne et le Mont de Sestrières."
—P. 91.

This route, by which Folard, in contempt of Polybius, carries Hannibal to the Alps, is now the direct course from Grenoble to Briançon, one of the most astonishing works of Napoleon. Those who have seen it may try to imagine how the Carthaginian army would have made their way from Bourg d'Oysans to the Lautaret at a time when nature had received no corrections of art. A knowledge of this line will be gained from Brockedon's illustrations—" Pass of the Mont Genevre." The journey from Grenoble to Briançon is also well told by Mr. Weld's " Summer Ramble, 1850."

There is no hint of this way in any ancient writings earlier than the Chart of Peutinger. The Chevalier, however, rejoicing in his own " experience de la guerre et un grande connaissance du pais," gravely instructs us, that it was the most usual and most frequented route of the Gauls into Italy, and therefore adopted by Hannibal. It is true that a good knowledge of several tracks qualifies a man for comparing them : but a great familiarity with one may rather disqualify him. So it was with Folard : his campaign in the Alps of France and Piémont had the same partial effect on his historical views that an acqaintance with M. Viso had on the Marquis de St. Simon, and a residence at Grenoble on my friend Henry Long, and the ownership of Lampourdier on the Comte de Fortia d'Urban. We shall meet the Chevalier again on his summit.

6. *Up the Isère to Le Cheylas.   Mr. Ellis.*

Distance.—Mr. Ellis, looking along the Isère for a beginning of Alps, found it at Le Cheylas, 33 kilomètres above Grenoble. In p. 89 he says : " The total distance from " Valence (or from the junction of the Rhone and Isère) to Le " Cheylas, is 87½ Roman miles." This gives 700 of the 800 stadia of Polybius : and I presume the principle of measurement is that which Mr. Ellis prescribes elsewhere ; " all the way along the very "bank," which, below Grenoble, is not uuimportant.

River, Plain, Cavalry.—We saw, *ante*, chap. 2, how Mr. Ellis acknowledges the river to be the Rhone, but urges that it *must be* the Isère. That effort may have distressed him : but, having passed Grenoble, he says comfortably, "The vale of " Grésivaudan from Grenoble to Le Cheylas, being perfectly " level, is quite adapted throughout to the action of cavalry." Treatise, p. 97. This is true ; but Mr. Ellis's track has a very brief intimacy with the vale of Grésivaudan. It would have been more to the purpose if he could have said, "The south " bank of Isère is quite adapted throughout to the action " of cavalry." Letronne and Larauza spoke rashly of its being plain below Grenoble. Possibly they felt excused for imagining what their eyes had not contradicted. Mr. Ellis, more cautious, does not apply "plaine riche et fertile" to the whole, and commends it only from Grenoble to Le Cheylas.

Is it enough, then, that the last 33 kilomètres of his march to the Alps are suited to cavalry ? The Allobroges of the history were contemplated as an object of fear before the march was resumed after the refitting : they are named as the cause why the prince of the island conferred on Hannibal his greatest benefit, by accompanying the march with his force through their country. Did that potentate cross the Isère with his troops, lead them through the embarrassed country which stands on the left bank below Grenoble, and effect the passage of the Drac, only that he might be ready to support Hannibal in the Grésivaudan during the few miles of plain which would occur before he turned into his Alps at Le Cheylas ? Mr. Ellis has at least avoided the example of Larauza, who, to give length to his mountain march, began to measure without a semblance of mountain to begin with. He has turned sooner into mountain to provide for the elongation. He says that he gains 26½ miles by it; so we may be

more indulgent to what he calls the length of his march in
the Alps.

Allobroges.—We have already examined the reasons which
make Mr. Ellis to place this people south of Isère in the time
of Hannibal. He has an additional reason in thinking that
Allevard was "the chief town of an Allobrogic district, from
" its appearing to preserve, in its own name, that of the Allo-
" broges." Accordingly, Hannibal goes that way to the Mau-
risne, taking possession of the town of Allevard. Treatise, p. 95.

N.B. I shall have strong objections to make to the system
of interpreting Polybius pursued by this critic ; but at present
confine myself to a short notice of the five requisites, such as
is given to every theory. When we come to the merits of
his own peculiar doctrines, they will need to be sifted.

7. *La Chavane near the Isère, opposite to Montmélian.*
Larauza. Ukert.

These two commentators are to be taken together, as objects
of criticism, because their ἀναβολή is the same. Though one
begins the 1,400 stadia at Tarascon, and the other at Roquemaure, they both desire to end it at La Chavane. Nothing
could have emboldened M. Larauza to suggest such a point,
but the pressing expediency of leaving a few miles to help
out the scanty complement of his next section, the distance
through the Alps ; and it happened that, from that point to
the end, Dr. Ukert took Larauza for his model.

It is most unreasonable to treat a village standing in the
plain as a beginning of Alps. There are earlier points in a track
up the Isère, where mountain might suggest itself, as between
St. Nazaire and Sassenage, after entering the department of the
Drôme. But, if a traveller along the south shore of Isère can
cross the Drac without encountering mountains, he cannot
pretend to find one obstructing his journey to Aiguebelle,
sooner than the defile at that place. There is undulation of

surface for the few latter miles. At Planaise, Coize, Malta-
verne, Bourgneuf, you are passing through an easy country,
not mountain ; there is no pretence of δυσχωρίαι till you have
passed through the defile. Brockedon says that the road is
not interesting till near Aiguebelle, at the entrance of the
valley of the Arc about five miles above its confluence with
the Isère. Larauza himself writes—" Le chemin va sans cesse
" montant et descendant à travers ces riantes collines qui
" se succèdent depuis La Chavane jusqu'à la croix d'Aigue-
" belle."

Along the River.—As I hinted in a previous chapter, Dr.
Ukert was not disposed to compromise himself as a scholar
by making the word ποταμόν to represent two or three rivers
in succession, or to have grammatical reference to any but the
Rhone. Nevertheless, while he deems the word to refer to
'Ροδανόν, he manages to march up the Isère. The word for
this river being in manuscripts "Icaras," not "Isaras," he
thinks that Polybius blundered upon both rivers above the
confluence, taking the Rhone for the Icaras, and the Icaras for
the Rhone ; that Polybius wrote of the Isère as bearing the
great name Rhone, and deemed the Rhone to be the tributary
under the name of Scaras. Such is the discovery of Dr.
Ukert; but I think there can be few, if any other, who do not
acquiesce in the good sense which has accounted for Scaras
being found in manuscripts. When Holstenius met with τῇ
μὲν γὰρ ὁ 'Ροδανὸς, τῇ δὲ Σκάρας (the rivers which form the
point of the island), he observed that the capital sigma, now
written Σ, is in some old manuscripts, C ; hence he supposed
that OICAPAC had come to be written CKAPAC,—IC being
made into K. Another version has been found in Ἀραρός,
which led Iac. Gronovius, in his edition of Polybius, to this
comment : " τῇ δὲ ὁ Ἀραρός—non est hujus fluvii ille cursus
" ut possit cum Alpibus et Rhodano insulam facere. Optimè,
" ὁ γεωγραφικώτατος Chiverius, lib. i. Italiæ, cap. 33, Isaras

" reponit : et acutissimus Holstenius errorem addit natum
" majusculis literis confusis CKOPAC pro OIKAPAC." Dr.
Ukert does not yield to this ; and says (ii. 588), " We dare
" not change the name Scaras, as the thing does not admit of
" proof, and we find in Gaul many names for the same river."
What then ? This might furnish Polybius with an excuse, if
he really gave the wrong name Icaras ; but it is not believed
that he did so. If he had written Scaras, he would have
written ὁ Σκάρας : but the manuscripts have τῇ δὲ Σκάρας, a
noun without its article. There is something, therefore, which
requires correction, and he who resists the correction of Holstenius should favour us with a better one. (See Schweighæuser's *Adnotationes ad Pol.* iii.)

Whatever might be in a manuscript, as the title of the
second river, the Rhone would still be the Rhone ; the Island,
which is identified by so many characteristics, would still be
the Island ; and the second river, under any name, must be
that which we call Isère. With all due respect for Dr. Ukert,
his professed allegiance to manuscripts furnishes no rational
excuse for his dogma upon ποταμόν. We give him credit, as
a scholar, for repudiating the constructions of the many other
critics, but the failure in their contrivances is in no degree
remedied by his own.

Ten days. Plain for Cavalry.—M. Larauza seems to apolo-
gise for the very slow march made by the army along his
river, the Isère ; and, for making it credible that such a march
could occupy ten days, expatiates on the formidable stream of
the Drac, as if it would be the one cause of a tardy progress.
But the apparently candid confession of this difficulty must
not lead us to blink the other objections to such a course ; it
should rather call attention to them. M. Larauza gives a
detailed and forcible history, pp. 88, 89, 90, of the ravages of
this torrent ; of the efforts made in the time of Louis XIII. by
the Maréchal de Lesdiguières, and in later times, to turn its

course and compress its inundations; saying at last, "Est-il
" nécessaire de dire qu'un fleuve de cette nature n'est point
" navigable ? "

Now, though there is no Drac nor anything like it in the
tale of Polybius, and though there is in that tale the characteristic of ἐπιπέδα, which is rather kept out of sight by
M. Larauza, I am ready to concede that, if the Carthaginian
army had gone up the Isère, they would not have found the
Drac navigable. For them to have got over it by any other
method than wading, vessels and rafts must have been brought
up from the Isère, either by land-carriage or by towing against
the torrent: and either mode would have required the favouring aid of the inhabitants; and, according to the history, the
foreign intruders apprehended from them the most vigilant
hostility. In the march to the Alps, after the refitting of the
force, this enemy, watching the opportunity to destroy, was
deterred from attack not only by the presence of the allied
force, but by the Carthaginian cavalry. What would have
been the terrors of cavalry, themselves struggling through a
series of intractable whirlpools ? Why did the Allobroges of
Ukert and Larauza tolerate the invaders in their march below
Grenoble, and acquiesce in their passage of the Drac ? Why
permit a progress which they had the power to arrest ? In a
line to and over the Drac, conflicts would have ensued worthy to
have been prominent among the casualties of the expedition.

The unfavourable nature of the country along the lower
Isère has been shown from the writings of opponents, General
St. Cyr Nugues, and M. de Lavalette, as well as from those
of our friends. Yet, while M. Larauza imagines, without
authority from the historian, the physical impediment of the
Drac, as the cause of slow progress, he shuts his eyes to the
want of cavalry ground which that authority requires, as
favouring the progress of the Carthaginians. At last, however,
he cannot help feeling that the exploit which he conceives,

namely the safe surmounting of such an obstacle as the Drac
in defiance of a hostile population, was worthy to find a place
in the history. So he accounts for the historian's silence
upon it. This is his solution, p. 91: "Il est certain que
" ce nom (Drac) ne c'est pas conservé dans la géographie
" ancienne, et que cette rivière paroît avoir été très peu connu
" des anciens: ce qui pouvait expliquer la silence de Polybe
" sur le fait de son passage par l'armée Carthaginoise." A
most indiscreet comment! It admits that such events were
events to be told; but suggests that Polybius was prevented
from telling them by the uncertainty of a name. Now
Polybius in the beginning of the narrative told us that he
should not attempt names in an unexplored country; not
that he should omit facts, when he was at a loss for a name.
He had no name for man or place, when he described
the passage of the Rhone: he had no name for man or
place, when he described the dangerous conflict which preceded the arrival on the summit: but such events stand
forth in their importance. If a river like the Drac had
crossed our path when Hannibal traversed the plain of
Dauphiné with the enemy hanging on his march, M. Larauza
would have seen it probable, that the forbearance of the Allobrogian chiefs would not have lasted to the Alps; but that
the armament which struggled against the floods would have
met also with human opposition.

Allobroges. I have already controverted the doctrines of
Larauza and Ukert on this head; which rest partly on the
perversion of words, partly on the supposed ubiquity of that
people, and partly on misrepresentation of history, including
their supposed migration northwards from the maritime district just before the time of Strabo.

There is one auxiliary comment, the merit of which belongs
wholly to Dr. Ukert. He writes thus: "Dass diese Völker-
" schaft früher ein grösseres Gebiet als später besass und weiter

" gegen Süden sich ausdehnte, als nachher, darf man wohl
" aus des Apollodorus Bekanntschaft mit derselben schliessen,
" der sie als die mächtigste Nation Gallien's schildert, und zu
" seiner Zeit war die Kunde der Griechen auf das der Küste
" nahe Land beschränkt." " That this people possessed a
" larger domain in earlier than in later times, and extended
" itself further to the south, one might infer from Apollodorus's
" acquaintance with them, who represents them as the most
" powerful nation of Gaul: and in his time the knowledge of
" the Greeks was limited to the country near the coast."—
Pp. 590, 591.

The works of Apollodorus, all but one short treatise called
Bibliotheca, are lost: and the statement here imputed to him
is known only from six words which occur in a work of
a much later period. In the surviving fragments of a Dictionary called ἐθνικά, or περὶ πόλεων by Stephanus of By-
zantium, are these words—'Αλλόβρυγες, ἔθνος δυνατώτατον
Γαλατικὸν, ὡς 'Απολλοδώρος. Hereupon Dr. Ukert argues
that, as the knowledge of the Greeks was restricted to the
country near the coast, the name of a great Gaulish nation
which reached the Greek Apollodorus, must have been the
name of a nation dwelling towards the sea. The argument
would be worth nothing, if applied to a time some centuries
earlier: for, from the period when a body of strangers founded
the city of Marseille, the reputation of a state which rejoiced
in the navigation of the Isère and the Rhone, might be carried
through commercial channels to the whole civilized world.
But who was Apollodorus, the Greek whose knowledge of the
Allobroges is deemed incredible? He was a learned Athenian,
born (see *Fasti Hellenici*, iii. p. 546) about the year 168 B.C.;
and who lived to about 88 B.C. He must have read of the
Allobroges as a boy in the schools; he would read of them in
the very history which we are examining, and not improbably
had acquaintance with the author. Where is the meaning of the
proposition that " the knowledge of the Greeks was confined

to the country near the coast?" This insinuation of ignorance
is surely injudicious. In the time of Apollodorus there was
full intercourse of knowledge between the great stations on
the Mediterranean : the plays of Terence, which tell the ways
of Athens, were acted when Apollodorus was in his cradle.
As to the Allobroges, whose very existence it is sought to
mystify, it was fifty years before Apollodorus was born, that
Scipio came within four days' march of that people, and
vainly hoped that they would give to his enemy the check
which he had failed to give himself: and it was nearly a
century later, when the account came that this same people
had been defeated in a great engagement, and, like Athens
herself, had submitted to the dominion of the victorious
republic. Dr. Ukert has been sorely pressed for grounds
of argument ; and, amidst historical and geographical perplexities, we see the climax of distress in this desperate appeal
to Apollodorus.

Such is the list of points, proposed by the writers named,
for beginning the march through Alps : we have put forth our
reasons for believing Polybius to have intended the Mont du
Chat. Before we reach it, we have taken leave of the
sovereign of the Island, wishing him a prosperous journey
home, not through a series of hostile nations, nor through
the prohibitions of unfavouring nature, but over undulating
plains, cultivated by those whom he claims as his subjects.
We pause with Hannibal at the ἀναβολή : the ἀναβολὴ πρὸς
τὰς Ἄλπεις, and the ἀναβολὴ τῶν Ἄλπεων ; for they are the
same thing. We pause with him πρὸς ταῖς ὑπερβολαῖς.
To this point our construction of the line of march is exempt
from an embarrassment, which belongs in some degree to all
rival theories : our beginning of Alps is unquestionably a
beginning ; our course over the plain of. Dauphiné has never
felt the contiguity of mountain. In approaching the Mont
du Chat, we recognise, in a way not to be mistaken, the
beginning or first ascent of Alps.

THE ALPS OF HANNIBAL.

PART V.

THE MOUNTAIN MARCH. ASCENT.

CHAPTER I.

Some theories are not worked out beyond their first Alps.
Those of the Cenis are laboured throughout their 1,200
stadia. Termini and distance. By the Little St. Bernard.
By the Cenis. By the Little Cenis. The events of each of
the fifteen days.

HAVING crossed the Rhone, and reached the beginning of
Alps, we look forward to the ultimate terminus, and have to
trace the march till it brings us to a country beyond the
mountains, the plain of Italy. This remainder of the march
should be about 1,200 stadia. Polybius says, λοιπαὶ δὲ τῶν
Ἄλπεων ὑπερβολαὶ περὶ χιλίους διακοσίους :—the heights of
Alps, being the residue of the march, about twelve hundred
stadia. This comprehends the entire passage ; the first Alpine
ascent, and the last Alpine descent. In the fifty-sixth chapter,
the act of transit is represented by the singular ὑπερβολή :—
" Hannibal arrived into the Padan plain and the nation of
" Insubrians, having performed the whole march from Cartha-
" gena in five months, and the passage of the Alps in fifteen
" days." The word is similarly used in c. 34, 6, and c. 47, 6.

The initial event is the forcing of the first Alps, in front of which we left the army on closing the discussion of our second question.   The final event is the touching the great northern plain of Italy at the point which gives escape from the barrier of the mountains.   The termini of such a march, as proposed by other commentators, must be considered : but the scope of inquiry into details will now be narrowed.   It would be impracticable to compare henceforward at each step the merits of every adverse theory, so minutely as has been done to the points at which they severally professed to reach the Alps. The advocates of the Cenis will claim a far greater share of attention than other opponents ; indeed they might be treated, as the only survivors in the contest.   If I have substantiated the march up the Rhone to the Mont du Chat, the advocates of the Mont Genèvre have broken down irremediably : but it is still open to the Cenisians, to confess the error of so soon deserting the Rhone, and to try their fortune in the Arc valley after a march through Chambéry.

There is this reason for attending to the pretensions of the Maurienne : arguments are attempted in detail throughout all parts of their progress to the plain, by Larauza and Ellis : and each invites an answer.   They have struggled elaborately to show their fulfilment of Polybian requisites ; on which the subscribers to other theories offer little or nothing to be controverted.   Truth will be better worked out, by directly opposing those systematised errors, than in sifting the confusion of writers who hardly express a reason for their opinions.

Moreover the theory of the Cenis has of late acquired some reputation of strength.   Dr. Ukert, who, as we have seen, argues against the Rhone, and follows Larauza through the mountains, is proclaimed by one most eminent as " defending " his theory with all the light that profound geographical " learning can throw upon the question."   Dr. Arnold, too, though not adopting the Cenis, has said that it suits the description of the march in some respects better than any other pass: it is not clear what those respects may be: but the remark, imperfect as it is, has given encouragement to those who sympathise with it.

Termini and Distance.   The Little St. Bernard.

It has been seen how the march up the Rhone, as told by Polybius, brings us to the beginning of Alps, at or near the village of Chevelu, in front of the Mont du Chat: here is one terminus.   Where then is the other, the exit from Alps and entrance into the plain?   In determining this point, we must attend to the author whom we are interpreting, as to time and space; cautious of the distinction between plain and mountain.

I have myself passed down the valley of Aosta: but in a state which prohibited all endeavour to notice where should be deemed the exit from the Alps.   I can only apprehend it from the writings of others.   In his second edition, p. 213, De Luc says, " C'est à St. Martin que finit la vallée d'Aoste, et " c'est à une demi-lieue de ce village que l'on découvre pour " la première fois les plaines de l'Italie.   On est sorti tout-à- " fait des montagnes que l'on est encore à une lieue et demie " d'Ivrée."   The Oxford Dissertation places St. Martin twelve miles below Verres: and it is said, p. 118: " St. Martin may " fairly be called the entrance of the Alps: for two secondary " chains of mountains, which run off at right angles from the " main chain, meet a little above it, and form a very narrow " pass, that closes the valley of Aoste as with a door.   The " descent, which is rapid the greater way from Aoste, ends " here; and between St. Martin and Ivrea there are no moun- " tains, but only a wide valley with hills on each side, and " Ivrea itself is completely detached, and stands in the plains." Settimo Vittone and Monte-Stretto, which are a little way forward, have been mentioned as points of perfect liberation into plain. In short, it is reasonable to say, that at or near St. Martin the Carthaginians hailed their escape from the mountains.

Roman armies used this way over the Alps within a century after it was visited by Polybius. The Itinerary of Antoninus gives the distances along the whole line in which our termini stand: that is to say, between Labisco (Chevelu) and Ivrea, which is below St. Martin and the two other points suggested. I give the stations on the route, adding the modern names. See Wesseling's *Vet. Roman. Itineraria,* and *Oxford Dissertation. Appendix.*

Labisco (Chevelu) to Lemincum	XIV	Chamberri
„ Mantala*	XVI	near Pierre d'Albigni
„ Ad Publicanos† .	XVI	Conflans
„ Oblimum	III	La Bâtie
„ Darantasia . . .	XIII	near Moustier
„ Bergintrum . .	XVIIII	Bourg St. Maurice
„ Arebrigium‡ .	.XXIV	Pré St. Didier
„ Augusta Prætoria .	XXV	Aosta
„ Vitricium . . .	XXV	Verres

$$155$$

Farther to St. Martin about   10

$$165 \text{ R. miles.}$$

I believe these official measurements of distance to be upon the whole excessive. One would suppose that an estimate of

---

* D'Anville suggested Montailleu: but it is negatived by the distance XVI: and one cannot doubt that a route from Chambéry up the Isère would always be carried by Montmélian.

† At Conflans (confluentes) the river Arly, probably the boundary of the Allobroges, falls into the Isère.

‡ Peutinger's Chart gives XII to the summit, in Alpe Graiâ: VI to Ariolica (la Tuile), and then XVI to Arebrigium—this X must be rejected.

distance through unknown mountains made by Polybius without any sort of mechanical aid, would be less accurate than an
official register made in a much later day. The βηματισταί
of Rome ought to have advantage over the adventurous
traveller. However, which was nearer the truth is a matter of
fact to be inquired. It can only be answered by comparison
with ascertained distances at the present day. Speaking from
what is now before me, I believe at present that the 150 miles
of Polybius comes nearest to the actual length of the mountain
march by the Graian Alp. The authors of the Dissertation
correct from their own experience some figures in the Itinerary
as excessive. Albanis Beaumont is referred to : but it is not
clear what sort of lieue he uses; and his estimates are not
applied to the Italian side. There is at present no official
itinerary : but now that Albertville is in France, we may soon
see the whole laid down in a *livre de poste*. In the mean time,
if we carry the measurement to about St. Martin, I expect that
about 1,200 stadia from the ἀναβολή is nearer the truth than
can be gathered from the Itinerary.

Termini and Distance.   Mont Cenis.

The termini, between which Larauza, followed by Ukert,
measures 1,200 stadia in the Alps, are La Chavane on the
Isère and Rivoli. See Larauza, 159, and Ukert, ii. part ii. 606.
La Chavane not being in the *livre de poste*, they take the
measurement from Montmélian, which is on the opposite side
of the river. La Chavane is an inadmissible point for the
beginning of Alps. There is no character which entitles it to
represent that critical point in the march. Wherever you
apprehend this point of division between the fourth and fifth
sections of the march, it must be marked by an ascent of
mountain : and, if a traveller is supposed to have arrived into
the vale of Grésivaudan without encountering Alps to chal-

lenge his advance, there are none to challenge him till he
comes to Aiguebelle.

The consequence of the mistake which I point out, is that,
on a scrutiny of M. Larauza's mountain measurement, we
must deny to him three postes out of the 28 which he reckons
from Montmélian to Rivoli, quoting them from the " Etat
général des Postes du Royaume de France, 1814," and reduce
them to 25. Also they must undergo a further reduction
near the other terminus, which is erroneous.   I believe that a
traveller is quite out of the mountains at Avillano, which is
1¾ postes short of Rivoli.   De Saussure, § 1,294, says of
Avillano, " C'est à peu près là que se termine la chaine
" des Montagnes qui bordent le côté méridional de cette
" vallée : la chaine Septentrionale, de l'autre côte de la Doire,
" se prolonge un peu davantage.   Mais de là jusqu'à Turin on
" ne rencontre plus de Montagnes proprement dites."   In
accordance with this, I am assured by one on whose observation more recently made I can safely rely, that at Avillano
you actually *debouche* into the open plain, the feet of the
mountains being bent back and pared away.   If these observations are just, the 28 are further reduced to 23½ ; and that
distance at most can be claimed by M. Larauza between the
just termini of a mountain march over the Cenis.

But, in addition to these corrections, we must remember,
that the object of our inquiry is not the number of French
postes, but the number of Greek stades.   A French poste was
vulgarly reckoned two lieues of 2,000 toises each, on which
estimate 23¼ postes would be 46,500 toises = 123 R. miles =
984 stades. But a poste is not 2,000 toises. The Oxford Dissertation says with great truth, p. 183 : " The post-book cannot be
" considered a fair criterion of mensuration ; for it is well
" known, that in mountainous countries the distances are
" always over-rated for the benefit of postmasters.   Thus, for
" instance, the post-book reckons three posts or fifteen miles

" (nearer sixteen) from Lanslebourg to the stage on the
"summit of the pass, whereas the real distance is not ten
" miles; and of course the old road, by which we ought to
" make our reckoning, would be still shorter." I find this
specimen of exaggeration to be practically confirmed by
M. Albanis Beaumont; he accomplished those three postes in
$3\frac{3}{4}$ hours: and $2\frac{3}{4}$ of those hours were consumed in the
montée to the Chalet de la Meut. In that montée his rate
was more likely to be two miles and a half an hour than four.
In Brockedon's journal he complains at an earlier part of this
same journey, of the extortion in charging distances : saying,
" At Modane our voiturier insisted upon resting : we walked
" on to Lanslebourg, fourteen miles, though it is stated in
" the French post-book to be four posts." No man would be
a better judge of his own rate of walking along a road than
Mr. Brockedon : he probably intends English miles ; so that
he was charged fully nineteen for what was really fourteen.
I believe that, if the mountain march over Mont Cenis from
Aiguebelle to Avillano were rightly measured, it would be
found not only not to reach 1,200 stadia = 150 miles, but to
be hardly more than 100 miles.

Termini and Distance.   Little Mont Cenis.

The termini of Mr. Ellis are Le Cheylas on the Isère and
Avillano. He deviates from the track of M. Larauza at Le
Cheylas : there quitting the valley of Grésivaudan, he moves
into the mountains, and bears up for Aiguebelle in a track
separated from that valley by a range of hills parallel with
the course of the Isère : by this he professes to reach
Aiguebelle in $26\frac{1}{2}$ Roman miles : he then makes it 106 miles
from Aiguebelle to Avillano. If he becomes mountainous
$26\frac{1}{2}$ miles sooner than Larauza, he brings out a result which,
though short of the estimate of Polybius, is nearer the truth

than those of other patrons of the Maurienne : and, if his theory can survive the more serious impeachments of its merits, we need not care for its defect in mountain distance.

Time with events of each day.

In order that my own comments may be intelligible, I will here state how I apprehend the army to have been employed in each part of its progress over the mountains from the ἀναβολή to the plain. Polybius says plainly, in c. 56, that the passage of the Alps had been effected in fifteen days. I believe him to mean what he says : and I interpret him by distributing the events which occurred in those days, as follows : the subject necessarily dividing itself into ascent, summit, descent.

1. Hannibal forces the pass of Alps, and occupies the town beyond it.

2. He remains encamped at the town.

3, 4, 5. The march is resumed, and continued for three days without interruption.

6. On the fourth day from the town, Hannibal holds conference with natives : makes treaty with them : receives supplies and hostages : they attend the march.

7, 8. The march proceeds, the false friends accompanying it.

8. Hannibal is attacked by the natives, when passing through a ravine ; and he stays back with part of the army about a certain White Rock during the night.

9. He reaches the summit early in the morning, and encamps.

10. He remains on the summit, and addresses the troops.

11. He begins the descent : comes to the broken way : fails in an attempt to get round it : encamps, and commences the repair of the road : which becomes practicable for horses by the morning.

12. The cavalry and beasts of burthen, with the chief part of the infantry, go forward : the work of repair is continued.

13. The work is continued; and a passage is effected for the elephants, who are moved on from the broken way.

14. The army continues the descent.

15. The advance of the army touches the plain.

CHAPTER II.

Ascent to the Little St. Bernard. The forcing of the Mont du Chat, and occupation of Allobrogian town. Army rests there one day. On fourth day of marching from the town, conference with natives, who attend them for two days. Bourg St. Maurice and environs. The Reclus. Ravine and Roche Blanche. Modern evidence. Melville. Brockedon. Arnold. Character of conflict. Summit reached on the morrow, being the ninth day of Alps.

THOSE who will examine the rise to the Mont du Chat from the plain of Dauphiné, and the precipitous descent on the other side to the level which leads to Chambéry, will probably acknowledge the scene to admit of the incidents related by Polybius on the first assault of the Alps by the Carthaginians.

In 1854, from the garden of my house at Aix, I had in constant view an indication of Hannibal's track : there is a notch in the upper line of the mountain ridge seen from that side of the lake, which announces a passage at this part of the Grande Chartreuse range. The ground on the Col has of course been greatly altered since it was visited by Polybius : within two centuries it probably was disturbed by the engineering of the Romans, who constructed a military way through this natural opening. Very great changes and improvements have taken place in our own days. Objects which called

attention in 1819 had ceased to be perceptible in 1854. Just
before I left Aix, my friend Wickham came over to me from
Geneva for a day or two : we went, a large party, across the
lake with our donkeys ; and, having passed the Col, turned to
the left under the brow of the mountain to a farm called La
Vacherie, from whence the young and active usually climb to
the Dent du Chat, and enjoy, if atmosphere is propitious, a
glorious view of Mont Blanc. My friend was greatly struck
with the magnificent road made since he had examined the
pass, by the King of Sardinia, and which, keeping near to the
precipice above the lake, affords by zigzags a convenient ascent.
He had made the journey with Cramer in 1819 in a two-horse
car : and, though it was evident to us where their track must
have been, it was evident only because it could be nowhere
else : not a vestige was perceptible to the eye, to show that a
road ever had been : on the contrary, it seemed impossible.

The Allobrogian town.

Commentators have desired to identify some known place
with the town to which the Allobroges had retired for the
night, and which after their defeat on the following day was
occupied by Hannibal. H. Long, who fights the battle at
Grenoble before he comes near to his beginning of Alps,
suggests La Tronche, which seems almost a part of Grenoble.
Larauza, p. 103, after entering the defile at Aiguebelle, says :
" Entre Argentil et Eypierre on aperçoit divers chemins qui
" conduisent aux villages jetés çà et là dans les montagnes :
" la ville prise par Annibal devait être située par là au milieu
" des monts qu'on a sur la droite, &c." Mr. Ellis, in his track
to the Maurienne, fixes upon Allevard. Wickham and Cramer,
after crossing the Mont du Chat, suggest Bourget. If called
upon to give a name to the town spoken of, I would say the
village of Bordeau : not because there are habitations there

now, but because the situation is just below the col of the
Chat. I do not, however, perceive that we need find any
modern place for representing the town to which the Allobroges retired; if in that day the Gauls of this district
resembled those who had already found their way into Italy
(and why should they have surpassed them in refinement?) :
" They dwelt in unwalled villages, not acquainted with arti-
" ficial comforts : with their beds of rushes and their chief
". diet of meat : practising only war and agriculture, they led
" simple lives : ignorant of other science or art, the wealth of
" each was his cattle and his gold ; as in all circumstances
" these were easy to be shifted with themselves at their
" pleasure."* The town whence issued the disturbers of the
march of Hannibal, has not only no claim to present identifi-
cation, but none to other commemoration of history.

March renewed after a day's rest.

No incidents are attributed to the first three days of this
onward march from the Allobrogian town : it proceeded
securely and without aspect of danger, (as we believe, through
Chambéry, and by Montmélian up the Isère,) till the coming
forth of the natives on the fourth day. All that we read is
very consistent with the region here spoken of : the booty that
was obtained after the defeat of the Allobrogian leaders was a
probable thing in the country near Chambéry : the country
forward was without difficulty ; and as far as Conflans, as
thought by some, it continued to be the country of the
Allobroges ; whose leaders, if any survived, might be satisfied
with the defeat which they had sustained. Mr. Brockedon
says that from Montmélian to Conflans the road ascends
through a succession of beautiful scenes ; that the inhabitants
are numerous, and the valley highly cultivated. The Oxford

* Polyb. ii. 17.

Dissertation says : " From Chambéry to Montmélian the valley
" is large and very rich ; and from thence to Conflans, though
" not quite so wide as the valley of Grésivaudan, it is still very
" large. For six miles before we arrive at Conflans the road
" is quite straight, very fine and broad, the country covered
" with fine wood when it is not under corn or vines."*

In this part of the progress there is competition between
the valley of the Isère above Montmélian, and the valley of
the Arc. They who will investigate the characters of these
two approaches to the main chain, will find along the Isère a
great degree of richness belonging to the most fertile and
most populous valley of the Alps. Along the Arc they will
notice variations in the degree of barrenness through a valley
poor in produce and inhabitants. This characteristic of the
approach to the Cenis is differently appreciated by those who
assert its claims. Larauza, seeing that the country traversed
must have been competent to support a population such as
the history tells, quotes from De Saussure a sentence or two
containing some faint idea of vegetation ; and so struggles to
bestow fertility on the barren Maurienne. Dr. Ukert confesses the sterility, and treats it as favouring the notion that
the invaders suffered from privations. Mr. Ellis regards the
fertility of a valley as a matter of inference rather than of
fact : and deduces its productiveness from the population of
the entire province to which it belongs in comparison with
that of other Sardinian provinces. Thus, as there is no
population on Mont Blanc or Monte Rosa, and a very small
one on the Great St. Bernard and other tracts within the very
large province of Aosta, he assumes the barrenness of the
Val d'Aosta from the population of the Province of that
name. Treatise, pp. 156-7.

* M. Replat's theory carries the march north-east from Conflans
to Beaufort, thence to the Bonhomme, and over the Col de la
Seigne down the Allée Blanche.

In applying time and events to the track which I support,
I will pause, as may be convenient, to compare it with other
tracks, in respect of any distinct topic ; but shall afterwards
separately point out any further objections to which these
may appear liable.

Conference with Natives, on fourth day of renewed march.

At Conflans we suppose the natives to have come forth with
tokens of peace and amity, and to have conciliated the friendship of the invaders, as told by Polybius in the 52d chapter.
From that place, now Albertville, we suppose the march to
proceed up the Isère by the usual road through Moutiers and
Ayme to Bourg St. Maurice. Some writers desire to fix
precisely the point of each night's encampment. I pretend
not to do this : I cannot even tell what progress they made
beyond Conflans on the day of the interview with the natives.
It would be vain to delineate each mile of the march, either
above or below the great bend of the river at Moutiers. The
circumstance of an important body of the natives coming
forth to meet them with professions of amity was likely to
take place on the confines of a new people, and Conflans
appears probable : but there are no incidents in the narrative
which mark the track by any special features of country, till
we draw near to the region of the main ascent. We only
know, that a portion of the natives were for two days accompanying the march, acting on the conspiracy which they had
formed : their purpose was to defer the onset till the march
should be coming to the extremity of the inhabited district.
It is to be presumed that the route in use would always
attend the course of the river : and this route, though in parts
difficult, afterwards became the line of the Roman way : the
Itinerary gives 34 miles from Ad Publicanos (Conflans) to
Bergintrum (Bourg St. Maurice): Darantasia (Tarentaise) is
about midway between those places.

Bourg St. Maurice and the environs.

We read that on the second day from that on which the
conference with the natives took place, the armament was
suddenly attacked in passing through a difficult defile. Now
it is clear that the conflict which here ensued must have been
near to the great mountain of the pass : for on the morrow
Hannibal was encamped on the summit, gaining it on the
ninth day of Alps. Thus the scene of this engagement is
looked for under the control of intelligible limits, being
clearly within a day's march of the summit, which Hannibal
must have intended to reach on the day when the attack was
made. There is also a particularity of circumstance in the
story of it, which may be expected not to suit the approach
to one mountain so well as the approach to another. Let us
endeavour to apprehend the nature of country and of the
movements ; and consider whether the facts related may have
occurred in the regions to which we assign them.

The traveller, before he approaches Bourg St. Maurice, has
been released from the closer contractions of the valley of the
Isère.   The place stands in meadow ground on the right bank
of the river ; and, as you go down towards it along the side of
the mountain below which it stands, you look forwards over
the town, when a mile or more distant, to that open ground
beyond it which has been called the plain of Scez, with the
Graian Alp beyond in the distance.   The oblong-looking surface of this plain, so viewed afar off, might be thought level :
but it has a decided acclivity : it may be a mile and a half in
length ; less in width.

I have the impression that, in so descending upon Bourg
St. Maurice, and looking over and beyond the town, there was
presented to the eye with some distinctness that seeming
plain, enclosed as it were in a frame of four sides. The Isère,
whose direction has been changed before it comes to Bourg St.

Maurice, may be called the under line : pine-clad mountains
make the opposite or upper side ; and a similar boundary is
continued on the right-hand side : while on the left is a bare
crumbling mountain, below which the Reclus is making its
way towards you. In the lower right-hand corner of the
picture is the village of Scez : in the upper left-hand corner
is the λευκόπετρον of Polybius. Carrying your sight over the
opening there, you have the Alpis Graia in the distance.*

After you have passed through St. Maurice, and are proceeding up the right bank of Isère, the Versoy torrent crosses
you from the left, bringing the waters from above Chapiu : and
presently the Reclus comes in, running directly towards you
from the Little St. Bernard : and being crossed, also falls into
the Isère : which river has bent his course towards you, from
the mountains above Scez, among whom his higher stream is
lost to the eye.

The Reclus.

The Reclus has risen under the brink of the summit plain
of the Graian Alp, and falling rapidly for some miles in a
chasm or trough between mountains that swell on either side,
it has at length to struggle through large masses of rock, now
confusedly piled together just under the White Rock, which
stands erect on the left bank, facing the precipitous ascent to
St. Germain : it escapes through a bridge : and, flowing on
under the mountain on its right bank with the plain of Scez
on the left, falls, as stated above, into the Isère.

The present travelling route from Bourg St. Maurice to the
summit, having crossed the Reclus just above where it falls
into the Isère, comes to Scez. There you leave the valley of
the Isère, and proceed diagonally over what I call the plain

* See, in Oxford Dissertation, sketch of the Passage over the
Little St. Bernard.

of Scez, passing northwards through the small village of
Villars, to the corner where the White Rock overhangs the
Reclus. The road crosses this river by the bridge close to
the end of that rock, and is carried in zigzags up the precipitous mountain on the other side: on which is placed the
village of St. Germain. It then keeps the high ground on
the right bank of the torrent, far above and out of sight of its
channel.

Since I rode up through St. Germain on a mule in 1854, I
have referred to Brockedon's portrait of the λευκόπετρον in
his "Passes of the Alps." He does not introduce the opposite
precipice with its church and houses : I conceive that, though
not so perpendicular, it rises the higher of the two. The
position which he took for making this drawing must have
turned his view not directly across the stream, but more to
the right beyond the village ; and perhaps the sketch was not
finished on the spot, but part left to be filled up from memory :
for I can hardly think that there exists the gentle ascent
which is represented on the right bank from near the level of
the torrent. Not that any impressions of scenery which I
may retain from that expedition can claim to be relied on :
but in this instance I feel confirmed by sketches of my
companion.

I see no reason that it may not always have been practicable for a pedestrian from Bourg St. Maurice to make his
ascent to the Graian Alp by keeping the mountain brow on
the right bank of the Reclus without ever crossing it ; or by
keeping the brow of the mountain above Scez without ever
recrossing that torrent. But the middle course over the plain
by the ravine and White Rock, is that to which the controversy directs our attention; being that which has been brought
into use by modern art, and which seems recorded as matter
of history 2,000 years ago. Believing that the army entered
that plain, and that there the assault of the barbarians took

place, we desire to note all circumstances clearly; though they may not all be essential for establishing that the march was over the Little St. Bernard.

The Ravine and Roche Blanche.

We read that the lateral attack, with rocks and stones, was made upon Hannibal's troops as they were passing through a difficult ravine; and that a large part of their force remained during the night near a certain white rock. The rock is obvious: the ravine is open to speculation: for, strange as it may appear, the ground has not, that I can learn, been surveyed so as to be duly evidenced. The tracks which suggest the idea of a ravine, $\phi\acute{a}\rho\alpha\gamma\xi$, are the channel of the Reclus itself, which runs at the foot of the rock; and one, which is supposed to have been the course of the Roman road behind the rock.

Neither of these passages has ever received a sufficient description in any published work; no modern author has ever reported himself to have explored either of them. Polybius may have been prepared with some information concerning a ravine and a white rock before he made his journey; such information having been first derived from Carthaginian prisoners, or from Italian friends of the invasion who had accompanied it. When he reached the scenes we speak of, he would himself have to conjecture which was the ravine where the van of the march was assailed; and we have to conjecture now, which was the place that his mind recognised, when he used the terms, $\phi\acute{a}\rho\alpha\gamma\xi$ or $\chi\alpha\rho\acute{a}\delta\rho\alpha$. I will advert to what has been said by modern writers on the two passages alluded to.

In the Oxford Dissertation, p. 91, the description is this:—

" On the left bank, just above the bridge by which the modern

" road crosses the Reclus, stands a high white rock of gypsum,
" called in the country universally La Roche Blanche. The
" Reclus runs under its side, and is confined in a very deep
" rocky channel. On the other side of the rock is a woody
" ravine, through which another small stream flows, which
" afterwards comes down through Villars to Scez. The
" remains of the Roman road made by Augustus have been
" discovered in the neighbourhood of Villars, and it probably
" went up this woody ravine in the manner laid down in the
" plan.* From the words used by Polybius, φάραγγα τινὰ
" δυσβάτον καὶ κρημνώδη, which apply extremely well to the
" bed of the Reclus, we might be tempted to suppose that the
" army had marched up this torrent: but this passage would
" have been so difficult, that I can hardly conceive it possible
" to have been accomplished. The Roman road, though very
" much exposed to the attacks of the barbarians, would have
" been more easy."

This statement invites comment on the two tracks mentioned.
Now that which is up the bed of the Reclus is, I conceive, at
the present day not only extremely difficult, but utterly impossible: yet it need not have been so 2,000 years ago. The
bridge is now just below the end of the white cliff; and the
traveller, in crossing it, hardly sees the river running to him :
for a high mass of large accumulated rocks, covering the
stream, prohibits all prospect in that direction. In the
precipitous ascent through St. Germain, I certainly do not
remember that I could see the torrent at all, as it flows to
that great obstruction : and, when we had attained the higher
ground above St. Germain, and were advancing towards the
Little St. Bernard, the channel was too deeply sunk below for
one to perceive the character of its immediate banks. I am
not aware that any investigator has scrambled down to it for
the purpose of examination ; but believe that our acquaintance

* Sketch of the Passage in that work.

with this φάραγξ is limited to the fact that there is now no entrance to it.

But this does not conclude the subject of inquiry: two thousand years ago the passage may have been free from the masses of rock by which it is now blocked up; these deposits may not at that time have been detached from the mountains and brought into their present position, where they are arrested by the narrowness of the channel between two precipitous sides. When these obstructions did not exist, the shape of this trough and the character of its banks onwards may have permitted the operations which the history describes: the immediate banks of the stream higher up may not be very steep; and the onward tread of man and beast need not have been limited to the soil which is covered by the waters. I would observe also, that the sides which were pre-occupied by the assailants must have been practicable: if very steep, they would not themselves have moved so nimbly along them : and, if very rugged, there would not have been due freedom for the rolling of rocks and the hurling of stones, which are the acts of hostility recorded.

On the 19th September, 1854, as I looked on the stream just below the bridge, it seemed, that one might have stepped across from one stone to another, without much wetting the shoes. I know not in what state it was a month later: but there was only one day of rain at Courmayeur in the interval to the 25th October, when my son walked over the mountain on his return to Oxford: the weather was rough, but no snow lay on the plain of the Little St. Bernard. On the 11th November, another friend, bound for London, took the same walk from Courmayeur, and had no snow in his path. They did not, however, notice the stream. It would be vain to insist on the particular state of this channel in the time of Hannibal, either in regard to rock or water: no one, that I am aware of, takes the trouble to examine it now : and I can fully believe, that the enormous rocks which blockade it have arrived since that period : it may be that neither rock nor water at that time prohibited the progress of the expedition.

As to the other suggested passage in rear of the White Rock, the sketch, in the Oxford Dissertation, gives the line of it, and shows the rounded and worn-out end of the Roche Blanche standing into the plain of Scez, and a second similar projection into it from the mountain behind the rock, at some distance to the south-east, with a line drawn between them to represent the Roman track. Afterwards, p. 95, they say : " It had been " in Bonaparte's contemplation to carry a new road up the " ravine where the Roman one passed, and we saw traces of " the preparations that had been made for it." When I passed through Villars to the bridge, I was wholly unconscious of this second promontory, or of any sort of opening in the mountain after passing Villars : my impending illness had subdued all energy, and power of scrutiny ; and I omitted to look out for it.

General Melville first noticed the White Rock, as illustrating the statement of Polybius. His notes have never been published, but M. De Luc, who had them, writes thus :*—" Ces " circonstances et une autre dont je vais faire mention, firent " juger au Général Melville, lorsqu'il traversa cette montagne, " que, dans le tems d'Annibal, la route ne traversoit pas le " torrent, mais qu'elle montoit le long de sa rive gauche. " D'après cette opinion, formée par la lecture de Polybe et " l'inspection des lieux, le général auroit voulu monter par " là pour examiner cette vallée de plus près : mais son guide " s'y opposa, en disant que c'étoit un vieux chemin très " mauvais,. abandonné depuis longtemps, et que les contre- " bandiers seuls fréquentaient : il ajouta, que depuis la route " actuelle qui suit la rive droite du torrent, il pourroit aisé- " ment juger de la nature de l'ancienne. Le Général Melville

* 2d edition. 1825. P. 173.

" remarqua, qu'en effet le local répondoit parfaitement à la
" description que fait Polybe d'un passage difficile au pied
" d'une montagne escarpée." I conceive this to refer to some
onward point high above the right bank, after you have left
St. Germain, and are beyond those heights which face the
Roche Blanche, and can look back to the exit from the second
ravine said to be behind that rock.

Mr. Brockedon has spoken of Hannibal's passage not only in
his admirable work on the " Passes of the Alps," but in other
publications. In a journal of an excursion in the Alps, third
edition, 1845, p. 148, after saying that "Hannibal passed around
and behind the Roche Blanche," he adds : " In the surveys of
" this pass which were made under Napoleon, in contem-
" plation of the formation of a carriage-road over the Little
" St. Bernard, the engineers were led to decide upon the old
" Roman road as the intended line." I remember hearing
Mr. Brockedon speak as having some acquaintance with that
ravine, if such it should be called : but I do not feel certain
whether he said that he had gone through it. I believe that
neither he nor any one has written on the interior of such a
passage. As to the *angustiæ* of the Reclus itself, all I know
with certainty is, that it is impenetrable now. A man might,
I apprehend, go forward and climb down to it, and make
examination of it. A day devoted to this task would be a
day well spent.

Such are statements made by modern authors, which seem
to affect the question on the ravine of Polybius. On the
λευκόπετρον, I should say that, whatever ascent of Alps may
pretend to be that of Hannibal, it ought to exhibit a rock
corresponding with that of Polybius : he rarely notices local
peculiarities, and, when he has pointedly marked an object
like this, we may expect it to admit of recognition at the
present day.

Some theories exhibit a λευκόπετρον : not all. M. Larauza

found it in the Rocher de la Barmette between Termignon
and Lanslebourg. Mr. Ellis found it in the rock of Baune,
between St. Jean de Maurienne and S. Michel; and we
accept the whiteness of those rocks on their reports. A
writer in "Blackwood's Magazine" of June, 1845, says that
he found it on the summit of Mont Cenis, "of magnitude to
be a place of night refuge to Hannibal"! Some see no
occasion to point out a white rock: M. Letronne, on behalf
of Mont Genèvre, intimates, Janv. 1819, that he could
find one for his theory if he tried: "Il n'existe point de
" passage dans les Alpes où l'on ne trouvât quelque roche
" blanche, puisqu'il y a de gypses blanchâtres sur tous les
" cols de la chaîne." M. Larauza says of this assertion:
" Elle est, je crois, fort hasardé : j'avoue, pour mon compte,
" que sur les points que j'ai parcouru en traversant soit le
" Simplon, soit le Grand St. Bernard, soit le Mont Genèvre,
" je n'ai remarqué nulle part de montagne de gypse dont
" la blancheur fut sensible." The Little St. Bernard is not
among M. Larauza's exclusions.

M. Letronne, however, seems to deny that λευκόπετρον is a
white rock : he relies on the translation by Schweighæuser,
" deserta nudaque petra," and says : " Il est fâcheux pour cette
" découverte du Général Melville, que dans Polybe le mot
" λευκόπετρον, qui revient plusieurs fois, soit pris comme le
" λεωπέτρα des autres auteurs, pour λεῖος λίθος, et ne signifie
" rien autre chose que roche nue, escarpée : c'est ce qui est
" prouvé surtout par un passage du livre X." "Revient
plusieurs fois" is a very rash expression : the followers of
M. Letronne are welcome to conceive that λευκός may mean
" smooth ;" but, whatever it means, it recurs in Polybius, not
" plusieurs fois," but only in that one passage x. 30. 5. He
is describing the progress of an army through a defile in
Hyrcania, obstructed by masses of rock fallen from precipices
on either side ; and he states that, while the heavy forces

were obliged to proceed along the bottom of the valley, an ascent δι' αὐτῶν τῶν λευκοπ'τρων was not impracticable to the light-armed troops. I have no authority to refer to for the character and colour of these Hyrcanian rocks : the presumption is that they were white, shining, conspicuous : they may also have been bare, and steep, and slippery. But λευκός vi termini imports none of these latter qualities ; any face of rock, not obscured by vegetable matter, whether it be gypsum, limestone, granite, or any other, is bare, uncovered ; but such is not the sense of λευκός ; the primary sense is " conspicuous," from λάω, video. The meanings "bright" and "white" are not far removed : those terms represent the effect of colour to the eye. Bareness may be a cause of conspicuousness ; but it is not sufficiently akin to the original sense that it should be represented by the same word. When a lady's arms are uncovered, you may apply the epithet λευκώλενος ; but we do not construe λευκώλενος "Ηρη, bare-armed Juno.

I believe that the word λευκόπετρον, as meaning an individual of a species, is found in no other author, and only in these two passages of Polybius. But we find the same combination in proper names ; and in such instances the names have been bestowed upon rocks or mountains, for the reason that they are white. There is λευκόπετρα on the coast of Italy, of which Strabo says, p. 259, ἀπὸ δὲ τοῦ 'Ρηγίου πλέοντι πρὸς ἕω Λευκοπέτραν καλοῦσιν ἄκραν ἀπὸ τῆς χρόας, " They " call the promontory, which you approach coasting southward " from Rhegium, Leucopetra from its colour." So λευκὰ ὄρη in Crete are reputed to have their name from their constant covering of snow. Theophrastus says, iv. 1, ἐν Κρήτῃ γοῦν φασὶν ἐν τοῖς 'Ιδαίοις ὄρεσι καὶ τοῖς Λευκοῖς καλουμένοις, οὕπερ οὐδέποτε ἐκλείπει χιὼν, κυπάριττον εἶναι, " They say " that in Crete the cypress is found in the mountains of Ida, " and in those called Leuca, which are never free from snow." Pliny, xvi. 60, describes those mountains in the same way—

" Quos Albos vocant, unde nives nunquam absunt." If
Polybius had lived a century later, and had been the friend
of Cæsar instead of Scipio, he might have applied λευκόπετρον
to the Dover cliff, and we should have construed λευκός white.
For the same sufficient reason the rock in question has been
called Roche Blanche.

Dr. Arnold on the Defile and White Rock.

On so important a matter as the scene of this engagement,
which we believe to have taken place when the armament
had quitted the Isère and was pushing on to the summit, the
views of Dr. Arnold must not be left unnoticed; for he has
expressed them on this latter part of the ascent. He prefaces
them with a fact which does not appear in Polybius, saying,
Hist. iii. p. 87 : " It appears that the barbarians persuaded
" Hannibal to pass through one of these defiles instead of
" going round it ; and, while his whole army was involved in
" it, they suddenly, and without a provocation, as we are told,
" attacked him." Now there is nothing in Polybius on
Hannibal's getting into a wrong course, or of his wavering as
to the line of march, or of the natives obtaining his confidence
and guiding the march. His feeling towards them is told in
συνυπεκρίθη τίθεσθαι φιλίαν πρὸς αὐτούς.   iii. c. 52.

Some may infer from the word καθηγεμόσιν, that these
natives must have become the authors of a track of march to
be adopted by the general, and may assume that they led
him into a false track, though no such fact is told. This is
not reasonable : the inhabitants of a country can be useful to
soldiers as to others, and may be called guides without being
the directors of a line of movement. Can we believe that
these barbarians were in the counsels of Hannibal? The
friends from the Italian plain, Magilus and his companions,
enjoyed his confidence ; they were pledged ὅτι καθηγήσονται

διὰ τόπων τοιούτων, &c. The useful spies, who ascertained the enemy's plans at the first Alps, also called guides, καθηγουμένοι, were in a trust superior to that of the barbarians of the Isère: it was policy to tolerate the attendance of the latter, and to put on the semblance of trusting them; but there is no hint that Hannibal ever ceased to suspect them, or laid aside his precautions. Who, then, can believe that they were allowed to interfere with the route of the army? On the wise direction of this all safety depended. Hannibal had those whom he could trust; and the entire narrative imports that he kept his intended track. If he had withdrawn his confidence from approved friends, and transferred it to the natives of the invaded valley, the success of treachery might have been realized at Scez, and the armament have been forwarded to destruction on the glaciers of the Isère.

Dr. Arnold may be considered as assenting to our march till it ultimately quits the Isère, though he is not prepared so to construe Polybius. He had examined these scenes more than once: and it would be interesting to know which he looked upon as the right path, which Hannibal was dissuaded from following. He seems almost to assent to the channel of the Reclus as that which he did follow: for he says in his own history: "At last Hannibal with his own infantry forced his " way to the summit of one of the bare cliffs overhanging the " defile, and remained there during the night." Polybius says nothing about "the summit of the cliff," but "cliff overhanging the defile" rather accords with Roche Blanche and the Reclus.

Dr. Arnold does not otherwise favour our λευκόπετρον: he says, iii. 480, note M.:—"I lay no stress upon the Roche " Blanche: it did not strike me, when I saw it, as at all con- " spicuous: nor does λευκόπετρον mean any remarkably white " cliff, but simply one of those bare limestone cliffs which are " so common in the Alps and Apennines." In this Dr. Arnold follows Schweighæuser and Letronne. But the rock is not limestone: I am assured that it is common plaster-stone; gypsum; hydrated sulphate of lime. I have had opportunity to get one for myself, and have specimens from H. Long and Brockedon. When broken, it has the whiteness of fine loaf sugar: and though the brilliancy will not be sustained under exposure to climate, we may think that a lengthened precipice of such material was well selected by Polybius to mark the scene which he commemorates.

It is curious, that the two ravines near the White Rock, whose existence is testified by the clearest evidence, and which invite the attention of every one who knows the controversy on the ascent of this mountain, should be so imperfectly explored. I cannot myself doubt that both were used by the combatants of 118 B.C. But the blocks of mountain rock which have come to choke up the trough of the Reclus, have, I suppose, dissuaded all from exerting themselves to the examination of its present state; so as to see what it would be without the rocks. As to the hinder ravine to the east, one would think that it must always have been comparatively easy; but of that also there is no published account. General Melville abstained from exploring it, and Mr. Brockedon, if he went through it, has never printed an account of his doing so.

Accordingly doubt may remain as to which of the two ravines is the defile where Polybius conceived the enemy to have made preparations for overwhelming the invaders with missiles. If some sensible man will make his abode for two or three days at Bourg St. Maurice or Scez, and will investigate the ground through both ravines, he may throw conclusive light on these difficulties. But the solution of them is by no means essential to our main question. If the Carthaginian army ever came to the site of Bourg St. Maurice, there was no choice on their further way to Italy.

Character of the Conflict.

Having collected some statements of modern witnesses on the scene of action, it is expedient to notice, in addition, the character of the conflict as seen in a few facts alleged by the historian, and to apply the tale of what was done by the combatants, whether in attack or defence, to the scenes we speak of. Polybius states that the barbarians assailed the Carthaginian armament on their march through a difficult defile; and that the heavy armed infantry, who were in the rear, withstood the onset and saved the army. Nevertheless a considerable loss was sustained: and he gives the reason why a great number, not only of men, but of horses and baggage-cattle, who were in the van, were destroyed: the cause was in the nature of the hostilities practised in the ravine, the stratagem of injury by missiles. This inflicted much loss: but the main onset was from the rear, and was repelled by the heavy troops—ἔστεξαν τὴν ἐπιφορὰν τῶν βαρβάρων. It seems that, before the column of march had arrived at the defile, a certain multitude of the barbarians had already occupied it, and taken post on the lateral slopes, so as to be able to inflict injury in the way described: these, who so got forward, had deliberately prepared themselves for handling their weapons, rocks and stones. It became then essential that Hannibal's heavy battalions, who sustained the weight of the enemy in the plain, should arrest their further ingress into the defile; not only by excluding them from the direct entrance, but by opposing their endeavours to get round by any way towards the head of the column which was moving onwards, and to prohibit any attempt upon the heights which skirt the plain behind the White Rock, or which belong to the other side of the Reclus. If the mass of the barbarians had not thus been kept back, the artillery which molested the advance in the defile would have received

continual reinforcements, and the passage would not easily
have been purged of their harassing assaults.

It is clear that the natives never attacked front to front: if
the dwellers on the Isère could have brought out their
strength in time to face the invaders, they would not have
done it: their object was plunder with the smallest risk to
themselves. Had they attacked at a lower part of the valley
of the Isère, there would have been danger of retaliation
upon their own possessions. The scenes were now passed in
which vengeance would have been injurious ; the strangers
were in view of the desired heights, and longed only to
surmount them with the least delay. If indeed you suppose
that the policy of the barbarians would have been to face the
advancing army, they had hardly the option of doing so.
This armament visited their valley as a sweeping pestilence,
and waited not : they saw it as it passed : they followed, and
following gathered strength : they chased a foe willing to fly,
themselves unable, had they desired it, to intercept the flight.

Thus the mass of the native force was necessarily in rear
of the invaders : and we must conceive the attack to be made
when the army, after a pause in the plain of Scez, was
moving from it, and had begun to thread the narrower track
where the enemy made preparations of injury. When the
danger began, the column was compressed in part within the
defile : freer and more elastic in the open ground behind.
The success with which the onset was here withstood by the
heavy armed troops is told by express words : but we are left
to conjecture how the fighters with rocks and stones were
disposed of: it is consistent with the narrative to suppose
that they were hunted out by the lighter troops, and at length
dislodged from their positions and overpowered by numbers.
Still the onward progress had to be guarded against fresh
intruders from each direction : and it was not before the
morning dawned, that the whole army had defiled on to the

open mountain. This sketch of the engagement will be found warranted by the words of the history : the main shock of arms was not in the ravine.

There is an incident in the narrative, which I think has been misunderstood : we read, ὥστ᾽ ἀναγκασθῆναι τὸν Ἀννίβαν μετὰ τῆς ἡμισείας δυνάμεως νυκτερεῦσαι περὶ τὶ λευκόπετρον ὀχυρὸν χωρὶς τῶν ἵππων καὶ τῶν ὑποζυγίων, ἐφεδρεύοντα τούτοις—" so that Hannibal was obliged to pass " the night, with half his force, about a certain white rock, a " tenable post, away from his horses and baggage cattle, in " reserve for their protection." My notion is that Hannibal so stayed back to withstand the weight and bulk of the enemy, which was always on his rear ; and to prevent them from making their way round and reinforcing that system of attack on the van with which the conflict had begun. I conceive that those first aggressors must have been rooted out from their positions of offence before the night came on ; and that the great business was to prevent a recruiting of that force from the multitude in the rear, where the enemy was most formidable in numbers.

The sentence in which περὶ λευκόπετρον occurs, seems to have been accepted, as showing that Hannibal, by his occupation of the summit of a cliff, protected the passage of the army during the night. In the Oxford Dissertation it is said : " The position of the Roche Blanche was eminently cal- " culated for the defence of this march : from hence Hannibal " commanded the whole plain of Seez, and was able to act " against the enemy, on the heights above St. Germain, as " well as upon those on the flanks of the road." Dr. Arnold writes : " At last Hannibal with his infantry forced his way to " the summit of one of the bare cliffs overhanging the defile, " and remained there during the night, while the cavalry and " baggage slowly struggled out of the defile." Hist. iii. 88. M. Larauza is so persuaded that the upper surface of a cliff is

the thing spoken of, that he considers (p. 115) half of the
army to have stood upon it at the same time.

Now it is probable that, after the struggle by which the
ravine must have been purged of its barbarian occupants, a
sufficient number of the Carthaginian force were posted all
about this rock, so far as it was possible to post them: and
one need not object to the conjecture that, while daylight
lasted, the archers and slingers might act upon a hostile force
appearing on the opposite bank. Still the idea which the
words ἀναγκασθῆναι νυκτερεύσαι περὶ λευκόπετρον convey
to me is this: that Hannibal kept possession, through
the night, of the surrounding ground to which this cliff
belonged, the ground outside the gorge and where the
enemy were most in force; and that, to give security to the
toilsome passage of the great armament, which was con-
tinuing its ascent from the defile and up the mountain, it was
necessary that he should maintain himself in the open ground
from which the passage was entered. There I conceive that
he passed much of the night under arms: and, as the other
portion of the army was struggling onward, there ensued a
discontinuance in the whole line of movement: but his communications ceased to be forcibly intercepted; and, by the
time that day had dawned, the assailants had melted away,
and the rearmost of the Carthaginians under their great
leader were free to pursue their onward course to the summit.

It may be that the epithet ὀχυρόν, *tenable*, has inclined
some to think chiefly of the upper surface of this rock, as a
position to be gained: but it need only import generally a
station of defence: the sentence has no word of movement,
and νυκτερεύσαι περί imports none. The rock probably was
always precipitous to the torrent: but we may not know
what was the form which it presented towards the plain in
the time of Hannibal, by the aspect which it presents now.
I conceive that some centuries ago it must have extended far

more prominently into the plain: at the moment when I passed, a good-sized cart was employed near the bridge in carrying away portions of gypsum which a labouring man was detaching and removing ; and our White Rock may have been subject to the daily spoil of house-decorators and others, ever since its neighbourhood came to have a human population, in the early Christian times when a Church was planted on the heights of St. Germain.

CHAPTER III.

Ascent to the Mont Cenis. Larauza. The Nine Days. Defile and λευκόπετρον.

Two theories only can here be said to challenge consideration : for, on the line of march through the mountains, Dr. Ukert is but a disciple of Larauza, translating him and his Itinerary. Larauza and Ellis must be controverted separately. They reach the valley of the Arc at different points : they quit it at different points : the λευκόπετρον of one is in special contradiction of the λευκόπετρον of the other : and they move over different summits.

Larauza placed the ἀναβολὴ ᾽Αλπεων at La Chavane : and, in doing so, desired to gain three *postes* into his mountain march. But a mountain march from the Graisivaudan up the Arc must be content to begin at Aiguebelle. The distance to it from La Chavane cannot be deemed space in the mountains, nor the time between them be reckoned as time in the mountains. The defile at Aiguebelle is the first point which, to M. Larauza coming up the valley of Graisivaudan, could represent the ἀναβολὴ ᾽Αλπεων. He says himself (p. 66) of all the previous ground from La Chavane,—" L'on n'est pas dans les Alpes."

But when M. Larauza gets to the defile of Aiguebelle as a
beginning of Alps, there is a question whether he finds such a
mountain as corresponds with that which the Allobroges had
to defend. We say that the Carthaginians fought their way
over a mountain. This M. Larauza denies : he calls it, p. 98:
" entrée des Alpes, et non la montée des Alpes." "Si le mot
" ἀναβολή désigne quelquefois l'action de traverser en montant,
" il peut aussi désigner celle de traverser en pénétrant." He
hardly tolerates the word as connected with the idea of ascent ;
saying,—" Polybe se sert en général préférablement du mot
ὑπερβολή (*vid.* cap. 53) pour désigner la montée des Alpes."
This is a mistake : the word ὑπερβολή is used twice in that
chapter, and in both instances means unequivocally the
heights themselves.

M. Larauza would have been more prudent, had he been
content with the metaphor by which ἀναβολή signifies a
beginning. Ascent is the beginning of transcent : you begin
your mountain by ascending it. The first onset of other things
is also called ἀναβολή : when we speak of "striking up" as
the beginning of a musical performance, we translate ἀναβολή.
In relating a fox-chase, if we had to find a Greek word for the
throwing off, it would be ἀναβολή : listening to the leading
hound one might say, as of the minstrel, ἀνεβάλλετο καλὸν
ἀείδειν.

M. Larauza might thus have had a pretence for beginning
his course of mountain march at Aiguebelle. But he strains
for more. Under the pretence of Hannibal preparing himself
for the mountain attack when he got to La Chavane, he
measures the mountain march from that place ; that is, by the
road back from Montmélian. Now, though Hannibal, for the
last day or two of the ten, might be laying his plan for forcing
the first mountain, the day of encounter with the Allobroges
was the first day of mountain, not the third. Larauza objects
here to the term "mountain," saying,—" Il s'agit non d'une

montagne, mais d'un défilé." When he reads that the Allobrogian chiefs were occupying τοὺς εὐκαίρους τόπους δι᾽ ὧν
ἔδει τοὺς περὶ τὸν Ἀννίβαν κατ᾽ ἀνάγκην ποιεῖσθαι τὴν
ἀναβολήν, he translates it, " les postes qui dominaient les
lieux par lesquels il fallait qu'Annibal passât." In this he is
countenanced by others who, in fixing the ἀναβολὴ Ἄλπεων,
disclaim mountain. My friend Henry Long translates ποιεῖσθαι
τὴν ἀναβολήν " to make a passage." M. Larauza also finds hi
theory of level ground to be strengthened by διῆλθε τὰ στενὰ
and διήνυε τὰς δυσχωρίας. He forgets that the narrowest and
roughest defile may be at a great elevation : the col or pass is
often in a depressed part of a ridge, though there is higher
ground on either side of it. In the present case the στενά of
the Polybian description are not on the flat level plain of a
river : the very contrast with the plain which they had quitted,
ἕως γάρ, &c. shows that they were now in mountain instead of
plain ; and we read that the army, after pervading the στενά,
continued its progress down a precipitous mountain. The
Allobroges, seeing with what difficulty the horses and baggage-
cattle of the Carthaginians were unwinding themselves in a
long line, were emboldened to close in with the line of march
(ἐξάπτεσθαι τῆς πορείας), and to fall upon them at many
points : and the effect of the attack shows the character of the
scene. Polybius says, that the loss sustained was not so much
from human conflict as from the hostility of nature : the
assault on the line produced a general shock, sending over the
precipices beasts with their burthens, and men also, amidst
the confusion caused by the rushing of wounded and affrighted
animals.

This tale is not well fitted to the pass above Aiguebelle.
According to Polybius, the occupation of the pass was gained
in the absence of the enemy, who had withdrawn to their
town. That success was achieved in the night; and at Aiguebelle the morning would have found the army in free meadow

ground. M. de Saussure observes, § 1191, that, if M. Abauzit
was right in thinking that Hannibal went up the Arc, his
battle with the Allobroges was probably between Aiguebelle
and St. Jean de Maurienne. He says, § 1187 : " Aiguebelle
" est un joli bourg, situé au milieu d'un terre-plein assez
" étendu." § 1191 : " La partie inférieure de la vallée de l'Arc,
" jusqu'à Aiguebelle, est large et à peu près droite. Presqu'
" en sortant d'Aiguebelle, on rencontre un grand rocher qui
" remplit à peu près toute la largeur de la vallée. Au-delà
" de ce rocher, on descend dans une jolie petite plaine de
" forme ovale, que l'on traverse suivant sa longueur ; et au
" bout de cette plaine, à une demi-lieue d'Aiguebelle, le
" chemin est de nouveau serré entre montagne et la rivière, au
" point qu'on a été obligé de le soutenir avec un mur." We
must remember also the marked incident of Hannibal and
his select body coming to the rescue with the troops who had
in the night occupied the posts of advantage. He made that
downward rush ἐξ ὑπερδεξίων, to put an end to the struggle :
and the combat into which he came down was itself carried
on at a great elevation ; for the damage which ensued was
mainly from precipice on the edge of which it was carried on.
Even when the enemy had been destroyed or dispersed, we
read of the difficulty with which the army was extricated
from the embarrassments of the passage. In M. Larauza's
scene of action, Hannibal would have charged into a meadow
on the banks of the Arc, the "jolie petite plaine."

Polybius writes that, after the crash of arms on the mountain, Hannibal overcame the perplexities and dangers of the
descent, and proceeded to the occupation of the enemy's
town : the army there rested for the whole of the next day.
Nature then became propitious to the advance of the invaders.
They could not have enjoyed that ἀσφάλεια in the valley of
the Arc. De Saussure, having mentioned the second gorge,
proceeds thus : " A cet étranglement succède une seconde

" plaine, après laquelle la vallée se resserre pour la troisième
" fois : mais il seroit trop long de détailler les nombreux dé-
" filés que l'on passe dans cette route, et de noter combien
" de fois les étranglemens de la vallée, et les sinuosités de
" l'Arc forcent à passer d'une rive à l'autre." M. Larauza proposes to comprehend into the scene of the engagement the
second defile mentioned by De Saussure, saying : " Nous ne
" verrions aucun inconvénient à y comprendre la seconde
" gorge que l'on traverse à une demi-lieue plus loin, et qui
" offre à peu près les mêmes caractères que la précédente."
Now there is an inconvenience : not that it is difficult to
imagine a fight continued into the second plain or into the
third ; but that such fact is not conformable with the history
which we are interpreting. Polybius speaks of one mountain
pass, and gives us to understand that Hannibal could hardly
have forced it if it had been duly defended ; that the enemy
lost the opportunity ; that the consciousness of having done
so disheartened them : but the visible struggle which the
Carthaginians had to make against local embarrassments encouraged the enemy at last to assault the long line laterally,
as it unwound itself from the pass. Hannibal was then provoked to sweep down from his own reserved position, and
extirpate human hostility : from that moment he met no
molestation for many days. If the route had been along the
Arc, the hostile leaders, when morning showed them to have
lost the advantage of the first *étranglement,* would have done
their best to make use of the second, or the third, or the
fourth. The route to Chambéry offered them no such resources : resistance had ceased from the Mont du Chat.

The Nine Days.

M. Larauza in his computation of time produces confusion
by a wrong use of the numeral adjective, third, fourth, fifth,
&c. I have in a previous chapter of this Part assigned to

each of the fifteen days of mountain its employment. At present we are considering the first nine of them. The first day of Alps was the day on which Hannibal, gaining his success at the Pass, pushed on to the enemy's town beyond, and occupied it. The second day he remained encamped there. He marched on from the town on the third day of Alps. On the fourth day of that renewed march, being the sixth of Alps, he fell in with a party of natives, with their symbols of peace, supplies, and hostages. The natives having accompanied the march for two days, made their treacherous attack, which was on the eighth day, and Hannibal reached the summit on the ninth day.

M. Larauza commits the following errors, not without an object. In p. 103, he calls the day during which the army was rested at the Allobrogian town, " le quatrième depuis son entrée dans les Alpes." According to Polybius, it was their second day of Alps. Then he says, " Le jour suivant, le " cinquième depuis son entrée dans les Alpes, il lève le camp, " et se porte en avant." This was obviously his third day, not the fifth of Alps. Then he says, p. 104 : " Il marche " tranquille pendant trois jours ; mais au quatrième (le " huitième depuis son entrée dans les Alpes) il se vit expose " aux grands dangers."— εἰς κινδύνους παρεγένετο μεγάλους.

This is a deceptive statement: the fourth day from the town is not the eighth day of Alps, but the sixth : and the deception is not only by calling it the eighth, but by with-holding the facts belonging to it in the enumeration, and substituting, as the fact peculiar to it, the occurrence of danger. The writer does not give the events of the day, but shifts his ground ; and in fact quotes only an observation of the historian which is introductory to the incidents which are coming, and insinuates the misconstruction of Polybius on κινδύνους, which has since been handled in a bolder way by Mr. Ellis. The day which Polybius designates as τεταρταῖος, is the day of the conference and treaty, the supplies and the hostages ; and, as Larauza makes this his eighth of Alps, he really leaves out of his reckoning the two in which the natives followed the march before the assault was made ; for on the ninth day of Alps, which followed the eighth, Hannibal was on the summit.

The object of such perverse interpretation can only have been to cure one error by another. M. Larauza having unduly brought two days into the ascent of Alps which did not belong to it, omits, by way of compensation, two days which did belong to it.

It is further obvious, that a misrepresentation, such as I desire to expose, is likely to escape detection, when the expounder is hashing up his criticisms on the texts of Polybius and Livy together at the same time ; and still more, if he is promoting confusion, by introducing his own ideas of local identity as if they belonged to one or other of the original texts : as in p 107 of M. Larauza : " Le huitième jour, c'est-à- " dire le quatrième depuis le départ de St. Jean-de-Maurienne " l'armée se sera trouvée," &c.   Here he gives account of the two days, which he has already excluded from his computation. N.B.—Dr. Ukert accepts Larauza's results : but has the discretion not to exhibit the reasonings on which they are founded.

The Assault and the λευκόπετρον.

M. Larauza suggests a rival λευκόπετρον within a reasonable distance from his summit, and fairly claims attention. As he travelled along the road, which is on the right bank of the Arc to Termignon, he descried, in coming towards Lanslebourg, a certain amount of gypsum rock on the brow of the mountain upon the opposite side of the river.   Thereupon he imagined certain operations of Hannibal, connected with this piece of gypsum, as the λευκόπετρον of the history.

The hypothesis is set forth in these words, p. 115 :—" I

" est impossible de n'être pas frappé de l'identité des lieux,
" lorsqu'après avoir passé Braman et Termignon, l'on arrive
" au défilé que l'on traverse à trois quarts d'heure de marche
" de ce dernier village, une demi-lieue en avant de Lans-
" le-bourg. Les divers détails de localités, fournis par
" l'historien, se trouvent rassemblés de manière à ne laisser
" aucun doute. La vallée se resserrant en cet endroit y forme
" une gorge étroite et profonde : le chemin se trouve bordé
" sur la droite par le précipice, au fond duquel coule le tor-
" rent de l'Arc : sur la gauche, par d'énormes rochers nuds
" et arides, souvent escarpés et roides, d'où les Barbares
" pouvaient écraser les Carthaginois obligés de passer im-
" médiatement au-dessous. A droite de la route, et de l'autre
" côté de l'Arc, se voit le λευκόπετρον, que j'entendis encore
" appeler, par les habitans du pays, le rocher blanc, ou le plan
" de roche blanche, quoique son véritable nom soit le rocher
" du plan de la Barmette.

    " C'est un rocher de gypse, paraissant d'une blancheur
" éclatante dans toute sa partie supérieure entièrement nue et
" découverte, tandis qu'au dessous, il est couvert de sapins,
" et présente, depuis le milieu jusqu'à sa base, sur un plan
" légèrement incliné, une espèce de talus qui se prolonge
" jusqu'à Thermignon, et où l'on fait venir du bled, du
" seigle et de l'avoine. Il est probable qu'Annibal remonta
" cette petite plaine pour venir se porter sur le rocher blanc,
" qui la termine et la surmonte. La partie supérieure de ce
" rocher offre un plateau assez étendu. Des gens du pays
" me dirent que Napoléon y avait fait passer un chemin
" practicable pour l'artillerie. Annibal auroit donc pu se
" porter là avec une partie de son corps d'armée, le reste
" s'étendant si l'on veut, soit sur le glacis qui se trouve en
" dessous, protégé par les bois de sapins qui couvrent cette
" partie de la montagne, soit encore sur la petite plaine qui
" descend du côté de Termignon. On voit que c'était là

" pour lui une position forte et sûre, de laquelle il pouvait
" protéger la marche de son armée, et atteindre facilement, à
" coups de flêches et de pierres, les Barbares qui se montraient
" sur les hauteurs opposées."—*Histoire Critique,* pp. 115, 116.

The portrait here drawn is quite intelligible : but I perceive
in it no coincidence with the story of Polybius, and nothing
that is probable in itself. M. Larauza conceives the army in
two parts, moving by parallel courses up the two sides of the
deep ravine which contains the river Arc : one part, having
the elephants and beasts of burden and cavalry, pursues the
present route along the precipice above the right bank, and
they are oppressed by rocks rolled down and stones thrown
from heights above them : the other corps d'armée marches
along the mountain side upon the left bank with Hannibal ;
and having reached the top of a white rock they fire across
the river upon the assailants over the heads of their suffering
comrades.   To this transmission of arrows and pebbles the
comment ascribes the safety of the army, and to this only :
for the description given shows the enemy to have been safe
against all other aggression.

Now, if we suppose in the archers and slingers of the Carthaginian army a precision of practice approaching to that of
modern artillery, still their efficiency would not be great after
darkness set in : while the enemy would continue to work
their prepared instruments of destruction upon the armament
passing under them with far less prevention by the loss of
daylight : they could still push over their fragments of rock.
In this theory of the combat, all personal conflict is excluded;
and the pressure of the barbarian mass on the rear, as told by
Polybius, is wholly forgotten.

M. Larauza does not suggest any crossing of the river by
the combatants during the engagement ; nor does he say that
the two corps d'armée, which he separates, I presume, at Termignon, could meet again till they got beyond Lanslebourg.

He does not appear to have examined the ground on the left
bank of the river; nor say, whether it is practicable to pass
quickly from one side of the Arc to the other: so that one division of the army could assist the other, save in the way which
he describes, by missiles. One is inclined to ask, would so
prudent a general have thus marched with columns so separated by the river? Does Polybius furnish a clue to such
tactics? does he attribute the safety of the army solely to
weapons discharged from a distance? I rather collect from
χωρὶς τῶν ἵππων, ἐφεδρεύοντα, ἐπιφοράν, and other expressions, that they had come to close quarters with the enemy,
and that the continuity of their line of march was broken, so
as to cause an interval between the van and the rear of the
column.

I get no information concerning such a track on the left
bank of the Arc from friends who have crossed the Cenis, or
from any source besides the comment of M. Larauza. He
did not himself pursue it, nor does he give description that
shows it practicable: but he reports that he picked up a story
from some *gens du pays*, that the route which he imagines,
had given passage to modern artillery:—his means of reference
might have induced him to search out the occasion when such
thing had or might have taken place. If that mountain brow
was ever chosen for the transit of French artillery to the Cenis
in preference to the usual track on the right bank of the Arc,
it ought to be the better line of the two: in which case
Napoleon, when this approach to Italy was the object of his
care, would have so established it.

M. Larauza looked out for a piece of gypsum within a moderate distance from the summit of the Cenis: and no one will
doubt that he saw one: the country abounds in them. But
while the existence of such white rock may not be denied,
his attempt to interpret through it the details of the Polybian
narrative, whether by obscure insinuations of modern events

or unexplained conjectures upon ancient ones, does not incline one to believe that this *plateau de gypse* ever bore the standard either of Hannibal or Napoleon.

CHAPTER IV.

Ascent to the Little Mont Cenis. Mr. Ellis and the Rock of Baune. The Combat. Evasion of the Text. Summaries. How Mr. Ellis shortens the reckoning of time. Two days. Two days more. His final argument for Baune. His progress from the Battle to the Summit.

MR. ELLIS'S mountain march is, as we have seen, from Le Cheylas on the Isère, by Allevard and La Rochette, to the Arc at Aiguebelle, and over the Little Mont Cenis to Avigliana. The leading novelty by which his theory is distinguished is this : that a certain white rock, which he has noticed in the valley of the Arc, above St. Jean de Maurienne and below St. Michel, called the rock of Baune, is the λευκόπετρον of Polybius. It has generally been understood, that the λευκόπετρον was at the foot of the final mountain steep, where Hannibal was attacked by the natives on the day before he reached the summit: the context is thought to show, that the combat took place on the eighth day of ascent, and that he gained the summit early on the ninth. Mr. Ellis maintains that the battle took place on the fourth day of ascent ; and as he admits that the summit was reached on the ninth day, he requires a march of five days from the rock to the summit. His Alpine route is from Le Cheylas to Avigliana (p. 89), given in detail p. 91.

Mr. Ellis seeks to avoid an error of M. Larauza, who reckons two days into the mountain march before he arrives at mountain. Mr. Ellis, on the contrary, seems to be two days

in mountains, before he allows mountain march to begin.
Striking from the Isère into the mountains at an earlier point
than Larauza, he gives a greater length to his Alpine march.
I have no knowledge of the scene of his combat with the
barbarians at the White Rock, beyond his own statement and
his own engraved plan. I therefore take his rock of Baune
to be white, and his plan of the ground about it to be correct :
I will first shortly notice his explanation of the character and
circumstances of the engagement, as told in the history. It
will then be necessary to explore his contrivances for sub-
verting the generally received chronology of the march,
requiring five days, instead of a fraction of one, between the
λευκόπετρον and the summit.

The Combat.

Having related the first onset with missiles by the barbarians
posted in the ravine, Mr. Ellis says (Treatise, p. 45) : " No
" danger was now to be apprehended on the rear : the heavy
" infantry there held the Gauls in check, and Hannibal was
" enabled to devote his personal efforts to the safety of the
" van. For this purpose it must have been necessary to gain
" possession of the heights above the slopes, where the
" Carthaginians had suffered so severely from rocks and stones.
" One half of the Carthaginian army, that is to say, about
" 20,000 men, were led on by Hannibal in person against the
" Gauls on the mountains, and succeeded either in driving
" them back, or in manœuvring so as to make them abandon
" their posts. The march through the ravine was performed
" during the night, which may have been about to fall when
" Hannibal took up his position on the heights. He probably
" thought that during the night he could draw his army off
" better from the Gauls in the rear. During all the night he
" remained in position, separated from the rest of the army,
" as it defiled through the ravine."

Mr. Ellis appears to think that, the danger in the rear having ceased, Hannibal and half the army went forward to protect the van. My impression is, that, the danger to the van having been removed or checked, Hannibal and half the army stayed back, to prevent a renewal of it through reinforcement coming to the enemy from the rear. Mr. Ellis thinks that the protection which the word ἐφεδρεύοντα imports was given by remaining in position on the heights through the night. I conceive that the word signifies the support given by a force in reserve; and such is the meaning of ἐφεδρεύοντων in the preceding sentence, where the arrangement of the column of march is explained. Mr. Ellis gives his opinion (p. 46) thus:—" The most remarkable circumstance the " narrative of Polybius contains, a circumstance which gives " an important clue by which the scene of this contest may " be found, is the fact of Hannibal's having posted 20,000 " men on the heights away from the rest of his army, and for " the sake of ensuring its safety. This circumstance at once " suggests the existence of practicable ground, above the " slopes on one side of the road, by no means usually to be " found in the Alps." It seems to me that the circumstances which give Mr. Ellis his clue are only to be found in his own engraved plan of the engagement, where Hannibal's 20,000 men are seen posted on the heights, and above them six substantial bodies of the enemy commanding their position from still loftier heights. The plan is drawn in much detail: but Polybius is not to be recognised either in the plan or the Treatise. The idea of νυκτερεῦσαι περὶ λευκόπετρον is excluded from both. The rock of Baune appears, stretching north from the Arc for nearly a mile : in the plain, lower down the Arc, is the track along which the elephants, cavalry, and baggage seem about to enter the fatal defile which runs from west to east below the end of the rock. It must be two miles further to the north, where Mr. Ellis's 20,000 men are

drawn up on the heights, and the enemy above them. If this
plan is to be regarded, it results that Hannibal, instead of
passing the night περὶ λευκόπετρον, marched away from it
two miles and more, in time to pass the night somewhere else.
Nevertheless Mr. Ellis thinks (p. 41) that the rock was
noticed as a natural monument of the battle fought around it :
that Hannibal remained encamped near the rock during the
fourth night, and arrived on the summit of the pass on the
ninth morning.

Evasion of the Text of Polybius.

Mr. Ellis announces in his Preface, that he " conducts the
" investigation on the principle of trying the claims of every
" pass by the text of the narrative of Polybius." His Introduction, which follows the two pages of Preface, begins with
supporting the same principle in detail. But it ends with
disclosing the design of differing from his model on the funda-
mental matter of the chronology of the march, by making a
new division of the greater part of it, changing the most important terminus, and disabling the reader from applying the
text of the historian.

Polybius, in c. 39 of 3d book, divides the whole march into
five sections, giving the termini of each : he states the fourth
to be from the passage of the Rhone ἕως πρὸς τὴν ἀναβολὴν
τῶν Ἄλπεων ; and the fifth, what remains, the passage of the
Alps to the plain of the Po. Accordingly, in the narrative,
Hannibal coming to the mountains, ἤρξατο τῆς πρὸς τὰς
Ἄλπεις ἀναβολῆς. Mr. Ellis, in his Introduction, begins with
correctly repeating the division of Polybius into the five stages,
saying (p. 4) : " They terminate, respectively, at the passage of
" the Ebro ; at Emporium ; at the passage of the Rhone ; at
" the foot of the first Alpine ascent ; and at the commencement
" of the plains of Italy." He gives its importance to the
terminus which separates the fourth and fifth sections of the

march, by adding,—" The last two of these stages, in which
" the passage of the Alps is included, are all with which this
" book is immediately concerned." In a discussion of distances which follows, he speaks of the ἀναβολή as the "ascent
of Alps"—" the commencement of the ascent of the mountains." He says (p. 5) : " The ascent of the Alps on the way
" to Italy means the place where the route first became
" mountainous, the point where the army was first obliged to
" ascend the mountains." He insists on this, so far as to say
that, though a different interpretation might be possible, it is
scarcely probable that any other meaning can be attached to
the expression of Polybius, τὴν ἀναβολὴν τῶν Ἄλπεων τὴν εἰς
Ἰταλίαν.

The reader is then informed, that the narrative will be given
in full from the passage of the Rhone to the arrival in the
plains of Italy, with the exception of three chapters and part
of a fourth. And I think that most readers would now expect
to find that the ἀναβολή of Polybius is to be recognised
throughout by Mr. Ellis. But it is quite otherwise. We soon
find (p. 6) that Mr. Ellis sets up a terminus of his own, in
preference to the ἀναβολή of the history. He makes that
very important point of the march to be, not the ἀναβολὴ
τῶν Ἄλπεων, but a town within the Alps,—the town to which
the enemy retreated in the night from their custody of the
εὔκαιροι τόποι, and which Hannibal occupied after his successful conflict on the mountain.* The variation must be a
studied, not an accidental variation. If it were without consequences, it would not be worth noticing. It suits Mr. Ellis's
special theory to fix his terminus two days more forward than
that of Polybius, which he has approved before. We shall see
presently that he drops two days out of the reckoning, and

* If we read on to p. 91, we shall learn the very town, " now ;
place of importance, and whose ancient name is traced in the
modern one."

afterwards dispenses with two more. He is meditating to construct an argument in which that change will be of importance. Not that Mr. Ellis writes in avowed correction of Polybius: he hardly informs the reader that he is making an alteration. But he does make it; the cause being, that his respect for the historian is superseded by his own theory of the Rock of Baune, and by a fancy on the Polybian style invented for aiding it. The variation itself is to make "a certain town" the terminus at the first Alps instead of the ἀναβολή: and the object of the change is to produce a five days' march instead of one of a few hours between the λευκόπετρον and the summit.

These consequences of Mr. Ellis's injurious meddling with the text—viz. the curtailment of four days in the earlier Alpine march—I will presently explain. I have fairly given the substance of his Introduction to some extent: the rest of the matter, which concerns Mr. Ellis's substituted arrangement, with his translation and summaries exhibited in capital letters, as they occur, are too copious for me to transcribe. I can only hope that the reader may be provided with the Treatise itself.

Mr. Ellis first says that there is a peculiarity in the style of Polybius: that, before entering into the details of an event, he gives a short statement or summary of the occurrences, and then narrates the circumstances at length: that the short summary serves as an argument to the succeeding and more detailed account: that in the portion of the history * which we are dealing with, there are seven summaries, which he shall distinguish by printing them in capital letters. He notifies the change which he makes in dividing the subject, thus: "The first division will consist of the march from the

* The portion which Mr. Ellis translates begins after crossing the Rhone, and, omitting some parts, ends with the assault on the Taurini.

" passage of the Rhone to the island : the second, the march
" from the island to a certain defile and town at the com-
" mencement of the Alps : the third, the march from the town
" to the neighbourhood of a certain λευκόπετρον ὀχυρόν, or
" ' strong white rock,' where the army encountered great
" danger from an attack of the Alpine Gauls : the fourth, the
" march from this rock to the summit of the pass : the fifth,
" the circumstances which took place while the army re-
" mained on the summit : the sixth, the descent from the
" summit of the Alps to the commencement of the plains of
" Italy : and the seventh (all of which will not be given),
" the march from the foot of the Alps to the country of the
" Insubrians."—Pp. 6, 7.

Having thus exhibited a division of his own in his own
terms, Mr. Ellis says : " These form the seven parts, into
which the narrative seems to be divided." As there is no
doubt how the narrative has been divided by Polybius, we
need not be diverted from it by the division that seems good
to Mr. Ellis ; unless it is proposed in preference to that of the
historian. As to the summaries, he does appeal to the historian. He says : " The correctness of the supposition, that
" this mode of narrative was adopted by Polybius, will be
" best seen by an inspection of the historian's own words."
I have inspected the historian's own words, together with Mr.
Ellis's translation of them, and have observed those which he
puts in capital letters as summaries, and the succeeding words
which he calls the more detailed accounts. I perceive two
summaries marked between the passage of the Rhone and the
Alps in c. 49 and 50 : those for the ascent and summit in
c. 52 and 53 : two for the descent in c. 54 and 56.

Let any reasonable man give attention to the first of these,
which Mr. Ellis takes from c. 49 of the 3d book. I ask, how
do the first words give a summary of events, explained and
detailed by the rest of the chapter ? It seems to me, that what

is called Summary, brings Hannibal to the island : in the rest,
we learn what he did after he got there. The first words of
the Summary state the march to the island; they tell us
what it is like, and how it is formed. The words which
follow, πρὸς ἣν ἀφικόμενος, &c., give facts which occurred in
his progress through the island, as he approached the Alps.
Besides the display of capital letters to give importance to his
summaries, Mr. Ellis would impress upon us that the other
facts are incidental, episodical, subordinate (pp. 22, 38, 39).
The island is to him only the scene of an episode, because he
intends to back out of it : he illustrates the episodical character
by a very inaccurate statement, and which would not support
his fancies, if it were true. He says (p. 23) : " Before pro-
" ceeding to relate the transactions at the island, Polybius
" arrests the march of the army at the confluence of the Isère
" with the Rhone, measuring the distance up to that point."
Polybius does nothing of the kind. Hannibal's distances have
not been measured since he left Spain ; and Polybius never
measures the march up to the confluence at all. If we desire
to measure it for ourselves, we must first refer to c. 39, when
Hannibal was still in Spain : we there read among the five
distances of the whole march to Italy, "1,400 stadia from the
passage of the Rhone to the beginning of Alps." There is no
mention of the distance, as Mr. Ellis alleges, before proceeding to relate the transactions at the island. After they have
been related, we shall read in the next chapter, that, having
in ten days advanced 800 stadia along the river, he began the
ascent. If we deduct this 800 from the 1,400, we recognise
that it must have been 600 from the διάβασις to the island.
The statement that Polybius, before relating the transactions
at the island, arrests the march at the confluence and measures
the distance up to that point, is a fiction.

 Those who will read Polybius's narrative of the march from
the passage of the Rhone to the arrival in the plain, will see

as straightforward a tale of events as is found in any other
history. Mr. Ellis bids us to expect that more than the
explanatory particulars which occur in all narration will
strike us as peculiar to this historian. But on examining the
portions marked with Mr. Ellis's capital letters, together with
the proximate sentences, we find no propriety in the designation " Summary ;" and sometimes a striking unfitness. A
careful reading of his Introduction, annulling the promise of
his Preface, which was " to try all by the narrative of Polybius," suggests no other object in the new division of matter
made by this explainer of Polybius, than to disfigure Polybius
and explain him in his disfigured state. The invention of
Summaries is chiefly subservient to the perversion of dates.

I am surprised that so marked and decided an interference
with the text should not have been distinctly avowed by its
author : and that it should be noticed only at the end of his
introductory chapter, the tenor of which is contradicted by it.
Though Polybius is thus slighted, his terms are nevertheless
used in the titles of Mr. Ellis's chapters : as,—" to the commencement of the ascent of Alps ; " and " from the commencement of the ascent of Alps." We do not there read " to the
town ; " and " from the town." And, in the discussion where
the town has first to be mentioned, it is only insinuated, that
it looked down upon the Carthaginian encampment ;—which
is in order to give it an early position in the Alps. For my
own part, I think it is to be inferred from the context of the
narrative, that the town was quite beyond the εὔκαιροι τόποι ;
and that, when the enemy had repaired to it for the night,
they were no longer in sight of the posts they had quitted :
also, that we must conceive the town to have been beyond
the scene of the conflict which ensued the next day. There
is no fair pretence for setting up the town to usurp the
character of terminus between the fourth and fifth sections
of the Polybian march.

Mr. Ellis does not speak out as impeaching the Polybian march, till he says (p. 32) : " The ten days' march from the " junction of the Rhone and Isère, must be taken as terminating, " not at the point where Hannibal left the Isère (Mr. Ellis's " ποταμός), but at the town of the Allobroges, which he cap- " tured after passing through the defile at the commencement " of the Alpine ascent." He proves this, by saying, "The fifteen days of Alps are *clearly* reckoned from the town." I say, on the other hand, that Polybius calls the terminus ἀναβολή ; and, when Mr. Ellis calls it " the town," it makes two days' difference in a reckoning on which his peculiar theory depends : and further, that, to support that theory, he finds it necessary to reject two more days, without a pretence that any fair critic will justify. All for the Rock of Baune.

This discord from Polybius which Mr. Ellis has invented is so pleasing to him, that he introduces " the town," when there is no need to mention it. In p. 54, he quits the summit with these words : " On the eleventh day after leaving the town, the Carthaginians began their descent into Italy."

In p. 64, he brings the town prominently forward in a journal which he presents of the whole march from the con- fluence of the Rhone and Isère to the plains of Italy ; stating it thus, in two parts : I. The ten days' march *to the town* of the Allobroges, including the halt at that place. II. The fifteen days' march across the Alps, *from the town* of the Allobroges to the commencement of the plains of Italy.

Before I say more on the shallowness of this Summary system, let me notice, as allied with it, the dangerous frame on which the Treatise is constructed. In the chapters where Mr. Ellis discusses the narrative from the passage of the Rhone to the plain of Italy, he lays down, from time to time, some condition with which a theory pretending to be based on Polybius ought to conform : the first is in p. 28 : the last in p. 63 : they are ten in number, and are put together at the end of the fifth chapter, following the journal ; which is framed according to Mr. Ellis's improvements on the text, or, as he expresses it, "elicited from Polybius." Having supplied all these conditions, and many minor ones, he points out, in chapter vi, that " there are four passes in which there is some *primâ facie* probability : " and that " the examination which "leads to the rejection of three out of the four will not be " long." Accordingly he disposes of them in four pages : chiefly for want of a view, for remoteness from the plain, and for the want of Taurini : and tells us in p. 73, " The Mont Cenis remains alone with likelihood in its favour."

The rest of the work, except what is given to Livy, is mostly devoted to examine whether the characteristics of the Cenis Pass are in accordance with the conditions derived from the narrative by Mr. Ellis. It might be expected that the conditions would fit them pretty well, having been made to order. I will mention the first and the last.

The first is this : " The commencement of the Ascent of " Alps must be at a distance of about 100 Roman miles from " the junction of the Rhone and Isère, reckoned along the " left bank of the latter river."—Treatise, p. 28.

The last is this : " The plains into which the road over " the pass enters, when it emerges on the side of Italy, must " anciently have been inhabited by the Taurini."—P. 63.

But I must not omit the fourth, which has brought the Rock of Baune into so much favour with him who discovered it. It is this : " The White Rock is nearly half-way, in point " of time, between the town of the Allobroges and the summit " of the pass."—P. 66. Mr. Ellis's town is Allward ; but we do not learn that name till chapter vii. pp. 91, 93. Mr. Ellis speaks of its present importance, and of its preserving, in its own name, that of Allobroges : he says it is six miles beyond Le Cheylas.*

---

* It is right to say that some have approved of these conditions.

It is now to be shown, by what series of contrivances Mr. Ellis makes the Rock of Baune to be the λευκόπετρον of Polybius. I will then attend him to the summit. His fifth Summary, which he calls "Circumstances which took place while the army remained on the summit," will belong to another head of my subject.

Two First Days of Alps removed by Mr. Ellis.

In the first chapter of this fifth part, I have allotted to each of the fifteen days which Polybius ascribes to the Alpine march, the work which belonged to it: and I believe such distribution of employment to be correct. When Hannibal is said to reach the summit on the ninth day, it means the ninth of the fifteen : this is required by the context of the narrative. I impute, that Mr. Ellis has thrown the chronology, and thereby the geography of the march, into confusion, by setting up a reckoning of his own against that of Polybius.

We reckon the fifteen days of Alps, by beginning with the day of storming the defile and forcing the passage along the edge of the precipices, and afterwards occupying the enemy's town. Hannibal stayed an entire day encamped at the town : this was his second day of Alps. He resumed his march on the third day of Alps. On the fourth day of that renewed march, he met a body of natives, and held conference with them. That fourth day of the renewed march was the sixth day of Alps. After the conference, the natives attended the march for two days before they made attack. The attack therefore was on the eighth day of Alps.

Mr. Ellis reckons the fifteen days of Alps, by beginning with the march from the town, and so omits the two first

In Mr. Ball's "Guide to the Western Alps," p. 54, they are commended as giving Mr. Ellis's arguments in a condensed form, and the author expresses his obligations for them to a Fellow of St. John's, Cambridge, who is also a member of the Alpine Club.

days of Alps. He makes the fourth day of that resumed march to be the fourth day of Alps : and prepares to make the very same day the day of the attack, which he will try to do, by omitting the two days for which the natives attended the army after the conference and before the attack.

We both profess to reach the summit on the ninth day. Our ninth day is the day following that of the assault, which was the eighth. Mr. Ellis's ninth day is the fifth day after that of the assault. Beginning his reckoning on marching forward from the town, he cuts out the day on which the army had fought its way over the mountain, and captured the town, and the day on which they remained encamped at the town. Mr. Ellis knows that τεταρταῖος imports the fourth day of the renewed march, and therefore was the sixth day of Alps : yet he merges those two first days of Alps into the previous march of ten days along the river. The excuse is, that Mr. Ellis cannot think Hannibal would have been so long in marching 100 miles. In so getting rid of these two days,* Mr. Ellis does not pretend to follow the history : on the contrary, he says (p. 32) : " The march of ten days ought to terminate where the march of fifteen days begins." It must have occurred to him, that after those ten days Hannibal ἤρξατο τῆς πρὸς τὰς Ἄλπεις ἀναβολῆς. Nevertheless, Mr. Ellis says, " It *must* be taken as terminating at the town of " the Allobroges : from this town the march of fifteen days " is *clearly* reckoned." So, as the two first days of Alps are found inconvenient to the Baune theory, he throws them away as being already reckoned in the ten.

Mr. Ellis corrects the chronology of Polybius thus (p. 33) : " It would be on the morning of the eighth day after leaving

---

* Some have suggested, that the first day of Alps should be deemed the previous day, in the night of which Hannibal with a select body occupied posts in the absence of the enemy. In that case, Mr. Ellis has omitted one day more than I charge him with.

" the confluence of the Rhone and Isère, that Hannibal
" encamped before the heights occupied by the Allobroges :
" on the same night he seized the abandoned heights : on the
" ninth the defile was passed, and the town captured : on the
" tenth the Carthaginians remained in the neighbourhood of
" the town." Thus Mr. Ellis ekes out his ten days of παρὰ
ποταμόν with forcing the heights of Alps, and enjoying a
well-earned repose in the Alps for the whole of the next day.

Mr. Ellis is well aware of his variance from Polybius—he
says (p. 33) : "Polybius estimates the length and distance of
" a passage of the Alps, from the point where Hannibal left
" the Isère (the ποταμόν of Mr. Ellis); so that it might be
" *natural* to expect that the fifteen days occupied in that
" passage would be reckoned from the same point." However, Mr. Ellis finds something still more natural : he proceeds—"But from the rest of the narrative, it seems *plain*
" that the fifteen days' march is reckoned from the town, the
" capture of which makes a natural break in the history."
Now, whether or not the critic be more natural than the
historian, the text has in express terms made the break,
where Hannibal, having left the river, ἤρξατο τῆς πρὸς τὰς
Ἄλπεις ἀναβολῆς ; and this accords with the division made
in c. 39, between the fourth and fifth sections of the entire
march.

Having ratified his doctrine by his three assertions,—1,
that it is clear ; 2, that it is plain ; 3, that it is natural,—Mr.
Ellis reposes at last on this additional circumstance, that it
is of no consequence ; as the space from his river to his town
is so trifling. He says (p. 33) : "This town no doubt was near
" to the Isère, and thus only a short distance removed * from
" the point where the march along the river terminated."
Proximity would be a poor ground of argument, if it were
true : our question here is on time, rather than space. See

---

* Mr. Ellis says six miles, p. 91.

what things were to be done : they stormed the mountain :
they achieved their victory after a severe encounter above
the precipices, and then occupied the enemy's town on the
other side. It required a day to perform this work : what
matters the distance? It was mountain work, not river work :
Alps, not ἐπίπεδα : and after this Hannibal rested for two
nights at the Alpine town. If these remarks are just, the
fourth day from the town cannot also be the fourth of Alps.
It was the sixth.

Two more Days cut out by Mr. Ellis's reckoning.

Mr. Ellis proceeds to dismiss two more days of Polybius,
in order. to accommodate the Rock of Baune. We have seen
how he converts the fourth day from the town into the fourth
day of Alps : but he almost surprisés us by announcing that
this same τεταρταῖος represents the day of the attack near
the λευκόπετρον. He says (p. 35) : " The attack took place
" near a certain strong white rock, and was made on the
" fourth day's march from the town." Again (p. 37) : " This
" day was the fourth : and the treacherous attack was the
" great danger which Polybius particularly mentions as
" having occurred on that day."

Now, the statement of Polybius is this : " Hannibal,
" having occupied the town and encamped, and remained there
" for one day, again marched on, and for some days following
" led the army through without interruption. Being already
" in the fourth day, he came again into great dangers." It is
then told how the natives, dwelling near the pass, meditating
treachery, met him, bearing crowns and symbols of peace.
They make plausible representations, furnish supplies of
cattle, and deliver hostages. Hannibal's policy is, not to
show his distrust of them : but he takes measures of precau-
tion, altering his order of march. The natives accordingly
attend the march of the army for two days ; and then make

their attack, when passing through a defile. As that fourth
day from the town was the sixth day of Alps, the day of
the attack was the eighth.

But Mr. Ellis, having turned the beginning of Alps into
the town, and the sixth day into the fourth, has only to
dismiss two other days, and to let his fourth day last till the
battle is fought. He feels encouraged to this by the words
of the history—ἤδη δὲ τεταρταῖος ὤν, αὖθις εἰς κινδύνους
παρεγένετο μεγάλους. His translation is "encountered dangers;" so he thinks that the bloody work has begun: he
exclaims (p. 39) :—" What then was this great danger ?
" According to the view we have taken, it was the treacherous
" attack in the neighbourhood of the rock. According to the
" general view, it was the meeting with the deputation of
" Gauls, bearing boughs and crowns. No great danger could
" be said to result to Hannibal from such an encounter, or
" such weapons."

Had Mr. Ellis so read Polybius as not to know that two
days intervened between the danger that the history points
out as belonging to the insidious designs of the natives,
shown on the fourth day from the town, and the explosion
of their schemes in the ravine? He insinuates (Treatise,
p. 36) that these two days were days that preceded that
fourth day. I will not do him the injustice to suppose that
he thinks so. If he does, I recommend him to read again the
passage in Polybius, or his own translation.

The evident object is to shorten the march to the λευκόπετρον, because he wants to swell the time which came after
it to the summit. The contrivance on which Mr. Ellis most
relies is the danger on the fourth day. He admits no idea
of danger short of the murderous assault, which was two
days later. In short, he does not recognise that a man can
be in danger of being killed till he is killed. So, as soon as
the word κινδύνος appears in the text, he deems the conflict

to have begun, and disregards the additional days which he knows will elapse before the first blow is struck. By such means the Treatise of Mr. Ellis professes to bring out the *real meaning* of the narrative, with *clearness, simply,* and *without confusion;* and to show that the interpretation usually received is *lax, strained,* and *without foundation.*—Pp. 40, 41.

Having thus condemned our construction of the text, Mr. Ellis gives his own opinion :—" The only satisfactory view " that can be taken of the Greek narrative is, that Hannibal " was attacked near 'the strong white rock,' on the fourth " day of his march from the town of the Allobroges." He presently clenches his argument, by showing that Hannibal passed that night in camp, and took five days more to reach the summit. "As therefore Hannibal remained *encamped** " near the rock during the fourth night, and as he arrived at " the summit of the pass on the ninth morning, the rock " must be situated nearly half-way between the town and " the summit of the pass ; nearly half-way, that is to say, in " point of time, for, in point of distance, the respective diffi- " culties of the way, above and below the rock, must be " taken into account. *Another condition* for the determina- " tion of Hannibal's route is thus obtained !"

Mr. Ellis, in his zeal for applying κινδύνους to produce the battle in his third summary, appeals for illustration to the use of κινδύνοις in his second summary. He says this :— " Polybius does not merely say that Hannibal had on the " fourth day to encounter great dangers, but that he had " *again,* on the fourth day, to encounter great dangers. To " what previous event does this '*again*' refer? Clearly to " the similar part of what has been given as the second " summary, where it is stated that Hannibal found himself " in a situation of the greatest danger. This danger, we " know, befell him, in consequence of the attack made upon

*We believe that he was under arms.

" him at the commencement of the ascent of Alps." This is
quite a mistake. No attack had been made. The situation
of danger in which he found himself is explained by Polybius
to be in the changing character of the country, by which the
cavalry lost its terrors ; in the departure of the allied force,
and in the enemy's occupation of the requisite pass. Hannibal was then outside the Alps. Danger threatened in the
circumstances related ; and he prepared to counteract it by
stratagem. The day of danger to which Mr. Ellis prema-
turely assigns the assault near the rock, and the day of
danger to which he appeals in the plain of Dauphiné, were
both exempt from actual conflict—one as much as the other.

Final Argument for Baune.

In my first criticism, written at Nice, I dwelt at some
length on these things, not without hope that Mr. Ellis might
acknowledge that the fifteen days occupied in the passage of
the Alps should be reckoned from the ἀναβολή, or beginning
of Alps. I showed him that τεταρταῖος was not the fourth
of Alps ; was to be reckoned from the town, and that it could
not be the day of the battle. In his defence (Journ. of Phil.
No. vi. 317), he puts his blunder on ἐνναταῖος into a new
shape, as follows :—

" After the halt at the town, the first period mentioned is
" one of four days (τεταρταῖος). At the termination of this
" period Hannibal fell into great peril. (The battle of the
" Rock, according to my view ; a conference with some Gauls,
" according to Mr. Law's view.) The point from which this
" τεταρταῖος is reckoned is not stated."

" The next date mentioned by Polybius gives a period of
" nine days (ἐνναταῖος). At the end of this time Hannibal
" gained the crest of the Alps. Nothing is said with refer-
" ence to the point from which this ἐνναταῖος is reckoned."

It is not safe to read these two sentences without a careful eye upon Polybius himself. "The first period" and "the next period" are terms of Mr. Ellis; but the periods are quite independent of one another. He proceeds :—

"I see here but two suppositions to adopt. The term of "nine days *must* be reckoned either from the beginning or "end of the four days. The latter supposition, the most "obvious, is inadmissible : the passage of the Alps could not "then be effected in fifteen days. As the term of nine days "*must* thus be reckoned from the same point as the term of "four days, we have only to determine from what point "τεταρταῖος is reckoned. On this the nine days, and, as may "easily be perceived on the perusal of Polybius, the fifteen "days also will depend. But τεταρταῖος is plainly reckoned "from the town." Camb. Journ. of Philol. ii. 317.

Never was a bolder specimen of the *petitio principii.* Our assent is begged to two miserable errors, without an attempt to substantiate them :—1. "The term of nine days *must* be "reckoned either from the beginning or end of the term of "the four days." 2. "It *must* be reckoned from the same "point as the term of four days." Each proposition is unfounded, and backed only by the favourite word *must.* Each numeral is, in truth, to be explained by its context. The reckoning of ἐνναταῖος has no relation to the reckoning of τεταρταῖος. The fifteen days stated by Polybius as the sum of the mountain march, comprehend the whole of that march, beginning with the ἀναβολή : and the ninth day, on which the summit was reached, is the ninth of the fifteen. It is not necessary that every numeral used during the mountain narrative should import some fraction of the fifteen. The word τεταρταῖος has no relation to the fifteen : it has its own special context, which explains it as the fourth from the town ; the point from whence he made a new start, αὖθις ὥρμα ; and therefore it would be the sixth of the fifteen. So in the descent, the word τριταῖος is a reckoning from the broken way, and expresses no fraction of the fifteen. But ἐνναταῖος is a part of the fifteen : the summit was attained on the ninth day of the effort to reach it, which effort began at the ἀναβολή. If common sense, exercised upon the meaning of words, did not interpret ἐνναταῖος, we might appeal to the translation of such ideas by Livy : nono die in jugum Alpium perventum est—quinto decimo die Alpibus superatis.

In the argument just considered, we have a fair specimen, not a solitary one, of a system of logic, worthy to be allied with the system of Summaries. When it is desired to establish anything very startling, you are given the option of some other extravagance, possibly more intense ; and when you decline that, you are held bound to the first. Here, wishing the ninth day not to be reckoned from the ἀναβολή Ἄλπεων, but from the town, according to what I consider Mr. Ellis's perversion of Polybius, he lays it down, that it must be reckoned from the beginning of the four days, which were from the town, or from the end of those four days. He attempts no proof of such necessity, and proceeds to assert that the latter alternative is the most obvious, but inadmissible : whereupon he adopts the other. Both alternatives are inadmissible : and the difference in value between them is but this—that Mr. Ellis adopts one, and nobody adopts the other.

If any should be misled by τεταρταῖος being called the first period, and ἐνναταῖος the second period, and should fail to detect the fallacy of the dogma, that the term of nine days *must* be reckoned either from the beginning or end of the four days, it may be useful to point out in plain words why both propositions are to be rejected as equally rotten ; and that we are not the better for being allowed the option.

The four days are conceded to begin with renewing the march on leaving the town ; and, if you reckon the term of nine days from the beginning of the four days, the four become included in the nine, and the whole gives a reckoning only from leaving the town (αὖθις ὥρμα). Thus the two first days of the Alpine route are omitted.

If you reckon the term of nine days from the end of the four days, you have a total of thirteen days, which is too much for reaching the summit, and too little for finishing the Alps.

In my adversary on these topics much is original, not only in his views, but in his style of combat, and I hardly know how to denominate it. In my first criticism on his treatment of τεταρταῖος, I objected (p. 22) to his not reckoning the two first days of Alps, which preceded those four days. I charged him with knowing the word τεταρταῖος to import the fourth day from the town, and not the fourth day of Alps : and I charged him (p. 24) with misrepresenting that day to be the very day of the assault near the Rock. I called upon him to meet that question. What is his answer ? He does not surrender the fatal error of τεταρταῖος intending the fourth day of Alps, or the day of the battle, or of its being five days short of the summit. But he is delivered of this proposition —" τεταρταῖος is plainly reckoned from the town." He produces this as a truth of his own ; and, as if I were a hesitating convert to it, adds, " I wonder Mr. Law did not perceive the consequences of *this admission.*" If Mr. Ellis should truly state the consequences of τεταρταῖος importing the fourth day of renewed march from the town, he would state them to be, that it denotes the sixth day of the Alpine march, the very day of the conference with the natives, and two days before the assault in the ravine. That assault was on the eighth day of Alps, and the next morning saw Hannibal reach the summit.

Mr. Ellis's Progress from the λευκόπετρον *to the Summit.*

Let us now attend this critic to the end of his nine days. After the battle of Baune, fought on the fourth day of Alps, he makes Hannibal encamp for the night near the Rock, and then saunter on leisurely towards the summit. As he has here to fill up a period of five days with what in truth only occupied a few hours, he has thought it expedient to make two additional summaries for that interval between the λευκόπετρον and the summit. I will give them as they appear with their details in Mr. Ellis's translation :—

Part of Chapter 53, *showing Fifth and Sixth Summaries, &c.*

HANNIBAL HAVING ON THE FOLLOWING DAY, WHEN THE ENEMY HAD RETIRED, REJOINED HIS CAVALRY AND BAGGAGE-ANIMALS, LED ON HIS ARMY TO THE HIGHEST SUMMITS OF THE ALPS, WITHOUT MEETING AGAIN WITH ANY CONSIDERABLE BODY OF THE BARBARIANS, ALTHOUGH PARTS OF HIS ARMY WERE HARASSED BY THEM AT VARIOUS PLACES ON THE ROAD.* For they, watching their opportunity, assaulted and carried off the baggage animals, sometimes from the rear, and sometimes from the van of the line of march. Upon these occasions, the elephants were of very great service : for the barbarians were so much alarmed at the extraordinary appearance of these animals, that they were deterred from attacking any part of the line of march where the elephants were to be found. ON THE NINTH DAY HANNIBAL ARRIVED AT THE SUMMIT OF THE MOUNTAINS ; AND, ENCAMPING THERE, REMAINED TWO DAYS, AS HE WISHED TO GIVE SOME REPOSE TO THOSE TROOPS WHO HAD ALREADY ARRIVED SAFELY, AND TO WAIT FOR THOSE WHO HAD FALLEN BEHIND. *During this period* many of the

* The idea of " various places on the road " is not in Polybius, though it is in Mr. Ellis's translation.

horses which had broken loose in their fright, and many of
the baggage-animals which had got rid of their burdens,
unexpectedly joined them in the camp, having followed apparently the tracks of the army.

As in our theory it is believed that the summit was reached
on the morrow of the conflict at the λευκόπετρον, Mr. Ellis,
being at war against that notion, offers this criticism (Treatise,
p. 48):—" It is necessary to notice an erroneous interpretation
" of a passage in Polybius, from which it has been concluded,
" that the battle of the rock took place on the day before
" Hannibal reached the summit of the Alps. The Greek
" narrative runs thus: τῇ δ' ἐπαύριον, τῶν πολεμίων χωρισ-
" θέντων, συνάψας τοῖς ἱππεῦσι καὶ τοῖς ὑποζυγίοις, προῆγε
" πρὸς τὰς ὑπερβολὰς τὰς ἀνωτάτω τῶν Ἄλπεων. In this
" passage it has been supposed that the words τῇ δ' ἐπαύριον
" are connected with προῆγε: and that Hannibal consequently
" gained the summit of the pass on the day after he fought
" the battle. Yet this supposition is unfounded: for all that
" the Greek implies as having occurred on the morrow, is the
" junction of the two divisions of the army."

Mr. Ellis has tried to make his English translation liable to
such a criticism, by annexing " the following day" to the
participle; not beginning the sentence, as Polybius does, with
τῇ δ' ἐπαύριον. But he is quite mistaken as to the Greek
narrative. Συνάψας does not monopolise the note of time.
τῇ δ' ἐπαύριον belongs to the verb, προῆγε; a word which
tells what Hannibal did on the morrow, after he had reunited
the parts of his force. In the same way, that term in the
44th chapter belonged to ἐξαπέστειλε: and will, in the next
coming chapter, 54th, belong to ἐνήρχετο. Mr. Ellis, however,
finds his grammatical perception strengthened by the reasons
which have been so effective on other occasions; namely, that
his own construction is most natural and clear. He would
have done better not to meddle with τῇ δ' ἐπαύριον; but to

have explained what are the places on his map at which he
supposes Hannibal to have halted between St. Julien and
Granges de Dervieux.*

Mr. Ellis makes one very true observation :—" The portion
" of Polybius's narrative relating to the march from the neigh-
" bourhood of the Rock to the summit of the Pass, is very
" short, and presents nothing of much consequence." It was
ingenious in Mr. E. out of so little matter to fabricate two
summaries. This Mr. Ellis has done. He must have observed
that the two together and the space between them are rather
bare of incident : so he adds to his English version " various
places on the road," not being in the original, and swells the
description with many things that had not occurred to
Polybius. We read in p. 48 of the Treatise :—

" Most probably they were merely the inhabitants of the
" several districts through which the army successively passed,
" who seized any favourable opportunity of plundering that
" occurred, without offering any organized resistance to the
" Carthaginians. It is by no means natural to suppose that
" ἐπαύριον is the same day as that indicated subsequently in
" the word ἐνναταῖος ; for the latter day seems clearly to be
" spoken of by Polybius as later than the former. Neither
" would any sufficient time be left, if this view were adopted,
" for the series of *repeated attacks,* and in *different localities,*
" which are *recorded* to have been made between the neigh-
" bourhood of the Rock and the summit of the Pass. The
" predatory attacks which the Carthaginians suffered were in
" all probability made by the *inhabitants* of the *several districts*
" through which they passed ; and the immediate neighbour-
" hood of the summits of the Alpine passes was not inhabited
" in the time of Polybius."

The last proposition is true : and therefore the several

* Places in Mr. Ellis's map ; one on the Arc, the other on the
Little Cenis, as the Durotineum of Pentinger's chart.

inhabited districts are a mistake. Mr. Ellis, being the inventor, as well as the recorder of the five days' march, has very naturally imagined tracts of countries through which it might be performed, and populations worthy to have contested the progress of the invaders. Alas! the several successive inhabited districts are of his own creation : " the various places on the road" are only found in his translation : the plunderers of the history were stragglers from the assailant mass of yesterday : the different recorded localities were the van, the middle, and the rear of a long column of march : and the series of repeated attacks which the Carthaginians suffered from the inhabitants, each district sending forth its predatory population, may be reduced, on a study of the history, to the occasional theft of a knapsack at one end of the column, or of a donkey at the other, during a few hours of struggle to the summit.

The words of the historian, unadorned by his interpreter, teach us this : that Hannibal having, in his wisdom, stayed back about the White Rock, till the advance had got clear of the defile, pushed on before daybreak for the summit, having reunited the different parts of his force, and the enemy being dispersed; and that, with only the annoyance of partial plunderers at different points in the column, he reached the summit on the ninth day. The few incidents which are expressed do, in fact, belong to and wind up the tale of the engagement : the dispersion of the enemy is the dispersion of those who attacked in the region of the λευκόπετρον : the reunion is the reunion of those who under that attack had become separated. These things, and the partial aggressions and pilferings, repressed by the terror of the elephants, all are incidents found in the one sentence, which, beginning τῇ δ' ἐπαύριον, is applied expressly to the morrow of the assault : we then read, 'Ενν αταῖος δὲ διανύσας εἰς τὰς ὑπερβολὰς, αὐτοῦ κατεστρατοπέδευσε καὶ δύο ἡμέρας προσέμεινε.

N.B.—If any should be surprised at the amount of confusion which we have been trying to unravel, I would refer to Mr. Ellis's own explanation for the cause of it. In accounting for the common opinion against his doctrine, that τεταρταῖος represents the day of the attack, he says : " The " difference of the two views arises from this cause : that, " while we have taken Polybius's narrative in this place to " consist, first of a summary statement of the events of four " days, and then of an explanation and a detailed account of " those events ; yet it has, on the other hand, been generally " supposed, that the whole is one continuous narrative ; or, " at all events, that no part of the details of the transactions " with the Alpine Gauls refers to the three days preceding " the fourth day indicated by τεταρταῖος." Treatise, p. 35. The statement is a fair one. The question of credit lies between Polybius Megalopolitanus, grave historian, on the one side, and an inventor of Summaries, on the other.

THE ALPS OF HANNIBAL.

PART VI.

THE MOUNTAIN MARCH. SUMMIT.

CHAPTER I.

Hannibal encamps on the Summit for Two Days. He calls his
Troops together, and addresses them. Evidence of Italy:
miscalled view. The Text considered. The following day
he begins the descent.

POLYBIUS says that Hannibal reached the summit on the
ninth day : that he encamped there and remained two days,
in the purpose of giving rest to those who were safe, and of
allowing time for those who were missing to come up.

De Saussure, speaking of the Little St. Bernard, s. 2,229,
&c., says :—" L'hospice, ou couvent, est situé dans un vallon
" en berceau, dirigé du Nord-Est au Sud-Ouest, large de
" trois à quatre cents toises dans le bas, partout verd, mais
" sans arbres ni arbrisseaux. La moyenne entre deux observa-
" tions du baromètre m'a donné 1,125 toises pour son éleva-
" tion au-dessus de la mer. Du côté du Sud-Est, le vallon
" qui renferme l'Hospice est divisé, suivant sa longueur, par
" une arrête étroite qui se prolonge du côté du Nord, à 3 ou
" 400 toises au-dessous de l'Hospice. Cette arrête produit
" un second vallon assez profond, parallèle à celui où est
" l'Hospice. En partant de l'Hospice pour descendre dans la

" vallée d'Aoste, on commence par monter une peute douce,
" qui aboutit au plus haut point du vallon de l'Hospice, mais
" ce point n'est que de quelques toises plus élevé que
" l'Hospice. Il est signalé, ou du moins il l'étoit alors par
" une belle colonne de marbre cipolin, veiné en zigzag et
" tiré sans doute des montagnes du voisinage. On voit
" ensuite, au-dessous de soi, sur la gauche, un petit lac ren-
" fermé dans un charmant bassin de verdure."

In the Oxford Dissertation, p. 96, I read this :—" The plain
" is about two miles and a half in length : it is, according to De
" Saussure, 1,125 toises above the level of the sea : it is well
" sheltered, and in the centre of it is a small lake." Brockedon's statement on the position of the lake I conceive to be
more accurate : he says (Passes, i. p. 7) :—" The lake of
" Vernai, or of the Little St. Bernard, does not occupy any
" part of the plain, but is situated far below it at its northern
" extremity, at the base of the mountains which form the
" north-west boundary of the Col." The extent of this plain
on the summit is well known, and defies the jealousy of
M. Larauza, who has ventured (p. 185) to pronounce it impossible for Hannibal to have encamped there. If comparison
be necessary, I believe that it has the advantage of being
sounder ground than his plain of the Cenis.

We may concur in the common belief that Hannibal
remained two days on the summit, which must mean that,
having reached it early in the morning of the ninth day, he
passed two nights there, and commenced the descent on the
eleventh day. Some might remark that, when he stayed two
nights at the captured town, the time was told by the words
μίαν ἐπεμείνας ἡμέραν; and that here we read δύο ἡμέρας
προσέμεινε. But in the two cases there was much difference
in the time for resting. In the first case there was but one
day of rest. Hannibal arrived at the town after a very severe
day's work to the whole army. The progress to it had been

over a very rough precipitous mountain, impeded by very hard fighting : he could not fail to rest after it ; and if the words μίαν ἡμέραν did not include remaining for the next day, they would have no meaning at all. On the arrival at the plain of the Little St. Bernard, there were almost two days for resting. That portion of the army which had gone forward, and for whose support Hannibal had stayed back the night before, may have reached the summit at or soon after daybreak ; and he himself promptly followed them. This day, though it succeeded a night of labour, was itself a day of repose, and must be counted one of the two, during which the army is said to have stayed on the summit : no one has contended that they stayed beyond the second night, nor is it probable : never was time more precious : it is easier to believe in a pause of two days and two nights, than in one of three days and three nights.

The Evidence, miscalled the View, of Italy.

One who should come to the reading of this history, not having already received any particular impression on the incidents of the mountain march, would, I think, not understand from it that the Carthaginian soldiers enjoyed a view of Italy from the summit of the pass. But probably most persons have read the story in their own or some other language before they read it in the language of Polybius, and may have received an impression that the invaders were indulged with such a view. Coming afterwards to read Polybius, they presume that his statement intends what they have heard of before.

The incident on which this notion is built, is an address of Hannibal to his soldiers, an incident which belonged to the one day of entire rest ; for Polybius, having related that incident and its effect, says, " On the next day he began the descent." Many a critic has assumed, but not, I think, by instruction of Polybius, that, when this address was delivered, the expanse of Italy was visible to the assembled army, and has fondly imagined the summit of his own theory to enjoy a special advantage for exhibiting it.

The Text considered.

Now what is the statement? Not that Hannibal in march halted his disheartened men at an eminence to enjoy a distant view in bad weather : but that, during the day of repose, he assembled them, and addressed them, having this resource or argument, the evidence, the manifestation, the assurance of Italy—*τὴν τῆς Ἰταλίας ἐνάργειαν*. This word, *ἐνάργεια*, though sometimes construed " view," has not in itself the meaning of " view." Although the word is founded on a quality which concerns the sense of sight, namely brightness or clearness, the proper force of it is clearness to the understanding. Such is the force of our own word " evidence," though by derivation it is more decidedly connected with the idea of sight. The certainty or distinctness which *ἐνάργεια* imports, may be a certainty obtained through ocular proof as well as other proof; but the word in itself does not signify " view." The other passages of Polybius in which the word occurs are these :—

> Lib. iii. c. xliv. 6, *ἡ τῆς παρουσίας ἐνάργεια τῶν ἐπισπω-μένων* : the clear fact of the presence of those who invited them on. When Hannibal introduced the Cisalpine chiefs on the morrow of the passage of the Rhone, this was the first topic of encouragement in his address to the soldiers. If *ἐνάργεια* signified " view," *τῆς παρουσίας* would be superfluous.

> Lib. iii. c. iii. 3, *πάντων δὲ τὸ ῥηθὲν ἐπισημηναμένων διὰ τὴν ἐνάργειαν* : all signifying their approbation of what was spoken, because of its manifest truth.

Hannibal had desired them to look around, and notice the favourable nature of the ground for an engagement. The truth of what he said was to be recognised by the eye: but ἐνάργεια is not a view of what he spoke, but the obvious truth of it. Lib. iv. c. xvii. 2, τοῖς λόγοις ἐπικρύψεσθαι τὰς τῶν πραγμάτων ἐναργείας : to obscure by words the evidences of things done. Lib. vi. c. xv. 8, δι' ὧν ὑπὸ τὴν ὄψιν ἄγεται τοῖς πολίταις ὑπὸ τῶν στρατηγῶν ἢ τῶν κατειργασμένων πραγμάτων ἐναργεία: through which (triumphs) the clear evidence of deeds performed by their generals is brought under the view of the citizens. The idea of view is expressed in ὄψιν, not in ἐναργεία. Lib. xvi. c. xxiii. 2, διὰ τῆς τῶν εἰσαγομένων ἐναργείας μιμνησκόμενοι τῶν προγεγονότων κινδύνων : remembering bygone dangers through the evidence of things brought forward. This, too, is said in speaking of triumphs. If Casaubon was right in conjecturing ἐναργείας, instead of the previous reading ἐνεργείας, yet the idea represented is evidence, not view; though visible objects were the means of bringing former calamities to mind.

As the employment of the word ἐνάργεια does not require us, indeed hardly permits us to render it by the term "view," the context of the narrative seems also to require the word "evidence." The history proceeds thus :—"For Italy has "been so placed* under the mountains which I have before "described, that, when both are contemplated together, the "Alps bear the character of citadel to the whole of Italy." The geographical character of the Alps as the barrier of Italy is adduced, as furnishing the topic of comfort to the

* Literally, *had lain,* or *had been placed.*

desponding soldiers, the description being suggested by the
historian's own observation of the course of Alps towering
above the Italian plain.   In this picture he rather has in
mind a view of the ramparts from the plain than a view
of the plain from the ramparts : the conception is that
the Alps have the character of citadel, and he portrays
them as the walls or defences of Italy, not expressing any
particular part of them, but speaking of the whole, which he
has described as ranging from the Sardinian sea to the
Adriatic.   He invites you to understand this natural defence,
and to appreciate the fact of surmounting it : he, the first
perhaps from Rome, who, in the pursuit of knowledge, had
completed the passage of the great bulwark, and contemplated,
as a soldier and a philosopher, its physical and military
importance.

This introduction enables us to sympathise in the consolation which Hannibal administered to his men : they who had
toiled for months to master the acropolis of Saguntum, were
to be assured that they had now mastered the acropolis of
Italy.   If, when he commanded their attendance, the expanse
of the Italian plain lay visibly before them, each man was
receiving through his own senses the argument of comfort,
and the assurances of his leader were superfluous.   As for a
specula, such as some have imagined for the scene of this
exhortation while they were in march, no such thing is offered
to us by the words of Polybius.   The encouragement was
administered to them in a scene surrounded with Alpine
heights : the important truth, that the citadel was gained,
that they had surmounted the source of one stream, and
attained the source of another, was to be impressed upon their
minds ; but it was not offered to their eyes.   This other
stream was the descending stream to Italy.   Nothing can be
so fitted to recruit the spirit and temper of the exhausted
traveller, as the sure knowledge of such a fact.   To feel this,

it is not necessary to have crossed the Alps. Let him, who
has only walked from Llanrwst to Bangor, reflect how he has
watched the point where he should cease to have a river for
his opponent, and begin to have one for his companion : that
point is evidence of the success of his enterprise, and that his
labour is not in vain.

Observe then the words, which tell the substance of Hannibal's address, in which he availed himself of this geographical
truth, applying it for encouragement and congratulation :
—" Wherefore, pointing towards the plain of the Po, and
" reminding them generally of the friendliness of the Gauls
" who dwelt there, and at the same time suggesting to them
" the very situation of Rome herself, he succeeded to some
" extent in confirming the spirits of his men."

Their attention was called to three subjects : the great
Northern plain into which they were about to descend ; the
favour of the inhabitants among whom they would arrive ; the
further object of their hopes, Rome. It will probably be
admitted, that two of these subjects were not represented as
objects of sight; and that we may translate ὑπομιμνήσκων
" reminding," and ὑποδεικνύων " suggesting." Mr. Ellis says
nothing on those words : but takes his stand on ἐνδεικνύμενος τὰ περὶ τὸν Πάδον πεδία ; saying : " This is of course
" the expression on which I relied to prove the fact of those
" plains being visible."—*Journal of Philology,* ii. 309. The
question then is—need this third topic of the address, the
plain of Po, have been at that time an object of vision, by·
reason of the word ἐνδεικνύμενος ?

If we regard the usual application of that word, there is
surely no such necessity. The plain of the Po had become
a familiar object of their desires, as well as the Gaulish alliance, and the Roman capital : and we find in his works six
other instances of ἐνδείκνυμαι besides this. In one of them,
it signifies to point out so as to induce ocular observation : in

one, the idea of sight is supplied by another word expressly
employed for the purpose : in the remaining four, it unequivocally means to show to the understanding.

Lib. ii. c. iv. 3, τῆς τύχης, ὥσπερ ἐπίτηδες καὶ τοῖς
ἄλλοις ἀνθρώποις ἐπὶ τῶν ἐκείνοις συμβαινόντων
ἐνδεικνυμένης τὴν αὐτῆς δύναμιν : fortune, pur-
posely as it were, showing her power to the rest
of mankind, by the things which happen to those.

Lib. iv. c. xxviii. 4, περὶ ἧς ἐν ἀρχαῖς ἐνεδειξάμεθα :
on which I have given explanation in the early
part of my work.

Lib. v. c. xvi. 7, πάντα ταῦτα μετ᾽ ἀποδείξεως ἐνδεικ-
νυμένου καὶ μαρτύρων· : having pointed out all
these things by demonstration and witnesses.

Lib. xi. c. ix. 8, ἐνεδείκνυντο τοὺς κεκαλλωπισμένους :
they marked out those who were finely dressed.

Lib. xviii. c. vi. 2. ἐναργῶς ὑπὸ τὴν ὄψιν ἐνδεικνύμενος :
pointing them out as clearly within view.

Lib. xxv. c. iv. 11, βουλομένοις ἐνδείκνυσθαι τοῖς Ῥωμαίοις,
ὅτι δι᾽ αὐτοῦ δυνατός ἐστὶ τὸν Φαρνάκην ἀμύνασθαι
καὶ καταπολεμεῖν : wishing to show the Romans,
that he is able of himself to repel and subdue Phar-
naces.

Such being the use of ἐνδείκνυμαι by Polybius, I think we
may be satisfied that in the sentence before us he did not
intend us to understand the exhibition of a thing actually
seen by the soldiers. If this had been meant, the words ὑπὸ
τὴν ὄψιν might have been added, as in the passage here cited
from the 18th book, and that cited before from the 6th book.
We may render ἐνδεικνύμενος "pointing out," or "pointing to,"
without implying a vision of the object by the persons assembled and addressed. Action probably accompanied the words:
the chief was encircled by his troops, seeing only those whom

he addressed, they looking only on their leader who addressed them : he enforced the topic of encouragement, pointing back to the horrors of the ascent, and forward in direction of the friendly stream which would guide them into the plain and the country of their allies. All this could be in a scene shut in with mountains and clouded with the dullest atmosphere. The historical fact is, that he made the effort of consolation : the consolation was, that they had gained the summit : for this to be owned and felt, he indicated to them, but not visibly to the sense, the subject plain.

CHAPTER II.

No practicable Summit gives a View of Italy. It is claimed for Monte Viso by St. Simon and the Anonymous of Cambridge 1830 : *for Balbotet, by Folard, who is followed by Vaudoncourt and Bandé de Lavalette : for the Cenis, by Larauza, the writer in " Blackwood's Magazine," and Mr. Ellis.*

SUPPOSE that the remarks which I have made are not assented to, and that the arbiters of Greek should adjudge ἐνάργεια to be "a view" in its most sensual import; an inquiry of fact will be opened. But it would be a fact for present inquiry: Polybius would not be responsible: we should claim the right to suppose, that, in his own journey through the Alps, he was not favoured with a transparent atmosphere, so conclusive of fact, as to warrant him in rejecting a current anecdote. He had no experience from which he could assert, that there is no practicable summit which gives a view of Italy.

The probability of finding a view is differently estimated by two classes of persons ; those who assume that Alpine elevation must necessarily give to the eye the command of all

surrounding country, as from the Malvern hills, or the tower
of Lincoln Cathedral, and those who believe that from the
summit of every Alpine pass, properly so called, such enjoyment is unattainable.   By a pass of Alps one must understand
a way not incredible for the passage of an army : there may
be parts of the main ridge so narrow that the eye may almost
from the same spot command a Savoy valley and a Piémont
valley : such places are accessible to the natives, and may
occasionally be penetrated by an adventurous traveller : but
no part which is so depressed as to be useful for armies or
merchandise can furnish a prospect which is not broken by
some course of mountain dividing one tortuous valley from
another.   I do not believe that at any period a large army has
come over the Alps by any course which is not now in the
limited list of great well-known passes.   The result of the
enterprising performances of the bolder tourists is, not to
show new practicable passes for large bodies of men, but to
prove their impossibility.

These comments are sustained by experience : if any lines
of passage practicable for an army could supply a summit
giving a view of the Italian plain, the discovery would have
been made manifest by some of the itinerant theorists who
have been searching for it during the last two centuries.
Though the discovery has not been made, instances may be
adverted to, in which critics of the march have more or less
imposed upon themselves by giving locality to this supposed
incident.   The passes which claim to be so distinguished are
not many.   The Great St. Bernard confesses not to see the
plain of Italy.   The Little St. Bernard and Mont Genèvre
also show no pretension to it.   Three passes only are to be
noticed, as put forward to assert the enjoyment of a view.

View. Monte Viso. St. Simon.

Viso is the Carthaginian summit of the Marquis de St. Simon, aide-de-camp to the Prince de Conti in the campaign of 1644 ; and it is adopted by the anonymous of Cambridge, who, in 1830, attacked Polybius and the Oxford Dissertation. It has appeared that the tracks which those critics assert, one drawn by Valence, the other by Grenoble, fall into one at Tallard on the Durance ; and that this comes to a beginning of the Alps in the valley of the Ubaye. One would think that any body of men, once touching the Durance, and on their way up that river to Italy and Viso, would make their way, not by ascending the river Ubaye. It is otherwise with these two writers : each conducts Hannibal south-west to Barcelonnette. Now, supposing a man to have got to Barcelonnette, his onward way to Italy would be by the Col d'Argentière, and down the valley of the Stura to Coni. Instead of that, they forward him from Barcelonnette to the Viso, and both their schemes of movement are curious. The Marquis does not quite know how he managed to get to Viso ; but he declares the fact : the other, knowing as little or less, and not going in person, has invented an impossible geography to make the thing clear.

Barcelonnette is about 22 miles up the Ubaye : and beyond this place the Marquis goes "jusqu'au col d'Argentière." Then, instead of letting Hannibal go down into Italy, he makes him to wander northwards upon heights of the main chain of Alps, till he finds himself on the Viso. The perception which the Marquis had of this interesting track is only to be told in his own words, which are these : " Quoique je ne sache pas " précisément quelle route Annibal s'est ouverte pour arriver " à la sommité des Alpes, je ne le perds pas plus de vue qu'un " chasseur qui, des hauteurs, laisse sa mente parcourir les " routes et les fourrées d'un bois à l'entrée duquel il l'a con-

" duite : il ne la voit plus, mais il l'entend au loin, et la
" rejoint aussitôt qu'elle quitte les fonds. Il me retrouve de
" même avec Annibal sur le Monte Viso, sans m'inquiéter de
" tous les détours où la fraude des ses guides, son peu de
" confiance en eux, et son manque de connaissance de l'in-
" térieur des montagnes, ont dû le faire errer pendant neuf
" jours." Perhaps the Marquis was not so long about it :
but he did not accomplish his object. He had been assured, that from the summit the plain of Piémont was to
be seen ; but he was unlucky in his day : " On me l'a
" montré comme on fait à tous les voyageurs ; mais je suis
" forcé à convenir que je n'ai pu la voir qu'en imagination."
He consoles himself with describing how far the Carthaginian
adventurer had been more fortunate : " Annibal, en arrivant
" auprès du Monte Viso, devient tout-à-coup un amateur
" ardent des montagnes. Il monta jusqu'à la sommité de ce
" pic inaccessible, pour jouir de la vue des plaines du Pié-
" mont, et pour les montrer à ses soldats. Il s'élève pour
" cela jusqu'à une hauteur que l'on croit être de 2,500 toises,
" et par conséquent supérieure à celle de Mont Blanc." One
is inclined to ask, how much of his speech was heard by his
troops ?

View. Monte Viso. Cambridge Anonymous.

The Englishman who has adopted Viso as the summit for a
view, finds a way to it for Hannibal not more happy than that
of the Marquis St. Simon. Having-performed the first Alps
in the valley of the Ubaye, he writes thus, p. 64 :—" After
" encamping at the town for a day, the army proceeds by the
" Chemin Royal up the valley of the Ubaye, and for three
" days their march is pursued in safety. On the fourth, the
" mountaineers in token of peace come forward, and purchase
" the good-will of Hannibal with an abundant supply of cattle.
" They gain their object by persuading him to accept their

" guidance through the rest of the passage. He is conducted
" by them from the valley of the Ubaye up the deep gorges
" of the river Guil away from the right path. The Cartha-
" ginians follow their guides into the difficult and dangerous
" ravine of the Guil, which proves fatal to a great part of the
" army. In the morning προῆγε πρὸς τὰς ὑπερβολὰς τὰς
" ἀνωτάτω τῶν Ἄλπεων, and early on the ninth day he reaches
" the summit of the pass of Monte Viso, about which he en-
" camps and remains two days." Then comes the eulogy of the
View; and then, without notice of intermediate points, Turin.

Now the path into which this writer states the Carthaginians
to have been seduced by the natives has no existence. After
more than three days' marches up the valley of the Ubaye, he
carries them up the gorges of the Guil. There are no such
gorges : the Guil torrent rising far to the north-west of the
Col de Viso, flows south-west, making its course to Mont
Dauphin, and so into the Durance. The valley of the Ubaye
never approaches the course of the Guil, though perhaps the
ranges of mountain, which send contribuents to one, may in
an opposite direction remotely contribute to the other. To go
up a gorge of the Guil towards Monte Viso, is impossible. To
go from the valley of the Ubaye up the gorges of the Guil is
impossible. According to the best maps, the most fraudulent
guide could not take you to the Viso from the valley of the
Ubaye up any gorge of the Guil.

The effort of this commentator was, not to interpret Polybius, but to interpret the Marquis de St. Simon. The attempt
was indiscreet : for the Marquis avowed that he could not
explain his own track : and yet he went in person, which the
Cambridge anonymous did not.

View from Balbotet.   Folard.

The Chevalier Folard, in his elucidations of Polybius,
invented this summit with its view. After coming over the

Mont Genèvre to Césanne, he studies the scene for Hannibal's
engagement with the barbarian enemy: he finds it near the
ascent of the Col de Sestrière; and calls it "le combat contre
"les Allobroges des Alpes Cottiennes." He says, "Il est
"difficile de pouvoir bien déterminer l'endroit où se passa
"cette grande action entre Annibal et les Allobroges. La
"connaissance que j'ai des lieux me feroit croire que ce général
"fut attaqué entre Sezanne et le mont de Sestrières. Le rocher
"où Polybe dit qu'Annibal passa une nuit si triste, se trouve
"là comme fait exprès, et existe encore." But the writer looks
beyond the Sestrière for Hannibal's summit: the march is
carried further forward along mountain tops, to make sure of
the best view. "Il gagna enfin le col de la Fenêtre qu'il avoit
"à sa gauche, par le haut des montagnes. C'est sur le plateau
"de cette montagne, où est aujourd'hui le village de Barbottet,
"qu'Annibal dut camper. C'est dans ce camp de Barbottet,
"qu'Annibal fit remarquer à ses soldats toute la plaine du
"Piémont, jusqu'au pais des Insubriens. Il n'y a que le seul
"endroit au plus haut du col de la Fenêtre d'où l'on puisse
"découvrir l'Italie." Tom. iv. pp. 90, 91.

The translation of Polybius by Dom Vincent Thuiller was
published in 1728 in six quarto volumes. The commentary of
Folard which belongs to it is to the text in bulk as about four
or five to one, the last volume excepted, which is without notes.
Certain reviewers had said:—"C'est dommage qu'on ne puisse
"pas lire de suite Polybe, et qu'il faille, pour ainsi dire, courir
"après le texte, qui se perd à chaque moment dans un abîme
"de Notes et de Réflexions." These remarks are complained
of in a preface to the fourth volume: but the criticism was
lenient, dealing only with material proportions. Other merits
might have been questioned, beginning with the title-page,
where the annotations are recommended for the improvement
of general officers. If all are equivalent to those which concern the ἐνάργεια of Hannibal, no subaltern could be the
better for them.

View from Balbotet. Vandoncourt. M. de Lavalette.

Though Chevalier Folard, as I believe, stands alone for the site of the first conflict with barbarians, and for the track in which he places it, yet before he brings Hannibal over the Genèvre, he is joined by other commentators, who, in the desire of a view, sanction the latter part of his labours with their concurrence. Two, who have tracked Hannibal up the Durance, and join the Chevalier at Briançon to cross the Genèvre with him to Césanne, having failed to discover a view of their own, follow him to regale their eyes with the prospect from Balbotet. These are General Vandoncourt, and M. Bandé de Lavalette. The general says (tom. i. p. 50): "Le neuvième " jour l'armée vint camper sur les hauteurs de l'Assiette :" and (p. 53): "M. de Folard est le seul qui a saisi le vrai point " du passage d'Annibal. Il remonta le col de Sestrières et " suivit la crête des montagnes jusqu'au col de la Fenêtre. " C'est du plateau qui domine le village de Balbotet, et qui " est en face de l'embouchure de la vallée de Pragelas, " qu'Annibal fit voir à ses soldats les plaines du Piémont : " c'est effectivement le seul endroit où l'on puisse avoir une " vue semblable : tous les autres sont masqués."

M. de Lavalette, unable to dispense with a view, says :— " Si, au lieu de s'enfoncer dans le vallée de la Doire au-dessous " de Cézanne, le voyageur franchit à droite le col de Sestrières, " il arrive bientôt sur le plateau de Balbotet : et là les plaines " du Po se dévoilent à ses regards. Il n'y a que ce point sur " toutes les routes des Alpes, d'où l'on puisse à une telle " hauteur découvrir et montrer l'Italie." This writer is, as I had occasion to show before, a conscientious critic : accordingly, having subscribed to this exploit in favour of a view, he is duly disturbed (p. 119) by the fact that Balbotet is no summit : "c'est là," he says, " une véritable difficulté ;" however, as no other point in the Alps shows the plain so well, he

is content to have his view in a wrong place, rather than not
have it at all.

View from the Cenis. Larauza.

The ingenious Larauza, in his effort to establish a view, has
said enough to show that there is none. In criticising the
plateau of Balbotet, he says, p. 188: "Qu'est ce qu'
" Annibal serait allé faire au sommet de cette montagne?"
May we not ask the same question concerning his own
eminence "au sommet du Cenis?" He proceeded from Susa
by the new road before day-break; and walking through
Jaillon and St. Martin, was for some time in expectation of
a view which he had conceived from the study of Lady
Morgan's "Italy:" but after a little discussion, he arrives at
this: "C'est donc au sommet du Cenis, et près du plateau
" où campa l'armée, qu'il faut chercher ce *promontorium* d'où
" elle vit les plaines qu'arrose le Po." Hereupon he quotes
from a work of 1764, by two Swedish gentlemen, saying:—
" Or, voici ce que dit Grosley qui, comme nous, fait passer
" par là le général Carthaginois. L'espèce de coupe que
" forme le plateau du Mont Cenis, est bordée de falaises très
" élevées, et ainsi il n'occupe pas, au pied de la lettre, le
" sommet de la montagne. C'est à mi-côte d'une de ces
" falaises, à la hauteur du Prieuré, qu'on découvre les plaines
" de Piémont, et c'est de là qu'Annibal put les montrer à son
" armée."

To this M. Larauza adds his own comment:—" Il est
" probable que cette Falaise que Grosley ne désigne pas
" autrement, est la montagne de Saint-Martin, qui se trouve
" en avant du petit Mont Cenis, formant la partie supérieure
" de la montagne de Jaillon, et située comme elle dans la
" direction de la vallée de Suse, à travers laquelle la vue
" débouche sur la plaine de Turin. Je le côtoyai à partir
" du petit hameau qui lui donne son nom, l'ayant con-

" tinûment sur ma gauche, et arrivé à la plaine du Mont
" Cenis, au-delà de l'auberge de la Grand-Croix, vers le
" quatorzième refuge, elle ne me paraissait plus que comme
" une colline très peu élevée au-dessus du sol. D'après la
" position de cette montagne, située tout à fait en face de la
" vallée de Suse, et n'ayant devant elle aucune autre montagne
" qui intercepte la vue, je conjecturais qu'en montant au
" sommet on devait découvrir la plaine ; ce qui me fut con-
" firmé à plusieurs reprises par des gens du pays avec qui je
" faisais route, et qui m'affirmèrent que du haut d'un rocher
" qu'ils appellent Corna Rossa, et qui se présente solitaire et
" détaché à la partie supérieure de la montagne de Saint
" Martin, on découvre Turin et toute la plaine. En me
" montrant la gorge qui sépare la cime de cette montagne de
" celle du petit Mont Cenis, ils me disaient que leurs anciens
" leur avaient raconté qu'un fameux général nommé Annibal
" était passé par là il y a bien long tems. Nous pouvons
" donc supposer très naturellement que ce fut là ce promon-
" torium d'où ce grand capitaine montra l'Italie à son
" armée."

We have here come to M. Larauza's own evidence touching
what he gathered from the *gens du pays;* and I will add what
appears from other writers concerning the Corna Rossa. De
Saussure, telling the observations which he made from the
Roche Michel, says : " Au couchant du Roche Michel, au
" dessus du village de la grande Croix, on voit un grand
" glacier, qui de la poste du Mont Cenis paroit le disputer
" en hauteur au rocher de la Fraise,* vis à vis duquel il paroit
" situé, mais je le crois moins élevé. De la Roche Michel
" nous le voyons abaissé de 68 minutes au dessous de notre
" horizon : ce glacier se nomme *Corne-Rousse.*" iii. c. 7, s.
1265. As this glacier was in view to De Saussure looking

* La Fraise is south of the Rocher de la Ronche, in the same
chain, and east of the southern end of the lake.

westward from the Roche Michel, it is strange that M. Larauza
should have conceived it in the track of Hannibal : for he
carries that track straight from Lanslebourg to La Grande
Croix, and thence through La Ferrière and Novalèse, not by
the heights of Bard or St. Martin, p. 137. He can only
bring Hannibal to such a spot by supposing a special excursion for the purpose.

There is further evidence on the Corna Rossa, and more
recent. They are mentioned by Brockedon, whose investiga-
tions of the region westward of the route over the Cenis will
be found in *Blackwood's Magazine*, of May 1836, p. 643. He
left the Vieille Poste on the Cenis, attended by his guide
Etienne, in the morning, not in the best weather ; and, crossing the summit of the Little Mont Cenis, soon turned off to
the left. Leaving the Val d'Ambin to the right, he went up
the valley of Savines, and came to the Lac Blanc. Here he
speaks of looking towards the Mont d'Ambin to the right, and
the mountain of Bard to the left ; and says of the latter :
" Its summit can be attained by a difficult path, leading from
" the lower lake of the Mont Cenis, and, passing by the
" Roches Rouges, the spot where Larauza says the plains of
" Italy can be seen : an assertion laughed at by Etienne, who
" had been there a hundred times, he said, as chasseur and
" guide ; and who observed, that the plain could only be
" seen from the Roches Rouges, when the Roche Melon, an
" enormous mountain on the other side of the valley of
" Novalèse, was removed." He said that, by climbing to the
glaciers of the Mont du Bard, in clear weather, the plains of
Italy could be seen over the Combe of Susa, and that the
view was very splendid ; but it required five hours' hard
labour to attain the spot : and was inaccessible after snow, or
in unfavourable weather.

Mr. Brockedon also reports his disappointment on a subsequent journey in not visiting the Corna Rossa, as he

intended. He says: " I looked out at five o'clock, and before
six every object was concealed in mist and cloud." He
proceeds: " Whilst I was at breakfast, I obtained information
" from a respectable old guide, who had twice ascended
" to the Corna Rossa with botanists and engineers : he denied
" that the plains of Italy could be seen thence." The state of
the weather having impelled Mr. Brockedon direct to Susa,
he here speaks of a gentleman of his acquaintance, who had
been for fourteen years engaged upon a survey of the Alps,
especially of those which divide Piémont from Savoy; these
duties had led him to the mountains above Bard : and he
said that from its glaciers the plain could be seen, but not
from the Corna Rossa, as the view from that is intercepted by
the Bois Noir, the mountain which flanks the Roche Melon.
Same work, Aug. 1836, p. 246.

Such is the information which offers itself on the Corna
Rossa. With M. Larauza, all geographical and optical difficulties are surmounted to his satisfaction by the traditional
knowledge of the *gens du pays* whom he fell in with on his
way, and who pointed out the gorge between the mountain of
St. Martin and that of the Little Mont Cenis as the passage of
this famous general " il y a bien long tems : "—" Nous pourrons
" donc supposer tres naturellement, que ce fut là ce promon-
" torium, d'où ce grand capitaine montra l'Italie à son armée."
" Ainsi" (says the amiable enthusiast) "tout se débrouille
" et s'éclaircit à mesure que nous avançons ! "

How susceptible of proof is he who is resolved to believe!
What! Hannibal and his army, after ascending from Lanslebourg, to find themselves in a gorge between the Petit Mont
Cenis and the Corna Rossa ! What could bring him there?
He could not collect his army on the Cornes Rousses in their
route from any one place to any other place : he gives them
a special expedition, utterly *extrà viam*, made from their
encampment on the plateau of the Cenis, an expedition made

for the purpose of consolation, but which would have exacted
from them a day's walk more severe than any which they
performed between the Pyrenees and the Po. The notion of
the general mutilating the short repose of the summit, even
by the trudge of half a mile up the snowy steep, for the
doubtful satisfaction of a view, seems too frivolous to find
place in this controversy ; but, observe, a young man and an
enthusiast goes from Paris to the Cenis in the very purpose of
ratifying the fact of a view ; he finds himself on the plateau
in a season which was not the end of October : he has faith
in the gorges and the falaises : there is every stimulus, and no
impediment to the process of ratification, save only the difficulty of the enterprise : and he abstains from the experiment.
Yet these very mountain steeps, when buried in snow, are to
be accepted as the holyday pastime of the African soldier, on
a day, his only day of rest, when drooping with toil and
privation !

View from the Cenis.　Anonymous.

Since Larauza made his fruitless search on the Cenis for
the prospect which he desired, two of our countrymen have
discovered points of view which have respectively given
satisfaction to themselves. A writer in " Blackwood's Magazine " of June 1845, gives us this information (p. 758) :—
" From the southern front of the summit of Mont Cenis, not
" only the plains of Piedmont are distinctly visible at the
" opening of the lower end of the valley of Susa, which lies
" at your feet, but the Apennines beyond them can be seen.
" To settle this important point, the author made a sketch of
" both on the spot, on the 24th October, the very time of
" Hannibal's passage, which is still in his possession."

If this sketch has a virtue that can settle a point of so
much interest, the owner should not enjoy it alone : in com-
passion to the literary world, let him, through Mr. Colnaghi,

give the public the benefit of his exertions, and allow the eyes of others to indulge in the same plain and the same Apennine which have charmed his own. No one will be severe on the performance, seeing the disadvantages under which it was executed. According to the writer, Hannibal, when down at the ἀπορρώξ, was within the circle of perpetual snow ; and, as the artist exercised his pencil on the anniversary in front of the summit, his fingers would be touched with frost, and lose their usual freedom. The cherished landscape has probably adorned the wall of his drawing-room, smiling under the title of ἐνάργεια, and having, as a pendant, the still more curious λευκόπετρον. That, too, would be an instructive novelty : for, amidst the variety of Cenisian discovery, this critic alone has found that landmark of Polybius on the summit of the Pass.

Mr. Ellis, in the " Journal of Philology," ii. 325, defends this unknown writer, as well as himself, and designates my notice of him as " uncourteous." Now, I did not doubt that he sketched what he saw; but I did doubt that he saw the plain of Italy and the Apennine from the front of the summit of the Cenis. If Mr. Ellis knows the spot, it is not through the article in " Blackwood." But it was generous in him to sympathise with one whose ideas are so opposite to his own. Their geography can hardly be the same : one discovers the λευκόπετρον on the summit of the Cenis ; the other, when he reached the Cenis, had left his λευκόπετρον five days' march behind.

View from the Cenis.   Mr. Ellis.

Mr. Ellis's theory of a view, lĭke his theory of a λευκόπετρον, is contrived by taking great liberties with time and space. From the Rock to the summit, commonly supposed to occupy a few hours, he has allowed a march of five days. His summit also is on a large scale. One expected an

encampment which should occupy the requisite extent of
ground about the Col of the Little Mont Cenis, and within
which the rest of a short two days, so much needed, might
be enjoyed. But Mr. Ellis finds his summit to be capable of
a second encampment, and contrives to occupy the one day of
pure rest in shifting the army more than seven miles further
on, besides other pursuits.

Among eighteen distances enumerated in his Treatise as
composing the march through the Alps, we read this in p. 91 :
" From Bramans to Col of Little Mont Cenis, 7⅔ Roman
miles. From Col to Grand Croix, 7 Roman miles." In the
Treatise, summit sometimes means Col, sometimes Grand
Croix. Mr. Ellis says, p. 50 :—" On the morning of the ninth
" day Hannibal at length gained the summit of the Pass.
" Here he encamped, and remained during the greater part of
" the ninth and *all the tenth* day, waiting for stragglers who
" had been left behind, and giving repose to his men after
" the toils and dangers of the ascent." Here summit seems
to mean the Col. When he says, p. 54, " On the eleventh
day the Carthaginians began their descent," Grand Croix is the
summit which they descend from.

Now certainly the notion of " encamping on the ninth day,
" and remaining all the tenth for repose and to wait for strag-
"glers," is not consistent with the army marching that very
day more than seven miles, besides making a lateral excursion
for a view. Mr. Ellis makes light of it ; only admitting that,
" by this movement to obtain the prospect of Italy, the position
" of the Carthaginian encampment would be *a little altered*
" from what it was on the ninth day." Indeed, after the
view he finds it not worth while to return towards the
Col : so, having retraced their steps through a depression in
the mountains, they turn round and walk on, in time to
make a new encampment around Grand Croix. This additional encampment, told in p. 118, is not only omitted by

Polybius, but does not appear in the journal or conditions of Mr. Ellis.

Such is his repose on the summit. In interpreting the history, we all encroach upon the two days of summit, in making a fraction of the ninth to be the first day : the tenth was the only day of unbroken rest. But Mr. Ellis's invention deprives the soldiers even of this : he converts that one day of rest into a real day of work; attributing to it the labour of disencamping, a march of many miles in deep snow, some being rugged untracked ascent after descent had begun ; and at last the making a fresh encampment for the night. Was this relief to the weary ? Did this help those who had lagged in the ascent, to rejoin the quiescent mass ?

Though Mr. Ellis's arrangements are utterly irreconcileable with Polybius, he has the merit of explaining whereabouts his own view is to be found : and I should expect that a traveller might walk to the spot on his instruction. He deals with a few miles of descent as the Polybian summit, to the part which overhangs the plain of St. Nicholas, guiding us to the view thus :—" On leaving the plateau of the L. Mont " Cenis for La Grande Croix, the path turns sharply to the " right, and eventually passes over the hills, at a point where " there is a depression in the chain. Turning to the south, " along the crest of the heights, from this point, so as to " ascend out of the hollow through which the path runs, and " thus arrive upon the long summit of the ridge, the traveller " will gain a prospect of Italy in the course of some five " minutes. The view is better seen from the southernmost " extremity of these eminences, a walk of a few minutes " further. The part of the hilly range from whence this " prospect is gained, and which lies to the south of the de- " pression through which the path runs, forms a ridge about " half a mile in length, without any definite head rising above " the general level of its summit. It presents a very steep

" slope towards La Grande Croix, and terminates, as before
" mentioned, above the plain of St. Nicholas, in a very lofty
" precipice. From the crest of this ridge it may be con-
" jectured that Hannibal pointed out Italy to his army."
Treatise, p. 115.

Thus instructed, we try to realize what a capital view Mr.
Ellis must have had, and how much Hannibal would have
lost if he had not wandered to it. Taking these *indicia* of
distance as affecting Mr. Ellis himself on a walking tour in
summer, this ascent of the ridge would not be serious—ascent
out of the hollow—some five minutes—a few minutes further
—ridge of about half a mile. The labour here depicted would
not be distressing to him, although it would require the
unpleasing change from descent to ascent : indeed the whole
half mile of ridge might not be wanted for a tourist, though
it would for an army : but in either case, whatever the distance
may be, it would have to be retraced from the ridge to the
point of depression, where the track emerged into the route
for La Grande Croix. But we are not estimating the excursive
energies of a tourist, but a superfluous effort exacted from an
exhausted army, and said to have been imposed for their
comfort, on the one day when all was rest and repose. The
severity of the snow is told by Polybius : the length of the
little walk is told by Mr. Ellis : the pleasure of the *extra
viam* we must imagine for ourselves.

And now, what was the display of Italy that rewarded the
soldiers when they got to it ? Mr. Ellis is the relator as an
eye-witness : and we would readily receive his testimony on
its merits, if he had plainly given it. He tells us what the
Carthaginians would have seen ; saying,—" The country seen
" would be the district to the east of the Po, and the south
" of the Tanaro, where the cities of Alba and Acqui are
" situated. This part of the plains is intersected by several
ranges of hills—one of which may be discerned from the

" point of view on the Mont Cenis, even after the hazes, so
" prevalent in the plains of the Po during a great part of the
" day, especially in summer, have effaced the prospect of the
" flat country. In the extreme distance the chain of the
" Apennines closes the view, and would have offered to Han-
" nibal the means of indicating the position of Rome."—P. 116.

So much for what the Carthaginians would have seen. But
we would rather know how much Mr. Ellis did see. On this
the particulars are scanty : he says,—" It is indeed only a
very small portion of Italy that is descried." This is his
fact : a fact which does not require him to have seen one
acre of what Hannibal referred to in his address, the plain of
the Po. But further Mr. Ellis gives us to understand, that it
was such a poor view, that the men would not have found
out that there was one, if Hannibal had not told them, and
himself helped their eyes to it ; and that, if it had been perceptible of itself, he would not have taken the trouble to make
a speech about it : accordingly it is suggested that the action
intimated by ἐνδεικνύμενος, was a natural gesture, necessary
for making a man to see something ; for that, if he could
have seen it of himself, Hannibal need not have helped him.
These are his words : " The existence of any extensive prospect
" does not seem to be required by the narrative. In fact, if
" we suppose the action, intimated by the word ἐνδεικνύμενος,
" to have been a natural, and not merely an oratorical gesture,
" we should be led to imagine that only a small part of the
" plains was visible : for to any very large expanse it would
" have been superfluous to direct attention. Besides, any
" prospect of Italy, however limited, would have been suf-
" ficient for Hannibal's purpose. It would have proved to
" the Carthaginians, by visible demonstration, that their ex-
" trication from the Alps was at hand, that the mountains
" were about to terminate, and that the plains of Italy were
" almost gained."—P. 116.

Here at last it is admitted, that Hannibal's object in addressing his troops was, to demonstrate to them that their extrication from the Alps was at hand. Polybius says, that this was done by words during the second day in camp. Mr. Ellis does not give that opportunity, and holds the general's oratory so cheap, that no demonstration short of a view would effect the object: so on the one day of repose he first makes them all march many miles down hill: and considering this not to be demonstration enough, he turns them up hill again, to make them quite comfortable on the subject. I apprehend that Hannibal made his demonstration at the time, and place, and in the manner stated by Polybius: Mr. Ellis's method, if it had opened to them a view of the plain which he shows it did not, would still have been superfluous, after their senses had taught it them by some miles of descent. If anything could then have unsettled their faith, it would be the senseless interruption of that descent, and carrying them up to an eminence foreign from their route.

By this process the demonstration would have been imperilled: if Hannibal had inflicted this toil extraordinary, and given nothing better in return than the dubious prospect of Mr. Ellis, each sufferer, whether private or field-officer, would have stigmatised, not perhaps without an oath, the folly of the proceeding. But common sense was not so precarious an attribute of the Carthaginian leader, that he should impose a task, which would have quenched, not enlivened, the nascent hope of emancipation.

In the narrative thus shaped, we do not recognise the value of Mr. Ellis's improvement, when, correcting the divisions of march made by Polybius, he gives this name to his fifth summary, "The circumstances which took place while the army remained on the summit of the pass." (Treatise, p. 7. Introduction.) The circumstances ought at least to be according to Polybius: and Mr. Ellis has said, in his own

abstract of events, p. 50,—" Hannibal at length gained the
" summit of the pass : here he remained during the greater
" part of the ninth and *all the tenth* day ; waiting for stragglers
" who had been left behind, and giving some repose to his
" men after the toils and dangers of the ascent." But when
Mr. Ellis's *circumstances* are detailed, they make his contradiction of the historian most glaring. Polybius does make
Hannibal encamp on the summit on the ninth, and remain
all the tenth, and says that the stragglers did come up. Mr.
Ellis does not. He encamps on the ninth, but waits no part
of the tenth : allows no time for those who were left behind :
pities "the languor of inaction," and gives no repose to the
men.

THE ALPS OF HANNIBAL.

PART VII.

THE MOUNTAIN MARCH. DESCENT.

CHAPTER I.

Descent from the Little St. Bernard. The disaster of e th first
day requires particular examination of circumstances told.
The same phenomena still occur in the ravine below La
Tuile. Arguments on the Descent from the Cenis. Larauza.
Writer in " Blackwood's Magazine," June, 1845. Mr. Ellis.

BY the recent snow, which concealed the irregularities of
the surface of the ground, and by the greater steepness of the
Alps on the Italian side, there were dangers attending the
progress in descent, which had not belonged to the ascent.
The great peril was, when they came to a part of the track
where the path lay along a steep mountain-side, but had then
been quite broken away for nearly a stadium and a half, so
that they could proceed upon it no further, and must have
had to turn back. Hannibal made an attempt to conduct the
army so as to get round the impracticable part of the track,
meaning to regain it where it was sound again. The attempt
was unsuccessful ; and it became necessary to encamp, and to
set to work at once for making the usual path passable : and
this was accomplished. The account of this calamity is
given in detail, and affords the hope that we may be able to

identify the scene of obstruction : for the description shows a local character, likely to be permanent, and still capable of recognition. Let us, then, with this view, examine the early descent from the Little St. Bernard, that we may be able to compare its characteristics with the incidents described in the narrative.

Descent from the Little St. Bernard.

The descent from the summit plain of this mountain is in a direction to the north-east. After about three miles or more of descent, the road crosses a torrent, which flows from left to right, being derived from many mountain streams, the largest that which has come from the little lake which was mentioned as below the summit. This torrent, after you have crossed it, receives one which has accompanied your descent on the right hand, and presently falls into a larger stream, which has come from the glacier of the Ruitor. This river I take to be rightly called the Baltea, throughout its course to Pré St. Didier : there it falls into the Doire, which is thence called Doria Baltea. The stream from the Little St. Bernard, which you crossed at a place called Pont Serrant, was running in a very deep hollow. Passing then over a small plain, with the ground swelling on your left hand towards the Cramont range, you come to the village of La Tuile, which seems to stand on both sides of the Baltea. At La Tuile the great steepness of the descent ends, and cultivation and pine forests soon begin. Not far onwards you come to the spot where the march of the Carthaginians, there carried along the mountain-side on the left bank, was arrested by failure of the path ; and this would compel those who had advanced so far to retrace their steps for some way, before they could turn down to the torrent along which Polybius intends that they had the hope to proceed.

Below the part where the path was broken away, the river runs in a deep narrow chasm, mountain rising on either side. The present road onward from La Tuile was made about eighty years ago : it never rises to the mountain-side on the left bank, but proceeds close along the river till it crosses the stream by a bridge, and is then carried up high along a rocky brow on the right bank, as related by De Saussure, who travelled it in 1792. At the time of General Melville's visit in 1775, the old track was still in use, keeping the left bank, and not crossing the Baltea. That old path was to the last liable to be broken away and destroyed by massive volumes of snow sweeping down from the heights. Now, as before, the avalanches are, in some years, arrested at the bottom of the ravine, and the snow sometimes remains there through a whole season, covering the bed of the torrent.

The tale as told of the labours of repair seems to indicate such a path : and one would say that, for the passage of the Carthaginian armament, not only was reparation required, but some improvement on what the path had been before. A road in such a place may be made by cutting a continued notch in the mountain side : the horizontal cutting gives a floor : the perpendicular cutting gives a wall.* If you make a path a yard wide, and then increase it to two yards, the labour of the second yard will greatly exceed that of the first, from the much greater height of the wall, and quantity of materials to be removed : and, if you further enlarge it to a width of three yards, the third yard will claim far more labour than the second. Accordingly we read that a horse-

---

* The method stated by Mr. Ellis is not of this rude kind : he supposes that the natural slope was not broken into ; but that the Carthaginians built up terraces outside of it from below ; and he says that this is still the mode of construction in the Alps : he saw fragments of an old terrace-wall near Novalèse, " such as Hannibal must have raised." Treatise, pp. 56 and 121.

path was soon accomplished : but much labour was required
to make it capable of an elephant. If indeed in the 218
B.C. the mountain-path in question had received no particular injury to make it worse than usual, some improvement
of it might still have been required for the passage of these
extraordinary visitors. It was an exigency never known
before on these mountains.

Those who were already in the mountain-side path, must
have returned to the sloping plain where it began, and where
presently the recampment was made. From this ground the
men and beasts were sent at first upon the masses of snow
which lay choking up the ravine itself. Here was the accumulation of solid snow which had survived from the previous season, now covered with snow lately fallen. Hannibal
hoped that by this course the army might be able to get
forward for the short distance to which the injury of the
regular path extended. This hope failed in the way which
Polybius explains. The Oxford Dissertation (p. 112) finds
a difficulty in understanding what were the perplexities
caused by the old snow, saying,—" It does not appear quite
" certain to which of the roads the difficulties occasioned by
" the new snow falling upon the old are to be referred : "
and it is suggested as possible, that Hannibal may have
endeavoured to turn the ravine altogether, by some road
which runs at the back of the rocks on the right bank, and
after crossing a chain of mountains, falls into a lower part
of the valley of Aosta, opposite to Morgés, below Pré St.
Didier. Nothing in the history corresponds with such a
notion : and I can see no difficulty in the text which should
provoke it. The accustomed track is represented as impracticable ; it was broken away, and there could be no width
to tread upon : hence it was impassable. The calamitous
details are given in explanation of the failure to circumvent
that broken part. After stating the great injury which the

road had received, Polybius says that Hannibal attempted
" to go round the bad places ; " evidently limiting the contemplated deviation to the necessity of it ; that is, that they
should avoid the stadium and a half to which extent the
path was destroyed, and get into it again as soon as they
could where it was not destroyed. The only *détour* which
suits these ideas and makes the incidents intelligible, would
be by the bottom of the ravine : and here only would be the
peculiar phenomenon which the narrative exhibits ; the under
floor of old snow, with its fatal slipperiness for the lighter
weight, and its tenacity for the heavier. Half an hour of
experiment or less must have proved the hopelessness of the
resource.

It is now more than 70 years since a new cornice road was
made on the opposite side of the chasm. But it is interesting
to know that he to whom we owe the development of truth
on the subject of our inquiry, crossed this mountain a few
years earlier, and himself trod in the footsteps of Hannibal
on that perilous mountain side. M. De Luc (p. 200), having
before him the notes of General Melville, writes thus :—
" Après que le Général Melville eut passé le village de la
" Tuile, son guide lui dit : A présent nous approchons d'un
" endroit très mauvais, qui nous donne beaucoup de peine
" pour le réparer toutes les années, parcequ'il est emporté au
" printemps par des avalanches de neige.—Lorsque le Général
" Melville traversa cette montagne en 1775, le chemin étoit
" fait de troncs de sapin placés deux à deux, suivant leur
" longueur, et applanis à la surface pour que le pied pût
" reposer de plat. Ce fut sur ces troncs d'arbre que le
" général, son domestique et ses mulets furent obligés de
" passer. Dans cet endroit le chemin suivoit avec une peute
" douce le côté escarpé d'une montagne, composé de rochers
" désunis et pouvant s'ébouler facilement."

Not long after this journey of Gen. Melville, the new road

was made by the Sardinian Government. De Saussure went over these Alps on 8th August, 1792, and states that, having passed the village La Tuile, he presently crossed to the other side of the torrent, which he also calls by the name La Tuile. " A dix minutes de la Tuile, on passe ce torrent, et on vient " côtoyer le pied d'une montagne dont les conches coupées à " pie sont d'une belle calcaire grenue, souvent recouverte de " mica. Le chemin est bon et assez large, mais sur une " corniche très élevée au-dessus de la Tuile. On voit là, sous " ses pieds, des amas de neige qui se sont conservés depuis " l'hiver, et qui forment des ponts sur ce torrent." iv. s. 2,232.

M. De Luc (p. 201) quotes M. Roche, author of " Notices historiques sur les Centrons," who visited this spot about two years before De Saussure, and reports that the snow of the previous season was lying in mass, coming nearly up to the level of the road. M. De Luc adds in his 2d edition that a friend of his own, passing this mountain in May 1822, saw this ravine almost filled up with snow, to a depth, as he estimated, of sixty feet, the torrent running beneath it.

Mr. Brockedon was on the same spot at the end of August, 1826 ; and found a large mass of snow in the ravine. Alluding to the incident of the baggage cattle becoming wedged in, he gives his own ideas thus :—" The water had " submelted the snow, and, as the feet found no support, the " beasts could not extricate themselves." Passes of Alps, i. ii.

The authors of the Oxford Dissertation, after a second study of these scenes, make the following statement, p. 109 :—" After " La Tuile, the modern road crosses from the left to the right " bank of the river and recrosses it about three miles lower " down. The old road remained constantly on the left bank, " and was obliged to be abandoned in consequence of the " numerous avalanches, which always fall from a pointed rock " that overhangs it, and which in the winter frequently carried

" it away. It is very remarkable, that that part of the old
" road which was most exposed to these accidents is about
" 300 yards in length, a distance agreeing almost exactly with
" the stadium and a half of Polybius ; and it appears that,
" from the very nature of the ground, it must always have
" been so exposed : for it is situated at the bend of the river,
" and immediately under one of the highest points of the
" Cramont and that chain of mountains which forms the
" south-east side of the Allée Blanche. From this point the
" ground slopes rapidly down to the river in a concave or
" funnel-shaped direction, the mouth of the funnel ending at
" the river, so that an avalanche from the top would be
" necessarily confined within the limits of the bend, and
" within the space of 300 yards. It appears, from the reports
" of the inhabitants, that this passage is peculiarly subject to
" avalanches : and it happens also that, owing to the narrow-
" ness of the bed of the river in this spot, and the precipitous
" nature of the rocks on both sides of it, the snow which is
" brought down in this manner from the Cramont, and which
" falls in immense masses into it, remains sometimes un-
" melted during the whole of the summer, and forms a natural
" bridge over the torrent for a considerable distance. Our
" guide told us that this had happened in 1816, at which
" time the snow formed a complete bridge over the river.
" The snow remained unmelted also in 1823. I took great
" pains to ascertain whether the snow ever remained un-
" melted the whole year round in any other part of the road,
" and I was assured that such an event never took place ;
" nor would it occur in this spot, were it not entirely sheltered
" from the sun by the extreme narrowness of the ravine and
" the great height of the mountains on both sides."

In these reports of safe witnesses we have plain evidence
on which to declare the conformity of this " mauvais pas " with
the " mauvais pas " of Polybius. The frequent visitation of it

by avalanches is proved as a fact. It is proved that they
continue to sweep smooth that mountain side; and that the
masses of snow deposited below often remain unmelted
through the following season, as had the snow which he
describes. In exhibiting this phenomenon as it offered itself
in the progress of Hannibal, Polybius speaks of it as proper
and extraordinary; importing, that the place was from natural
causes liable to the incident, and that this had now befallen it
in an unusual degree. And the evidence of our own times,
which has been adduced, strikingly shows how the avalanche,
annihilating any artificial track in its downward rush, is
received into the chasm beneath, and often perseveres to
occupy it in defiance of a summer's warmth. These proofs of
identity receive satisfactory confirmation, when we see that
the distance of the spot from the edge of the plain of the
Little St. Bernard corresponds with the distance that is to be
inferred from the narrative ; and that the extent which Polybius ascribes to the dilapidation of the road agrees with the
usual scope of the mischief as known at this day. It may
well be believed that, after a total disuse of the track for
70 years, that mountain side is now worn so smooth as not to
suggest that it can ever have afforded a path at all.

Descent from the Mont Cenis. Larauza.

M. Larauza cites with some approbation a notion of Letronne, which is this : that the old snow may not have been
much older than the new snow ; that snow usually begins
to fall at the end of September ; that on this occasion it was
probably earlier ; and that we may presume the slippery
under-surface to have been six weeks old when Hannibal
passed, which was about the 26th October, and to have
acquired a consistency ; inasmuch as the early snow of
autumn is the most ready to freeze. His conclusion is this :

" Lorsque cette neige déjà ancienne eut été recouverte par
" de la neige toute récente, ainsi que le dit Polybe, les Car-
" thaginois purent la prendre pour de la vieille neige, restée
" là depuis l'année précédente."—*Journal des Savans*, Dec.
1819. Larauza, however, diffident of the value of this conjecture, finds for himself another excuse in the difficulty of
identifying the place. He thinks that, even if the Carthaginians were right in their belief of the last winter's snow,
we cannot reasonably expect evidence for discovering the
place of it now : he says that, according to Polybius, " c'était
" un phénomène accidentel, singulier, extraordinaire, et non
" pas propre de ces montagnes : ce n'était pas un fait habituel
" et caractéristique du lieu." Now the words of Polybius
are, τὸ γὰρ συμβαῖνον ἴδιον ἦν καὶ παρηλλαγμένον : peculiar
to the place, and now to an unusual degree : ἴδιον fully
imports that which M. Larauza says it does not—" caractéristique et propre :" it does not mean "accidentel" or "singulier:"
and παρηλλαγμένον means "more than usual," an idea very
different from "accidentel." It is reasonable then to inquire
whether such incident of a place is confirmed by experience
in the probable part of any suggested route. Experience
does not testify masses of superannuated snow choking up the
trough of a defile and bridging it from one side to the other,
in the descent from the Cenis. Experience does testify this
phenomenon in the descent from the Little St. Bernard.

M. Larauza (p. 140) supposes that Hannibal, having in
his descent reached the plain of S. Nicolas, followed the
old route, now abandoned, which attended the left bank of
the Cenise by La Ferrière and La Novalèse : he himself
went up, as we have seen, by the present post-road formed
by Napoleon, through Bard, Molaret, and S. Martin : the
old line he did not explore. The higher part of it between
that plain and La Ferrière is liable to the visitation of violent
avalanches ; so much so that, more than a century ago, a

covered way was constructed by the Sardinian government
for the safety of travellers on the right bank of the stream,
built with solid masonry, and reaching for some distance
along the steep mountain side. When this was made, it
superseded the prior track, which had been on the left bank.
De Saussure, who was there in 1780, says, after passing the
plain of S. Nicolas and before coming to La Ferrière,—" On
" laisse à droite une grande gallerie, couverte d'une forte
" et solide voûte : cette gallerie a environ 300 pieds de
" longueur sur 15 de largeur : on l'a construite pour servir
" de passage aux voyageurs, lorsque le chemin comblé par
" les avalanches devient impraticable." iii. s. 1250. The
same account is given by Alb. Beaumont : and Mr. Brockedon
describes the ruins of that once useful work, which was
blown up on the completion of the new road by Napoleon.

M. Larauza, fancying that these facts tend to identify the
Carthaginian track, exclaims : " Les avalanches, si communes
" et si considérables en cet endroit, cette longue voûte con-
" struite pour en garantir, n'expliquent-elles pas cet éboule-
" ment de terres qui avait interrompu le passage ? " The
answer is, that this covered way is very good evidence of
the frequency and violence of avalanches ; but that it is no
evidence of the fact which distinguishes the subject of our
inquiry. Any spot of ground may be subject to avalanches,
if the shape of the ground above it is such as to conduct
volumes of snow towards it. But a place the most subject
to be so visited, need not be subject to an endurance of the
snow throughout the year : this will depend upon aspect and
exposure to the sun's influence. The "voûte" makes us believe
in the avalanche against which it was to give protection :
it does not make us believe, that the snowy masses continued
to defy the ordinary action of a summer's warmth.

One who confidently asserts, in the descent from the Cenis
or any other pass, the scene of so great calamity to the Car-

thaginian army, is not entitled to be silent on such a topic as this. Although the mass of snow which Hannibal found in the chasm was not a thing of regular occurrence, still it was likely to be repeated: the same promoting causes would tend to the same result. A hollow funnel-shaped slope in the mountain-side, which confined within particular limits the downward rush of a great mass of snow in one year, would operate in the same way if an unusual rush should come in another year; and the deep chasm below, screening the mass from melting influences, would have the same preserving effect. Such disposing causes, existing in the permanent features of nature, together with the effects of those causes, are things capable of evidence; and in the route of the Little St. Bernard that evidence has been supplied. masses of the last year's snow, occupying the chasm and concealing the torrent that drains beneath, are testified for the years 1792, 1816, 1823, and 1826, by the distinguished travellers to whom I have referred, while such evidence is utterly wanting between the plain of St. Nicholas and La Novalèse. The Swedish traveller, who favoured the hypothesis of the Cenis, is silent upon such phenomena. Both De Saussure and Albanis Beaumont seem to have travelled by the old Novalèse road, and would have noted such a circumstance had they become acquainted with it. M. Larauza himself, though eager and curious, did not explore the ancient track, nor does he report any knowledge gained on this subject: he listens to the tales of the *gens du pays* as he went along the new road, and retails the nonsense which they amused him with, about Hannibal cutting down trees "pour combler la vallée." Those natives, if they could be primed by a few conversations about old snow under new snow, would soon establish the very spot on either road, and explain it to the next comer.

Neither Letronne nor Larauza represent Hannibal trying to

circumvent the "mauvais pas" by carrying man and beast
higher up the mountain; they saw, at least, that the old
snow was "au fond de la gorge." One invents for the Carthaginians a blunder on the age of the snow, and the other
fails in his translation of the history; but there is nothing
extraordinary in these casualties of criticism. Our English
critics are more adventurous.

Descent from the Cenis.   Writer in "Blackwood," June, 1845.

This writer has already been referred to, as having discovered the λευκόπετρον on the summit of the Cenis, and
sketched the "View of Italy" from the southern front of
the summit. On the "mauvais pas" which embarrassed the
descent he thus expresses himself, p. 758 :—" The steep and
" rocky declivity, by which the old road formerly descended
" to the valley of Susa, corresponds perfectly to the famous
" places mentioned both by Livy and Polybius, where the
" path had been torn away by a recent avalanche. This
" place in Mont Cenis is immediately below the summit of
" the pass, and may now be seen furrowed by a roaring
" torrent, amidst dark ledges of rock. The corresponding
" chasm on the southern side of the Little St. Bernard is
" below the reach of avalanches." He then supplies this
version of the Polybian narrative :—" The way on every side
" was utterly impassable, through an accident of a peculiar
" kind, which is peculiar to the Alps. The snows of the
" former years, having remained unmelted upon the mountains,
" were now covered over by that which had fallen in the
" present autumn, and, when the soldiers' feet went through
" the latter, they fell and slid down with great violence.
" This shows the place was within the circle of perpetual
" snow, whereas that on the Little St. Bernard is much below
" it, and far beneath any avalanches." June, 1845. P. 758.

This is not a happy edition of Polybius. The history,

speaking only of the way by which Hannibal tried to get round the broken path, says of the snow, ταύτην ἀδύνατον ποιούσης τὴν πορείαν : the translator writes, "the way on every side was impassable." In the history, the circumstance noted as the cause was peculiar, ἴδιον, to the way which Hannibal attempted : in the translation it is "peculiar to the Alps." In the history, it is peculiar to the one particular place, because of the fresh snow lying there upon the snow of a former season ; the translation changes a particular thing into a general one, telling us, that the snows of the former years had remained unmelted upon the mountains.

After all, one would expect that the sinister incident, if applied to Alps generally, might belong to the Little St. Bernard as a part of the Alps, especially as the elevation of that mountain is 75 toises higher above the sea than that of Mont Cenis. But the author has his contrivances for raising one and depressing the other : on his "famous place by " which the old road descended to Susa, and where the path " had been torn away by a recent avalanche," he reports that it is "immediately below the summit of the pass," and "within the circle of perpetual snow ;" while our corresponding chasm, the ἀπορρώξ at La Tuile, is pronounced to be "much below that circle, and far beneath any avalanches." It is indeed below that circle : his famous place also is and was below it. But it is not a consequence of that position, that it should be exempt from avalanches. Happy would it be for the mountaineer, if he could reckon on such security ; his cattle and his crops live not above the snow-line ; but he has to witness and to deplore the destroying avalanche.

Descent from the Little Mont Cenis. Mr. Ellis.

We rejoin Mr. Ellis : who, as we may remember, having (p. 50) brought Hannibal to the summit on the ninth day, and encamped him there to *remain the rest of that day and*

all the tenth, forgot his engagement, and turned the tenth into
a day of hard work instead of repose. We proceed through
two more summaries : and find Mr. Ellis performing the task
of exploring the old line of descent by the course of the
Cenise torrent through La Ferrière and La Novalèse to Susa.
He describes the track on the left bank of that torrent, which
was abandoned a century ago, when a new mule-road with
protecting masonry was constructed on the right bank under
Emmanuel III. This, too, is now obsolete : the traveller to
Susa uses only the safer road, through Bard, Molaret, St.
Martin and Jaillon, which diverges from the old one in the
plain of St. Nicholas, below La Grande Croix. In the old
track Mr. Ellis professes to have ascertained by inspection the
very scene of Hannibal's disaster, and to have found the
place where the path was broken away from the precipitous
mountain side, on the north of the hollow that holds the
river about a mile below La Ferrière.

The calamity of the path, which all understand to have
been along a steep mountain-side, and the rupture of it which
arrested the march, present the same topics to all inquirers.
All must try to explain the attempt made to circumvent the
part which, for a stadium and a half, had become impassable ;
and to say where the snow of a former season was still
remaining ; and to understand the causes which prevented
the army from proceeding on the surface of it ; and whether
the attempt at circuit was made by first moving in one
direction or another from the point where those in advance
were brought to a standstill. All know too that, in this
inquiry, a question has been made on change of climate. Mr.
Ellis gives a portrait or plan of the scene, to aid us in understanding the movements as he apprehends them.

The words which most claim explanation are, πρῶτον
ἐπεβάλετο περιελθεῖν τὰς δυσχωρίας. What was this experiment? How did they get to the place of it from where

the rupture of the path had arrested their progress? And, when their experiment failed, how did they get from it to the place of encampment? for the encampment was made before they set about the repairs. I have supposed, that they first retreated to the open ground from which the mountain-side path had begun; and that they then tried to pass along the trough of the torrent in which the old snow was found to lie ; and that, failing in this, they turned back to the open rising ground, made their encampment, and issued from thence to the work of repair.

Mr. Ellis discusses the circumstances of the ἀπορρώξ, when he is explaining Polybius in order to deduce conditions of congruity, and thus introduces us to the scene, p. 59 : " When-
" ever a man, descending a mountain where there is no track,
" finds his progress arrested by arriving at the edge of a range
" of precipices, he naturally creeps along their summit, till
" he finds a gully breaking through them from above, and
" affording him a tolerably safe passage down to their feet.
" A course of this nature would not improbably be that adopted
" by Hannibal : although it must, in his case, have been of
" an easier kind than is usual, as he would never have at-
" tempted to bring his whole army—men, animals, and baggage
" —down by such a line as might be taken by an unen-
" cumbered traveller. When Hannibal's attempt to make a
" circuit was frustrated, and he found himself obliged to halt
" and repair the broken path, he is said to have encamped
" περὶ τὴν ῥάχιν—back of a ridge—' dorsum montis.' "

Mr. Ellis discusses the same circumstance, when he is accommodating his theory to his conditions from pp. 119 to 128 of the Treatise. In order to give us his views relating to the ruptured path, he seems to have placed himself on the right bank of the Cenise, and taken a sketch which, being engraved, offers an elevation of the whole mountain-side that was facing him, and which includes more than the extent of the stadium and a half for which the usual path had become impracticable. One would expect here to see the point where Mr. Ellis supposes the progress to have been prohibited, and from which those who were in advance would have had to turn back. But the plan does not indicate the part where advance became impossible, and retreat necessary, nor does it show how they got to the scene of the disaster by which the attempt at circuit failed : neither does it appear how they proceeded from it to the place of encampment, after failure of the attempt. If these positions had appeared in their relation to one another, the author's views would at least have been intelligible.

A plan drawn for explaining the casualty of the ἀπορρώξ ought to express these things, if it is expected to assist our apprehension of the author's meaning : and the obvious excuse for Mr. Ellis not marking them, is that he was undetermined where to place them. But then why publish a portrait without the necessary features ? There is the mountain side, with a blue line carried down it to represent Mr. Ellis's gully : there is a zigzag line, meant to represent a track along the mountain-side. Nothing helps to the position of the important points : the arrest of the progress; the intended circuit, and its calamities ; the place where they then made encampment, from which the work of repair went to the damaged road. All is important to illustrate his theory.

The author's want of conception on the scene he desired to delineate for others, appears by his own statements. In p. 60, he says : "The account naturally leads us to look immediately " above the broken path for an encampment partly extending " over a ridge-back." We may look for it ; but it is not to be seen. Then, in p. 125, Mr. Ellis states it to be probable, that the ῥάχις of Polybius is about half a mile to the south of the Cenise, where a rill of water runs in a hollow parallel to the Cenise, with a ridge between them extending from west to east. And when this has been put forth as the ῥάχις, a third place, very distant from it, is suggested : "The fields " through which the Cenise flows between La Ferrière and " the commencement of the broken precipice would have " afforded in themselves a considerable space of ground for the " encampment." Thus explicit and satisfactory is Mr. Ellis's theory of the ἀπορρώξ. He criticizes the historian (p. 59) for using the article τήν with ῥάχιν the first time he employs the word, and attributes the inadvertence to Polybius being personally acquainted with the country. On some things he is satisfied with his own evidence, as when he says, p. 121 : " The old road, still remaining, forcibly recalls the narrative " of Polybius : it is in many places supported on terraces, such " as Hannibal must have raised along the mountain-side."

In the explanations of περιελθεῖν there is a characteristic difference between the process conceived by Mr. Ellis, and that which is understood by us. In his idea the circuit which Hannibal contemplated was down a precipitous gully : we apprehend that it was along the declined channel of a stream. His old snow stands high up and exposed on a mountain side, facing south. Ours lies in a low bottom, shielded from the sun throughout the year. This competition was not brought to notice in his Treatise : nor did he disclose, that evidence had ever been brought forward on the "mauvais pas" of the Little St. Bernard. Mr. Ellis took pains to wield his own deductions : but declined to measure them with the facts of a rival theory.

That other hypothesis had been long before the world. Mr. Ellis was aware of the evidence of General Melville, reported by De Luc ; of the facts of De Saussure and others to the same point, viz., the accumulation of the snow in the bed of the torrent below La Tuile, which still from time to time occurs ; and the pointed comments of the Oxford Dissertation. Nevertheless his Treatise did not contain a hint that

the route of the Graian Alp had pretended to supply a site
for the calamity of the broken way. This silence was the
more remarkable, as he discussed the matter largely himself,
not forgetting the old snow or the subject of the snow-line ;
and alluded to certain writers, as if they agreed with him :
to Gibbon and Arnold, and to Evelyn, mentioned in Arnold's
note M which refers to Evelyn.   Yet the rival pretensions of
the broken way, which had been so thoroughly asserted for
the route of the Little St. Bernard, are not alluded to in the
Treatise of 1854.

My criticism, written at Nice in 1855, caused that silence to
be broken : and in 1856 Mr. Ellis noticed me in the " Cambridge Journal of Philology," vol. ii. 327.   He reluctantly
admitted the fact, that the Baltea torrent is sometimes filled
up by the snow of a former winter.   On this fact, verified by
so many eye-witnesses, his words are: " I am ready to acknow-
" ledge, that the circumstance which Mr. Law mentions has
" sometimes occurred."   Then, instead of excusing himself in
his defence, for having shirked these facts, he blames me for
not dealing with the old snow more largely ; saying this :
" That no permanent snow is now found on the route of Mont
" Cenis at the place where I have supposed Hannibal to
" have met with it, is a circumstance easily explained by the
" change of climate in the Alps, a fact supported by the
" authority of Gibbon and Arnold, and proved by the
" testimony of an eye-witness, that of Evelyn.   Of these
" witnesses Mr. Law takes no notice : there is not a word of
" Gibbon and Evelyn, and but a slight remark (p. 59) about
" Dr. Arnold."

If I had cared for their evidence, I could not have dealt
with these witnesses at Nice.   Mr. Ellis's Treatise had
accompanied me from England : not so the works of Gibbon
and Arnold and Evelyn.   I directed the criticism only against
Mr. Ellis ; and I gave it to the printer immediately on my

return to England in April, 1855. But let us see what Mr. Ellis's witnesses have to say.

Mr. Evelyn reports the Simplon, one of the lowest passes, as covered with snow in September, 1626 : to this fact, which may happen in any year, he was an eye-witness. His account ("Memoirs," i. p. 220) is this: "That there were on " the summit a few huts and a chapel; and population " enough to bully his party on their spaniel killing a goat. " He says that a multitude came and disarmed them, and " kept them prisoners till masse was ended : then came half a " score of grim Suisse, on which they were glad to make " payment and escape; being told that their way onward had " been covered with snow since the Creation." Such is the philosophy of the snow-line : and yet my credulity does not accept, even on the testimony of the eye-witness, that the Simplon in 1626 was. with its chapel and congregation, on a summit of perpetual snow.

Gibbon says, in Chapter ix., to which Mr. Ellis refers, " Some ingenious writers have suspected that Europe was " much colder formerly than it is at present." He admits that two circumstances tend to confirm their theory : 1. That the Rhine and the Danube were often frozen over and capable of supporting enormous weights. 2. That the reindeer was a native of the Hercynian forest; which is said on the supposition that the reindeer was the " bos cervi figurâ " of Cæsar, "cujus à mediâ fronte inter aures unum cornu existit." Gibbon adds, "The modern improvements sufficiently ex-" plain the causes of the diminution of the cold : these " immense woods have been gradually cleared, which inter-" cepted from the earth the rays of the sun." Surely this has no bearing on the Alpine snow-line.

Mr. Ellis appears surprised that I made but a slight remark upon Dr. Arnold : and I am surprised that Mr. Ellis alluded to him at all. My remark was this : " Though I

" entertain the truest respect for Dr. Arnold, and a high
" admiration of his history of Hannibal's campaigns, yet in
" all that he has said of the invading march I find nothing to
" commend: on this point of the snow-line of Polybius, as
" on some others, I quite differ from him." Mr. Ellis was
then the special object of my criticism: he is not now; and
I shall comment on Dr. Arnold with equal freedom. But
why should Mr. Ellis pretend to care for the opinion of
Dr. Arnold? They do not agree. Dr. Arnold says that the
old snow of Polybius was " no accidental patch." Mr. Ellis
says, that " it was clearly an isolated patch." Dr. Arnold
placed the ἀπορρώξ of Polybius above the snow-line. Mr.
Ellis says that there is no reason for imagining it. Having
so brought their opinions into contrast, I may say this.
Thinking Dr. Arnold wrong on the snow-line, I must think
Mr. Ellis right in differing from him. But in the application
of their opinions, I do not think Mr. Ellis has the advantage.
Both resist our theory, in which the permanence of the old
snow is accounted for by its lying in a deep ravine, not
exposed to the sun: both disallow that argument. Dr.
Arnold has the better excuse : he disregarded it, being under
a delusion on the snow-line. Mr. Ellis has not that delusion
to palliate the blunder. His " isolated patch" flourished
through a summer under exposure to a southern sun, not
having perpetual snow to protect it.

The question between our old snow which occupies the
trough in which a stream is used to run, and Mr. Ellis's old
snow which is an isolated patch half-way up a mountain,
is almost a question between horizontal and perpendicular ;
between level and precipice. A rapid stream cannot be quite
a dead level : but it is opposed to precipice. Mr. Ellis does
not seem alive to the difference. His phenomenon displays
itself in an erect gully, where man and horse can acquire no
footing, and must roll down the mountain : ours lies in a

trough at the bottom of a defile with mountain on both sides ; but it was so slippery and otherwise injurious, as to prohibit a march. Mr. Ellis, in his defence,* instead of confessing his own sins, imputes them to me, and gives vent to this sage exclamation : " How does this snow in the bed of the torrent help " Mr. Law ! how could it possibly cause men to slip down the " precipices at the foot of which it lies !" I never sought the aid of such nonsense. It is Mr. Ellis, and no other, who would circumvent the " mauvais pas " by slipping down a precipice : he it is, who conceiving his gully to be spoken of by Polybius (whom he represents, Treatise, p. 59, as personally acquainted with it), construes ἐπιπολὺ κατωφερῶν ὄντων τῶν χωρίων, " for the declivity was one of excessive steepness." Κατωφερής signifies "declined," not " precipitous:" and ἐπιπολὺ κατωφερής is not " excessively steep :" ἐπιπολύ signifies " mostly "—" for the most part." There may be declivity in a line of railroad ; not precipice : it may be κατωφερής, but not κρημνώδης. Mr. Ellis's notion is somewhat akin to that of Livy, for which he is so roughly handled by Niebuhr ; namely, for turning the three half-stades of length into three half-stades of height. Lect. ix. vol. i. p. 173.

CHAPTER II.

Hannibal, having completed the passage of the Alps in Fifteen Days, came down boldly into the plain of the Po and the nation of Insubres. c. 56.

κατῆρε εἰς—*came down into.*

OUR opponents, unable to say that a man, entering Italy by the route of Susa or of Pinerolo, would come down into the

* Cambridge Journal of Classical and Sacred Philology. Vol. ii. p. 327.

Insubres, struggle against the words of the history : and first
they pretend that κατῆρε εἰς does not signify " came down
into :" they have discovered, that this expression does not
import the arrival at an object, but an inchoate movement in
the direction of it.

M. Larauza challenged the translation of M. De Luc, " entra
dans le pays du Insubres," calling it " une traduction évidemment fausse :" and he adds, "Nous nous bornerons à remarquer
" que le Grec ne dit nullement qu'Annibal entra dans le pays
" des Insubres, mais qu'il se dirigea vers ce pays, εἰς τὸ τῶν
" 'Ισόμβρων ἔθνος." One who could so translate, has very
naturally the additional merit of making an imperfect quotation.   The term κατῆρε εἰς is applied by Polybius both to the
plains and the Insubres.   M. Larauza exhibits it as applied to
the Insubres only : he may have felt that it would be absurd
to assert that Hannibal, who in the previous sentence was said
to have reached the plains, " se dirigea vers les plaines :" so he
suppressed the plains in expounding the sentence.   This was
not fair : he should also have contended, " que le Grec ne dit
nullement qu'Annibal entra dans les plaines : " but for this his
courage failed him.

Other critics, since M. Larauza, have tried to misconstrue
this simple expression.   In the work of 1830 on Hannibal's
passage by " A Member of the University of Cambridge," the
author objects to the translation " descended into," and says
this (p. 77) : " The word κατῆρε must here, as it frequently
" does in Polybius, simply mean ' he marched ;' and the entire
" passage must refer to the ulterior and eventful circum-
" stance of his bold movement into the plains of the Po,
" and his first encampment in front of the Roman army in
" the territory of the Insubrians.   Should there be any surprise
" at the peculiarity of this arrangement of matter, the follow-
" ing passage will show that in Polybius it is not unexampled.
" In the 35th chapter of the 3d book Hannibal is described as

" crossing the Ebro, and there parting with some of his troops
" —τὴν δὲ λοιπὴν στρατίαν ἀναλαβὼν ἦγε διὰ τῶν Πυρηναίων
" λεγομένων ὀρῶν ἐπὶ τὴν τοῦ 'Ροδανοῦ διάβασιν. All the
" latter part of the sentence has reference, as in the instance
" above, to an ulterior event."

This illustration is inadmissible, though we shall find it
adopted : καταίρω is never so used. The passage cited as analogous occurs thus : Polybius, having explained Hannibal's
proceedings after crossing the Ebro, having told how he discharged a portion of the troops, and committed another
portion to the command of the general who was to remain in
that country, says of Hannibal : " Taking with him the rest
" of the army lightly equipped, he led them on through the
" Pyrenean mountains for the passage of the river called the
" Rhone." Now see the weakness of imagining an analogy
between ἦγε in this place, and κατῆρε in the other. In
these words of the 35th chapter the historian, having brought
Hannibal across the Ebro, exhibits the scope of a portion of
march about to be performed ; and the notice of the passage
of the Rhone is the notice of an ulterior event, which will
be long after that to which ἦγε διά is applied.

Ἦγε διά tells an initial proceeding ; and for that reason it
is wholly unlike κατῆρε εἰς. But the want of prudence in
this anonymous critic is equal to his want of discernment :
he not only exhibits, as corresponding expressions, those
which have no correspondence, but he proves that they have
none, by adding these words : " For in the 40th chapter he
" is again crossing * the Pyrenees : and in the 41st he arrives
" at the passage of the Rhone—ἦκε μετὰ δυνάμεων ἐπὶ τὴν
" τοῦ 'Ροδανοῦ διάβασιν." Here his error exposes itself : it is
this expression ἦκε ἐπί, which is analogous to κατῆρε εἰς, not
the words of the 35th chapter. Each of those expressions
tells an accomplished fact ; one bringing Hannibal to the

---

* ἐνεχείρει ταῖς διεκβολαῖς τῶν Πυρηναίων ὀρῶν.

Rhone, the other bringing him to the plain and the Insubres.

Another patron of this false construing is Mr. Ellis. Not that in his published translation he adopted "se dirigea vers" from the French critic, or "he marched to" from the anonymous of 1830 : he prudently rendered κατῆρε εἰς "descended into." But two years afterwards, on defending himself in the "Journal of Philology," ii. 329, he condescended deliberately to adopt the error of his Cambridge predecessor, and borrowed his false illustration, saying this :—" The words, κατῆρε

" τολμηρῶς εἰς τὰ περὶ τὸν Παδὸν πεδία καὶ τὸ τῶν Ἰσόμβρων
" ἔθνος, may be compared with ἤγε διὰ τῶν Πυρηναίων
" λεγομένων ὀρῶν ἐπὶ τὴν τοῦ Ῥοδανοῦ καλουμένου ποταμοῦ
" διάβασιν, xxxv. 7. Yet Hannibal does not actually pass
" the Pyrenees or reach the Rhone till several chapters
" further on. Does any one believe that either of these
" events occurred twice ?" The answer to this wise question is, No ; the transit of the Pyrenees occurred once, and is told once. The reaching the Rhone occurred once, and is told once : it is not told by the words ἤγε ἐπί of chapter 35, when Hannibal had crossed the Ebro, and it is told by the words ἧκε ἐπί of chapter 41. Mr. Ellis must be aware that καταίρω εἰς never meant to march or set out for a distant object, and that it always imports "to come to," "to reach," "to arrive at." An old lexicon of Budæus aptly quotes from the 5th book of Polybius, κατῆρε μετὰ τοῦ στόλου παντὸς εἰς Κόρινθον, illustrating the effect of the words with "Huc ubi delati portus intravimus."

τὰ περὶ τὸν Πάδον πεδία—*the plain of the Po.*

Some advocates of a Taurine pass are persuaded that the historical statement, that Hannibal came down into the plain of the Po, accords with their theory, because the Turin of Augustus is on the Po. If the town sacked by Hannibal could be traced to that site, which it is not, this expression would not help to place it there. The meaning of τὰ περὶ τὸν Πάδον πεδία is too clear to be controverted. Every pass into Italy from the Brenner to the Col di Tende, leads you to the plain of the Po. The words signify, by the express definition of the historian, the great northern plain of Italy, bounded by the Alps, the Apennine, and the Adriatic. When we read that the potentates, Βασιλίσκοι, who waited upon Hannibal after his passage of the Rhone, had come ἐκ τῶν περὶ τὸν Πάδον πεδίων, we recognise the large application of the term. The πεδία, so often named by Polybius, comprised not only Cisalpine Gaul, but a large portion of Liguria and of the Venetian States, districts quite away from the stream of the great river, whose course divided the plain and gave its denomination. Senigaglia is said to be παρὰ τὸν Ἀδρίαν ἐπὶ τῷ πέρατι κεῖσθαι τῶν περὶ τὸν Πάδον πεδίων. Polyb. ii. 19, 13.

General St. Cyr Nugues limits the scope of this large term to the very banks of the Po itself. Being an advocate for the Mont Genèvre, he gives as a reason for declining the line of Susa, and seeking the Po at a higher point than Turin, the purpose of recruiting his army "sur les bords" before he attacks that place. He says, p. 19 : "Prenons la carte, et " suivons le cours du Pô. Ce fleuve, sorti du Mont Viso, " coule du midi au nord jusqu'à Turin. Nous lisons qu' " Annibal fut obligé de faire reposer plusieurs jours son " armée ; qu'il ne put éviter de prendre la capitale des Taurini. " Il est naturel de conclure de là qu'il descendit sur les bords " du Pô à quelque distance de Turin."

A still more curious conception of the plains is that of M. le Comte de Fortia D'Urban, whose singular theory will be noticed in Part X. He writes, p. 14 : "Après avoir franchi " le Tesin, Annibal fut entré dans les plaines du Pô : c'est " encore la vérité." Many others, among them M. Larauza, when they have occasion to express the idea of the Plain, say "plaines qui bordent le Pô ;" or, " plaines qu'arrose

" le Pô." For avoiding the risk of error in giving too narrow
a construction, it is but to say simply plain, or plains of
the Po.

The Insubrians—τὸ τῶν Ἰσόμβρων ἔθνος.

It is well that Polybius has applied the word of arrival,
not only to the plain as the terminus of the march, but also
to that nation of the plain, whose friendship and co-operation
welcomed the approach of the invaders. He promised in
c. 36, that he would make known πόθεν ὁρμήσας Ἀννίβας,
καὶ τίνας καὶ πόσους διελθὼν τόπους, εἰς ποῖα μέρη κατῆρε
τῆς Ἰταλίας : he now announces into what nation of Italy
Hannibal came down ; namely, among the Insubres. Unless
this statement is rejected as unmeaning, it results that he
came down the valley of the Doria ; for neither the people
of the Cenis nor of the Genèvre can be reconciled with it.

Our adversaries, however, though not pretending to reconcile Polybius with their own schemes, find a geographical
difficulty in ours. Polybius has said (lib. ii.) that, on the
first immigration of Gauls into Italy, nearly 200 years before
Hannibal, certain tribes called Lai and Lebecii, settled on
the Po in the parts above those which were occupied by the
Insubres. Accordingly it is objected, that a descent by the
valley of the Doria would have led into the former peoples,
and not into the Insubres, who were lower down the Po and
whose capital was Milan : and that, if we suppose him to
have come down into the Insubres, we are bound to introduce him by the Simplon pass or the St. Gothard.

It is very true that, if we want to bring him down upon
Milan, we must suppose him to have crossed the Simplon or
the St. Gothard. But we do not desire to bring him down
upon Milan : we know not that he ever was at Milan. We
desire to find meaning in the words of Polybius : he it is,
who has related that Hannibal came down into the nation
of Insubres. Those who profess to swear by Polybius, and

desert him at every step, are false disciples : an honest interpreter seeks, not to throw aside the author's words, but to
find sense in them. Was not the Insubrian the great leading
state among the Gauls, prominent in their resistance to Roman
encroachment? In the record of the first irruption, Polybius
says of them ὁ μέγιστον ἔθνος ἦν αὐτῶν : and they survived
the extinction of all the rest. True it is that Milan was their
capital, founded long before the time of Hannibal; and that
their proper original territory did not comprise the plain near
Ivrea, which received Hannibal's first encampment. But who
can resist the probability, that minor tribes who had first
settled in that plain, and were probably still its occupants in
name, had become subordinate to their more powerful neigh-
bour? Is it any stretch of imagination, to believe that Insubrian chieftains and an Insubrian force should be on the
banks of the Doria to welcome the approach of their illustrious ally? Besides being in hostility to the Romans, the
Insubres were themselves at war with their neighbours the
Taurini. Is it strange, that the historian, whose narrative
has contained no name of a people, besides Allobroges, during
the entire march from the Pyrenees, should now, on reaching
Italy, select, as fittest to be named, the great leading State of
the confederacy against Rome, by whom the Carthaginian
advent was so eagerly expected? Polybius was not writing
in controversy : he had no thought of the track becoming
subject to dispute : he was not defining it, to avert the quib-
bles of future ages. In the plain assertion that Hannibal
came down into the plain and the nation of Insubres, he
states a broad fact of history, whose truth is intelligible save
to those who have a purpose in perverting it. If Polybius
had written that he came down into the Cisalpine Gauls,
this quibble could not have been made : but the chief geographical inference would have been the same ; namely, that he
came down the valley of Aosta.

It is obvious that among the Gaulish adversaries of Rome, in the second Punic war, there must have been political subjection ; that Lai, Libui, and Lebecii, with other of the original Gaulish tribes, had in the lapse of two centuries become subordinate to a greater State, whose forces were free to watch the coming of their expected deliverer, whether on the banks of the Doria, the Po, or the Tesia. It is in unison with all prior notices of the Insubres by Polybius in his account of the preparations for war in Cisalpine Gaul, that he should have them in mind as the prevailing power in the region where Hannibal found the plain.

Which of these minor tribes deserved to be distinguished as the ally of Hannibal? Surely at the time in question, the Gaulish population of the district were serving under the Insubrian banner. A very few years later, they were serving under that of Rome. But no exploits are celebrated under their name. In the details of Roman aggression, the smaller tribes of the original settlers are not among the recorded victims. The names of surrounding nations appear in the annals of Roman conquest ; triumphs are celebrated over Ligurians ; over Cisalpine Salassians; Comensians; over Insubrian Gauls. Lai, Libui, Lebecii, have no rank as enemies of Rome. They belong to the history of Italy ; because they made part of the tale of the great irruption. Names of no importance are just mentioned by Polybius and Livy : they find a place in the catalogues of Pliny and Ptolemy, as now in the maps of D'Anville or Walkenaer. But they are unseen as actors in the affairs of nations: and the land in which they settled became at last an integral part of Roman possessions, without record of their annihilation to tell that they had been.

The supremacy of the Insubrians vindicates the κατῆρε of Polybius without more. Whether the same small tribes which squatted in that district two centuries before, were still tenants of the ground where Hannibal encamped, and put his men into hospital quarters among friends, while he waited for them to become fit for service, is quite immaterial. Their condition was restored before they were led to action ; and it was restored on friendly ground.

Mr. Ellis does not reply to what I have said, but only to what I have not said. In my first criticism written at Nice I stood, as now, on the supremacy of the Insubres. But it is a point which he has never noticed. He lays down peremptorily the identity of the Insubres with the modern Milanese, and trumpets upon it thus : " That the country of " the Insubres corresponded to the modern Milanese is in " accordance with the opinion of all geographers, Mr. Law " excepted. Polybius, in spite of Mr. Law's prohibition, " obstinately persists in considering the Milanese as the Insu- " brian country."

Mr. Ellis is aware that the Mediolanum of the Insubres became the capital of Lombardy ; and he may believe that, from before Hannibal to the late expulsion of Austrian power, there has been the same territorial consolidation of the dependencies. But it would be prudent to moderate his notion of the immutability even of their confines. I will not enter upon so large a field. I care not whether a place of interesting association, Cremona, belonged to the Insubres : a point on which there is diversity of opinion. As to what Mr. Ellis says of our theory at the other end of his Milanese frontier, that it supposes Hannibal to have turned back from the Milanese to besiege Turin, and that the early settlements of the Insubres reached to the Doria and the Orco, I never imagined any such thing; nor believe that Hannibal was ever on the site of Turin ; or that it then existed. The notion of turning back is a great mistake. The order of events was this : Hannibal arrived among his friends on the Doria, whom Polybius rightly calls Ἰσόμβρων ἔθνος :

among friends the army recovered its condition. This done, they attacked the adjoining people, the Taurini, divided only by the Orco or the Po. Having chastised them, Hannibal advanced against Scipio.

This crotchet on the Insubres must have received Mr. Ellis's peculiar attention : he gives it out in his Introduction as one of his Seven Summaries, but hardly makes up his mind, whether it shall be a summary or not. In p. 60 he says : " There is little doubt that the passage concerning the " Insubrians, is one of Polybius's succinct accounts or sum- " maries, and that it merely states the direction and end of " a march, the details of which are afterwards to be given." In the next page he says: " It is not necessary to take it " for granted, that the passage relating to the Insubrians is " a mere summary :" and he tells us (p. 7) that he shall not give us the whole of it. Thus the seventh Summary is left to take its chance : and, as the plains and the Insubres are never mentioned again during the campaign, we cannot be expected to recognise an Insubrian summary.

CHAPTER III.

On the Time employed in Descent. Many, and among them the Oxford Dissertation, differ from De Luc, who supports Polybius. Dr. Arnold on the Snow-line : his scruples on the Salassi.

Dr. Liddell on the Time.

DISTINGUISHED writers have blamed Polybius for his allotment of time in telling the march through the mountains. Dr. Liddell writes thus :—" In seven days after Hannibal began " the ascent, he reached the summit. Polybius says *nine* " (iii. 53, 9). But this must include the two days' halt at the " top of the pass. For the descent occupied at least *six* days

" (compare iii. 55, 8, with 56, 1); and the whole passage took
" *fifteen* days (56, 3)."

I abide by Polybius : his ninth day of ascent is as clear as
words can make it. Hannibal was two nights on the summit,
one of them being the night following the morning on which
he gained it. This gave only one integral day of pure rest;
and I hope it will be seen, that he marched again on the
eleventh day, and touched the plain on the fifteenth. The
eleventh, twelfth, and thirteenth days represent τρισί in
c. 55, 8, and the fifteenth day represents τριταῖος ἀπὸ κρημνῶν
in c. 56, 1. See *ante*, part v. c. 1, for the employment of each
day.

Dr. Arnold on the Time.

Dr. Arnold thought that the descent could not be effected
in the time allowed by Polybius. He says, in a note to
p. 91 :—" I have little doubt as to Hannibal's march up the
" Tarentaise; but the val d'Aosta puzzles me. According to
" any ordinary rate of marching, an army could never get in
" three days from the Little St. Bernard to the plains of
" Ivrea." Now Polybius relates no such fact as the army
getting in three days from the Little St. Bernard to the plains
of Ivrea. Τριταῖος signifies " on the third day " of the progress made on liberation of the elephants from the precipices,
and is applied to the arrival of the head of the column in the
plain. It is consistent with the narrative that, when this last
event took place, the tail of the column of march was
between Aosta and Verres.

The Oxford Dissertation on the Time.

The arrangement of time which Polybius has expressed is
not only disputed by opponents, but has been embarrassed by
ourselves. De Luc arranged the five days of descent very
accurately according to the words of the history. Second
edition, 1825.

A few extracts will give his notion of this chronology, pp. 212, 213 :—

" Le 11ᵉ jour fut employé à descendre au village de la Tuile, à tenter de passer sur la vieille neige qui couvroit le torrent de la Tuile, et à commencer la réparation du chemin éboulé.   Une partie de l'infanterie traversa ce mauvais pas le même jour.

" Le 12ᵉ jour la cavalerie et les bêtes de somme passèrent et se distribuèrent dans les lieux qui leur offroient des pâtu- rages et des fourrages ; les plus avancés durent arriver jusqu'à la ville d'Aoste.

" Le 13ᵉ jour au soir, le chemin dégradé fut achevé pour les éléphans qui arrivèrent à Pré-Saint-Didier.   Pendant le même temps l'avant-garde de l'infanterie et une partie arri- vèrent à Nuz, qui est à huit milles d'Aoste.

" Le 14ᵉ jour cette avant-garde se trouva au village de Montjoie et à Verrex.

" Le 15ᵉ jour entre Saint-Martin et Ivrée.—On est sorti tout-à-fait des montagnes que l'on est encore à une lieue et demi d'Ivrée."

Thus De Luc supports the fifteen of Polybius.   The O. D. would have it eighteen.   As we agree, that the descent was commenced on the eleventh day of Alps : any ambiguity must attach to the events of that and the four following days. They assert that the descent could not, consistently with the history itself, be made in those five days.   The question, then, between us is this : whether Hannibal reached the plain on the fifth day of descent, which is in accordance with the total fifteen ; or on the eighth, which is in contradiction of it.

The following view of the subject is given in the Oxford Dissertation, second edition, 114–116 :—" The descent pro- " bably commenced on the eleventh day, one day for the " passage of the cavalry makes twelve, and three for the

" elephants fifteen : and this is the number of days which,
" according to Polybius, he employed in passing the Alps.
" Having performed the passage of the Alps in fifteen days,
" he descended boldly into the country of the Insubres, and
" the plains about the Po. This statement is, however, rather
" inconsistent with the account in the beginning of this very
" same chapter, which says that, having assembled his army
" after the passage of that difficult piece of road, which had
" delayed him for four days, he descended, and reached the
" plains in three days' march from the broken ground, which
" would give eighteen days instead of fifteen. I think that
" there can be very little doubt that we must read eighteen
" days instead of fifteen, and that the 150 miles are to be
" completed at the commencement of the plain, and at the
" spot where the army was encamped. Indeed, the enumera-
" tion he makes of the losses sustained by the army, and the
" recapitulation of the march, are not made till after the fact
" of their having reached the plains has been stated ; and
" there can be no doubt, upon his own showing, that eighteen
" days must have elapsed before this event took place. It is
" possible that he might have intended to leave out of the
" account the three days employed in making the road for the
" elephants ; but I think it more probable that he meant,
" that in fifteen days the chief difficulties of the passage were
" overcome, and that he entered into a friendly country."

It seems to me that Polybius is here ill construed. As to
the notion of ending the fifteen days when the chief difficulties
were overcome, while the 150 miles expire many miles further
on, it seems quite inadmissible ; as is the other suggestion,
of omitting three days from the middle of the reckoning.
Such ideas are prohibited by the context : time and space
must begin together and end together. If it is true that upon
Polybius's own showing the passage occupied eighteen days,
it follows that he made an unhappy blunder in naming fifteen.
But the truth is that, in this criticism, the narrative has been

misapprehended : Polybius does not say, as imputed, that " the difficult piece of road delayed Hannibal for four days :" his text does not warrant you to say, " One day for the passage " of the cavalry makes twelve, and three for the elephants' " fifteen ; " neither does it express, as my friends report, " He " reached the plains in three days' march from the broken " ground." The cause of error is, that they accept every notice of time as cumulative : they conceive that Hannibal, having failed in his attempt to circumvent the place, encamped and did no more on that first day ; that he made the road for the cavalry on the next day ; that he constructed one for the elephants in three days *more,* and that he brought the whole army into the plain in three days *more.* I propose to show, that not one of these propositions is expressed by or justly deducible from Polybius ; and that his notices of time, fairly interpreted, are consistent with the fact that Hannibal touched the plain on the fifth day of descent, being the fifteenth of Alps.

The Oxford Dissertation, p. 112, tells the story thus :—" In " whatever way the attempt to turn the pass was made, the " troops were finally obliged to encamp at the entrance of it, " and, in all probability, in the plain on which La Tuile " itself is situated. The *next* day was employed in making " a road good enough for the passage of the cavalry, and " three days *more* in constructing one for the elephants." This imports, that nothing more, besides encamping, was done on that first day, after failing in the experiment upon the old snow which covered the bed of the torrent, and that the business of repair was only begun on the following day. The text of Polybius tells a different story : he says : " Where- " fore, abandoning this hope, Hannibal made his camp near " the edge of the mountain,* having cleared away the snow " that lay there ; and then, turning out his force ($\tau\grave{a}$ $\pi\lambda\acute{\eta}\theta\eta$) " reconstructed the path along the precipice with much

* Probably where the ground begins to swell towards the Cramont.

" painful toil; and so in one day made good a passage fit
" for horses and baggage-cattle. Wherefore, carrying these
" through at once, and having pitched his camp about those
" parts which had as yet escaped the snow, he forwarded
" them away to the pastures. He brought up the Numidians
" in successive gangs to the building of the road; and it was
" with difficulty, and after severe work, that he got the
" elephants through in three days."

From this narrative it appears to me, that the most vigo-
rous application of strength for clearing a passable track along
the damaged line on the mountain side, was made on the
same day which saw them leave the summit; that the prompt
transit of man and horse, evident from εὐθέως διαγαγών,
confirms the activity which I am supposing; namely, that so
much success must have attended the exertions of that first
day, that the pass would be ready for all but elephants the
next morning. This view of the subject accords with all
probability, as it does with the text. The difficulty which
seemed to defy the progress of the expedition, must have
offered itself to the head of the line of march within two or
three hours from the time when the army was put in motion,
which we may presume to have been, as on other occasions,
at daybreak—ἅμα τῷ φῶτι. The plain of the summit is
about two miles in length: and the first movement of the
column is to be dated from near the brink of the descent.
From thence they would reach the place of obstruction in
about four miles. The attempt to proceed along the bottom,
where the new snow lay upon the snow of the previous
winter, and so to circumvent the stadium and a half of
ruptured road along the mountain slope, was made by those
who first arrived in order of march. It was disastrous to
those who made it: but soon proved hopeless of success;
and the known character of Hannibal for prompt decision
assures us, that he did not fail in that promptitude under

circumstances which placed in immediate peril the existence
of his army. The narrative in terms exhibits instant action,
not idle postponement to another day. After describing the
attempt to get round, how it failed by the slipperiness of the
older surface when stepped upon through the soft fresh snow,
and how the weight of the cattle made them to break in and
become fixed, Polybius says, not that Hannibal pitched his
camp and went to sleep, but that he pitched his camp and
then set to work in earnest with all hands.

A small portion only of the army can have got down to
the scene of difficulties, when Hannibal commenced the effort
to vanquish them. If the text had spoken less plainly, one
would still ask—why presume delay in such a crisis ? Every
man in the army had become accustomed to apply himself at a
moment's notice to the encountering, by all personal labour, of
rocks, rivers, ravines, and every natural obstacle. If the night
of this first day was not such as to prohibit all operations, we
may be sure that relays of men were digging and clearing
throughout that night, and that not day only was devoted to
this vital struggle. As to the actual transit of the cavalry,
the words of the history best consist with the notion that they
went through early on the morning of the second day, the
labour which enabled them to do so having been applied on
the first day. The tenor of the narrative shows, that on that
second day Hannibal advanced his encampment to a part
which remained free from snow, below the scene of reparation : and the next note of time is, that the elephants were
got through with difficulty in three days of hard work and
suffering. But why three days *more?* The work done in
favour of the horse was work done in favour of the elephant.
It was a continuous process : ἐξῳκοδόμει and οἰκοδομία are
terms equally applying to all parts of it. The hardships
signified in κακοπαθήσας, and predicted of the three days,
belonged as much to the earlier labour which availed for the

horses as to the further exertions which were to liberate the elephants. Hannibal did not, after making a narrow road for the smaller animal, begin another road for the larger animal. It was the same path made wider. The first day's work gave a horse-path : the work of the second and third days gave it width for an elephant.

I insist therefore that the terms μιᾷ and τρισί, introduced as they are into this narrative of the descent, do not warrant the addition of one and three to the day of starting, so as to make five spent in vanquishing the obstruction. And I claim of those, to whom the author's meaning may seem doubtfully expressed, that they will lean to a construction that shall make him consistent with himself. I certainly think, that you best consult the context of the narrative, if you believe that the labour which liberated the elephants, being the labour of three days, was undergone on the eleventh, the twelfth, and the thirteenth days of Alps. If the descent began on a Monday, the κρημνοί were vanquished on the Wednesday. And now, to close the reckoning, it is to be shown that Hannibal would touch the plain of Italy on the Friday.

The scheme of reckoning, to which I am taking objection, after stretching the three days of reparation into five, gives three days more for reaching the plain, so making altogether eight : this is by virtue of the word τριταῖος, as if the word signified "in three days :" but such is not the force of the word : the expression of Polybius is, τριταῖος ἀπὸ κρημνῶν ἥψατο τῶν ἐπιπέδων—in the third day from the precipices Hannibal touched the plain. Those who require "three days more," exclude the day on which the repair was finished, and on which the elephants passed away from the scene of obstruction. But that day is to be reckoned as one of the three : if I have quitted London on a Wednesday, I am τριταῖος ἀπό London, in my third day from London, on the Friday : and this is so, whether I began my journey at day-

break or in the afternoon. In the 52d chapter all understand in τεταρταῖος the fourth day of movement from the
town. If Polybius had there filled up the expression as he
has the one before us, and had written τεταρταῖος ἀπὸ
πόλεως, you would not have understood four days more
besides the day of quitting the town. Πεμπταῖος ἀπὸ
Πισῶν imports the fifth day of navigation from Pisæ. So
τριταῖος ἀπὸ κρημνῶν imports the third day of progress
from the "mauvais pas :" the actual day of quitting it being
included in the reckoning. That day was the thirteenth day
of Alps : the progress of the beasts would not be delayed for
one unnecessary moment, and the day which overcame the
κρημνοί must be deemed the first ἀπὸ κρημνῶν, the day of
escape from them.

The first day from the precipice being thus the thirteenth
of Alps, it follows that Hannibal was τριταῖος ἀπὸ κρημνῶν
on the fifteenth day : and our case is proved, though not
to the satisfaction of those, who say that this would have
required an impossible degree of speed. Let us then
inquire what it was that happened on that third day. What
means ἥψατο τῶν ἐπιπέδων ? Are we to understand that
the whole army arrived into the plain on that day, elephants
and all, with the Numidians and whatever force had been left
for extricating them ? By no means. I do not conceive that
any one portion of the army, unless perhaps Hannibal and
his personal staff, was both at the place of precipice on the
first of those three days, and in the plain on the last. It may
be that he superintended in person the safe extrication of the
elephants : and he may have been among the first in the
plain. But the words of the history require neither. In the
narrative "Hannibal" and "the Carthaginians" are often
convertible terms : and the words here employed are correct
and intelligible, even if on that third day his head-quarters
were remaining at Aosta or Verres. They do not import that

the Carthaginians, as a mass, had occupied the plain; nor do they import any speed of movement measurable by a rate of walking. No time is predicated for the duration of an act. Τριταῖος gives date to an event by its distance from a prior event. We learn from it that the touching of the plain by those who first touched it took place on the third day of moving from the precipice by those who last left it.

The statement, of Hannibal collecting his force and coming down, συναθροίσας ὁμοῦ πᾶσαν τὴν δύναμιν κατέβαινε, seems to have been looked upon, as aiding the notion of the army making a given three days' march between the two termini. To me they only convey the idea, that, from the moment when the rescue of the elephants was secured, and the hesitation which might be caused by the detention of the extreme rear was removed, the progress as of an army was again brought into full activity, and the continuity of the column of march restored. Συναθροίσας certainly suggests the idea of bringing bodies of men from various directions into one central mass. It can mean no such thing here. A centre supposes radii: the only radius here was the onward line to Italy. It is not credible that the soldiers were allowed to disperse themselves into the lateral valleys. During the short time which intervened between the passage of men and horses and that of the elephants, the cavalry and a good portion of the army were moving forwards, into and down the main avenue to the plain; a sufficient force remaining to conduct and protect the work on the mountain. One cannot believe that this numerous host stood still, all waiting for the elephants. The richer part of the valley, about and below Aosta, must have been greedily sought; so that, when the compulsory halt of the rear had ceased, and the advance was again the advance of all, ass uggested by Συναθροίσας, &c., the leading squadrons may have been as near to the plain which they sought as to the summit which they had left.

There is one critic who seems to think that the horses and smaller beasts remained on the mountain, until the elephants were released from their detention. The anonymous of Cambridge (p. 17), in one of his efforts to correct others, undertakes to interpret the words ταῦτα μὲν εὐθέως διαγαγὼν διαφῆκε πρὸς τὰς νόμας ; and he conceives, not that the cavalry were sent down by Hannibal to the valley, but that " he turned out " the tired cattle to pasture, of course under cover of the " entrenchments, where they would be as safe as by the walls " of a fortified city."* Hannibal had better care of his horses than to send them to graze in the fresh mountain snow, when a rich valley promised provender at a few miles' distance. As to their shivering under the favour of Alpine entrenchments, I doubt that the mountain regions witnessed any entrenchments at all.

I believe I have rightly explained the proposition that Hannibal on the third day from the precipice, touched the plain. On the first of those three days there was no whole army at or about the precipice : on the last of them there was no whole army in the plain. Those who have been startled with the extraordinary speed of a great army transferring itself from the summit or from La Tuile into the plain of Italy in three days, must be told that the words of the history do not contain such an idea : they do not exhibit 26,000 men disgorged from the Alps ; they represent rather those who were at the head of the column stepping out of mountain into plain. This event was the earnest of triumph over the great barrier : and, when interpreters of Polybius, after telling the day of the elephants' liberation, quote as a thing not credible, that in three days more the armament was encamped in the plain, they would report more truly, if they said that on the third day of that liberation, Hannibal

---

* Dissertation by a member of the University of Cambridge. 1830. P. 17.

touched the plain. Ἅπτομαι imports the contact of the end of a line with another body; as when a rope hangs from a beam; so here, when the foremost point of a long thin line of march, threading the way through mountains, first gains the expanse of plain which is beyond. When at Newmarket or Epsom the winner's nose is at the post, the word for that crisis is ἅπτομαι. Hannibal won his race and defeated the Alps, when his foremost banner waved in the Dorian plain.

This notice of time may be thought tedious and minute. I have desired to show, that Polybius is free from the contradiction which is imputed to him : his words may not be clearly apprehended on a first reading. But, after reasonable attention, they cease to be obscure. To my mind they import that the Carthaginian armament commenced the descent at daybreak on the eleventh day of Alps, and met with an obstruction that same morning; one day's labour enabled all but the elephants to proceed on their march ; three days' labour, not three days more, was required before these could move on with the force which had remained with them. On the third day of their liberation, being the fifteenth day of Alps, the invaders hailed the plain of Italy.

Dr. Arnold on the Snow-line.

The bold writer, who ventured to suggest the pass of Hannibal to have been one by which you may pass from the higher Arc into the Vale of Vin, could not have escaped the necessity of committing the Carthaginians to tracts of enduring ice and snow. But one was hardly prepared to find that predicament engrafted on a more sober theory. If Hannibal transgressed the snow-line, à fortiori the earlier Gaulish invaders, who trod the Great St. Bernard, must have done so. But, after studying the perils of the snowy regions in the tales of modern adventurers, moving two, three, or four together, with the complement of professional guides, one listens with distrust to an invasion of these solitudes by a party of thirty thousand men with arms and accompaniments ; and, when one of high attainments and respected authority presses the fact for our acceptance, it claims grave attention.

In Dr. Arnold's "History of Rome," iii. c. 43, we read as follows :—" Hannibal was on the summit of the Alps about " the end of October : the first winter snows had already " fallen ; but two hundred years before the Christian era, " when all Germany was one vast forest, the climate of the " Alps was far colder than at present, and the snow lay on " the passes all through the year." He says further in the note : " It is clear, either that Hannibal passed by some " much higher point than the present roads over the Little " St. Bernard or Mont Cenis ; or else, as is highly probable, " that the limit of perpetual snow reached to a much lower " level in the Alps than it does at present. For the passage " of the main chain is described as wholly within this limit ; " and the ' old snow ' which Polybius speaks of was no acci- " dental patch, such as will linger through the summer at a " very low level in crevices or sunless ravines ; but it was " the general covering of the pass, which forbade all vegeta- " tion, and remained alike in summer as in winter. How " great a contrast to the blue lake, the green turf, the sheep " and cattle freely feeding on every side, tended by their " shepherds, and the bright hues of the thousand flowers, " which now delight the summer traveller on the Col of the " Little St. Bernard !"

I believe these notions to be erroneous. It seems to me, that we need not desire any higher point than the present track affords over this mountain, nor assume a change of climate for reconciling that track with the history. I do not understand that Polybius describes the passage of the main chain, or any part of it, as within the limit of perpetual snow; and I believe that the old snow spoken of was just that which Dr. Arnold says it was not, "such as will linger "through the summer at a very low level in crevices or "sunless ravines."

Let us examine the narrative, and consider whether Polybius intended "that the passage of the main chain was really within the limit of perpetual snow." Such an impression has been caused by these words of the historian : "They "(the elephants) had come to be in a wretched state from "hunger; for all the highest tops of the Alps, and the parts "reaching up to the heights, are utterly without trees and "bare, because of the snow remaining continually, both "summer and winter." This notice of the unproductiveness of the high Alps is called for, in showing that the elephants were in a miserable plight by want of food. Constant snow, it is said, causes the higher Alps to be without trees and naked—ἄδενδρα καὶ ψιλά. These negative terms are not sufficient to characterise the pure mass above the snow-line ; and we look to context, to know with what degree of strictness συνεχῶς ἐπιμένειν is to be received. If, in a philosophic discussion of the temperature and measurement of mountains by De Saussure or Forbes, we should find it laid down that snow remains constantly on a particular summit, our thoughts would advert to the snow-line. But Polybius was not so employed : what he says of bareness and barrenness, and the cause of it, is introduced only as accounting for the fact that the elephants were in a very bad plight by the time when they escaped from their detention. Those beasts might well be out of condition, without being above the snow-line : the last possible day on which any supply of provender can have been obtained, was before that of the barbarian attack : if any had been got then, still five days at least elapsed, in which their stock of food received no reinforcement.

We may well believe that the Graian Alp in 218 B.C. pro-

duced no store for their supply. The same is true of that
mountain at this day, and, I should think, of all the rival
passes, though they too do not reach the snow-line, and some
are far milder than the Little St. Bernard. This fact is
quite consistent with the sheep and shepherds that delight
the eye of the summer traveller, the cow pasturing by the
waters of the blue lake, and the gentians and rhododendrons
known to smile on the margin of glaciers. In Hannibal's
time there were probably no residents between Bourg St.
Maurice and La Tuile, perhaps not higher than Pré St. Didier ;
and, if the elephants at La Tuile had to rely on provisions
grown in the country above that place, their lives were unquestionably in danger. The cause imputed is climate :
passes of Alps, Grimsel, or Graian, have at no season a sure
vacation from.snow : hence barrenness and bareness of surface ;
hence the risk of starvation to a large animal coming from a
milder region. Such cause and such effect the historian
imparts in the words under consideration. Knowing something of the Alps, and writing for those who knew nothing,
he meant to tell that the cold and snow, to which those
higher regions are always subject, prohibit a vegetation that
will meet an unusual demand for the support of animal life :
but he had no intention to describe the full incident of perpetual snow, nor was the snow-line of the philosopher present
to his mind.

It seems to me, that every circumstance of the story which
Polybius tells, proves that the old snow was not "the general
covering of the Pass." It is only said to have been met with
in the attempt to circumvent the ruptured path, which was at
a level far below that of the summit. We know that the fall
is much steeper on the Piémont side than on the Savoy side.
If there was perpetual snow at this part of the descent, there
must have been perpetual snow for a considerable tract of the
ascent : if the ἀπόρρώξ was within the snow-line, the λευκό-

πετρον can hardly have been out of it. And yet snow is not
commemorated in the ascent: the arrival of the army at the
summit, their encampment, and the waiting for stragglers to
come up, has all been told before ever the idea of snow is
introduced into the story: it is mentioned then, as a new
cause of gloom and dejection to the suffering soldiers: "Snow
" having by this time become collected about the tops of the
" mountains, for the setting of the Pleias was at hand."

Seeing that snow is only introduced at this period of the
narrative, as a proper incident of the season, first causing
alarm after they had reached the plain of the summit, one
can hardly suppose that the perils of the ascent had been
aggravated by struggles above the snow-line; indeed, when
snow is first spoken of, it is only said to be collecting about
the mountain peaks, περὶ τοὺς ἄκρους. In the descent we
read of it as a special and grievous embarrassment: it is put
in contrast with the perils of the ascent. The history says
that they hardly fell in with an enemy; but that the loss
was nevertheless almost equal to that of the ascent, from
the bad ground and the snow which concealed the stepping-
place from view. He who wrote thus, cannot have conceived
any portion of the track of ascent to lie above the snow-
line.

As to the actual summit, Dr. Liddell, as well as Dr. Arnold,
has apprehended perpetual snow. Having stated, i. 342, the
halt on the summit, he says: "It was now near the end of
" October. The last year's snow, frozen into ice, lay thick at
" the top of the Pass." Dr. Arnold predicates perpetual snow,
not only of the summit, but of parts far below, that is, of the
mountain slope to which the ruptured path belonged. If
this were so, the whole Carthaginian armament must have
been for three days and nights above the snow-line, and a
portion of it, including the elephants, for a longer period: it
fairly raises the question, whether the old snow of Polybius

was an accidental patch or the general covering of the pass.

Can there be doubt on such a question? The phenomenon of old snow under new snow is noted by Polybius, not in the path of descent, not where they found the path to be broken away, but only in that place by which Hannibal tried to get round the broken path. It is there that he gives a minute description of incidents dangerous to men and cattle, caused by the soft fresh snow melting under their tread, and having beneath it the hard old snow. By these incidents the hope was frustrated of circumventing that obstruction to the march, the extent of which is defined. The phenomenon was purely local; and, when Hannibal was compelled to desist from his experiment, he encamped. This encamping was not impeded by old snow under new snow : he cleared his ground without difficulty, because that singular embarrassment did not interfere with this proceeding, which only required the removal of snow lately fallen. We observe also that on the next day, when the road was sufficiently repaired for all but the elephants, the camp was shifted to a part beyond the 300 yards of injury, which had escaped the snows altogether— περὶ τοὺς ἐκφεύγοντας ἤδη τὴν χιόνα τόπους.* Polybius says that, straightway carrying those through, εὐθέως δια- γαγών (that is, all but the elephants), and encamping on those places, Hannibal sent them away to the pastures : he then set the Numidians, by relays, to the construction of the road.

It seems that the account of this obstruction to the march, so related in the history, did not reconcile Dr. Arnold to the

---

* The Oxford Dissertation gives this translation, p. 224 : "when " these were immediately led down to the plains which were free " from snow, and sent to pasture." The freedom from snow is predicated by Polybius, not of the pastures, but of the scene of encampment.

idea of a chasm holding the accumulated snow : and it is true that, however strongly suggested, no Greek word is employed, which represents the particular thing. But is there any other explanation, consistent with the history ? Dr. Arnold for himself gives this statement. Hist. iii. c. 43 : " At last, they came to a place, where an avalanche had " carried away the track altogether for about three hundred " yards, leaving the mountain side a mere wreck of scattered " rocks and snow. To go round was impossible : for the depth " of snow on the heights above rendered it hopeless to scale " them. Nothing therefore was left but to repair the road."

According to this statement, no attempt to go round was made ; and, if it had been made, it would have been by scaling the heights above. Now Polybius relates that an attempt was made : he gives a most particular description of the attempt, with the causes of its failure : and it is quite clear to me, that the attempt was made, not by the heights above, which would have been a change from bad to worse, but by the hollow beneath. This was found impracticable, because a thing had happened there, namely, the fresh snow with the last year's snow under it, which was ἴδιον καὶ παρηλλαγμένον ; proper to the spot, and unusual in its degree. This circumstance is stated as the reason for desisting from the attempt : it could not be ἴδιον, if all surrounding parts had been above the snow-line ; it would then have been the permanent and usual predicament of the mountain. The description, together with the facts, is only intelligible, as of snow abiding in a hollow chasm between mountains. The encampment of the first day, the new encampment of the second day, and every incident of the story is inconsistent with the notion that this mountain was within the limit of perpetual snow ; and compels us to see that the old snow of Polybius was precisely that which lingers through the summer in a sunless ravine. Such is the trough of the Baltea torrent at a short distance below La Tuile : and from time to time, in these our days, the place continues to tell its own tale.

Dr. Arnold on the Salassi.

The non-resistance of this people contributed to make Dr. Arnold incredulous of the Little St. Bernard. He says, p. 90 : " After the two days' rest the descent began. Hanni-
" bal experienced no more open hostility from the barbarians,
" only some petty attempts here and there to plunder : a fact
" strange in itself, but doubly so, if he was really descending
" the valley of the Doria Baltea, through the country of the
" Salassi, the most untameable robbers of all the Alpine bar-
" barians." In the note M. we read : " The Salassians of that
" valley were such untameable robbers, that they once even
" plundered Cæsar's baggage, and Augustus at last extirpated
" them by wholesale. And yet Hannibal on the Italian side
" of the main chain sustains little or no annoyance." Dr. Arnold might safely have credited this freedom from annoyance in the Val d'Aosta. Strabo, indeed, reports the plunder of Cæsar's baggage by the Salassi. This people held out bravely against the domination of Rome. Why should they at any time have been unwilling witnesses of the advance of an enemy to Rome? Some Gauls on the outer side, and Inalpine nations whose country was invaded, had been hostile to this strange force, having no sympathy with, and not comprehending the object of the expedition. But in the valley of the Doria Hannibal found himself in what may be called the great Gaulish duct into Italy. Niebuhr, speaking from a quotation of Cato by Pliny, classes the Salassi among those who composed the great irruption of Gauls through the Alps ; and supposes them to have remained in those mountains and mountain valleys when others advanced through the last barrier onward to the plain.*

* Translation. Hare and Thirlwall, ii. 335.

Why should not the masters of that valley, though fierce and given to plunder as mountaineers, have sympathised with rather than counteracted the designs of their brethren in the plain? Some plunder might be made by individuals; but all probability is in favour of the Salassi being as a nation friendly to the Carthaginian invasion. The passage of Strabo that we are referred to, telling the last struggle for independence made by their descendants against the tyranny of Augustus, leads us to believe that they would at any time be inclined to the Gaulish confederacies against Rome, and, at the time we speak of, to that which was ripened under the auspices of Hannibal.

CHAPTER IV.

On Passes between Little St. Bernard and the Cenis.
Brockedon. Albanis Beaumont.

WHEN Dr. Arnold expressed his disbelief of the speed which he understood to belong to the descent as told by Polybius, he was waiting to learn, whether by further ascending the Isère beyond Scez, there might not be found some track through the chain of Alps, not quite so far northward as that of the Little St. Bernard, and by which the march would be shorter from the summit to the plain. In the same note he proceeds to say : " I have often wished to examine " the pass, which goes to the actual head of the Isère, by " Mont Isèran, and descends by Usseglio,* not exactly on " Turin, but nearly at Chivasso, where the Po, from running

---

* Usseglio here is a mistake : this place is on the Chiara above Viu.

" N. and S., turns to run E. and W." This accords with what he
had said in July, 1830: "The Little St. Bernard is not at the
" source of the Isère, but some miles below it. If Cramer's
" statement fail anywhere, I have always imagined that it
" was here, and that the army might possibly have followed
" the Isère higher up than he imagines, and descended into a
" valley which would take them more directly down upon
" Turin. The passes between the Little St. Bernard and Mont
" Cenis are almost the only points which I believe have not
" been examined."—*Stanley's Life*, letter 18.

That note may have been written long before the history
to which it is appended. The curiosity expressed concerning
intermediate tracks was reasonable, especially in one who had
a distrust of the pretensions of the Little St. Bernard. That
curiosity would have been satisfied with information given in
Blackwood's Magazine of January, March, April, May, and
August, 1836, as " Extracts from the Journals of an Alpine
Traveller." That traveller was Mr. Brockedon, one who, as a
resolute and persevering explorer of Alpine tracks, had no
equal. I heard of his death when I was at Aix in 1854:
and deeply did I, with many, deplore his loss: he was a man
as much respected for his talents and varied attainments, as
he was beloved for his amiable and friendly nature. I am
not aware that the instruction contained in those extracts is
to be found in any of the works published with his name.
Many passes over the main chain are there explained,
between the Little St. Bernard and the Mont Cenis: and that
which is particularly pointed to by Dr. Arnold, as going by
the actual head of the Isère, receives an ample notice, such as,
if read, would have erased that pass, the Galèse, from the list
of possibles, to Dr. Arnold's mind.

There are many passes into Piémont, both from the valley
of the Isère above Scez, and from the valley of the Arc above
Lanslebourg. From the former, there are the Col du Mont,

known to Mr. Brockedon, and the Col de Clou, both carrying you into the Val Grisanche, down which you come into the Val d'Aosta at Livrogne : the summits of these two passes are at about the level of the snow-line. Higher up the Isère, you may turn over the Col de Réme, from whence the Val Remy takes you into the Val d'Aosta at Villeneuve. Pursuing the Isère to his source, and ascending his glacier, you come to a difficult and dangerous pass, by which you arrive at the sources of the Orco, whose courses will bring you by Courgne to Chivasso. This is called the Galèse : Mr. Brockedon knew it well : that glacier lay before him, when he turned from La Val to cross the Mont Isèran, which stands on the Savoy side, having at its south-eastern base the early stream of the Arc. On the Piémont side, he was more than once at the same point near the source of the Orco : on one occasion he returned, and went north from Ponte, walking over the Col de Reale and the Fenêtre de Cogne to Aosta : on another, after surveying Mont Isèran and the surrounding peaks from the crest of the ridge, he proceeded some way down the glacier itself ; and returning, not quite to Ceresol, went over the Mont de Nivolet and by the Val Savaranche to Villeneuve. If the summit of that Isère pass approaches, as we are told, 11,000 feet, and the details of difficulty deserve the credit which I fully give to them, we may rest assured, that the crags of the Galèse would fatally arrest the progress of a company of infantry, even with the amplest supplies, and the fullest exemption from human hostility. No armament will ever rest on that backbone of ice.

The passes of the main chain from the Arc above Lanslebourg I believe to be five : of these, the three more southern courses, the Col du Lautaret (called by some L'Autaret), the Col d'Arnas and the Col du Colarin, are mentioned in the Extracts I have spoken of : one higher up I see in the maps as Col d'Insea : and the highest of all, Col Girard, is sanc-

tioned by the authority of Mr. Brockedon in "Selections
from the Diary of a Traveller in the Alps," given in *Fraser's
Magazine* for February, 1839. The most southerly of all
these, in his Journal of January, 1836, before mentioned,
Mr. Brockedon has given an account of as explored by
himself; the Col du Lautaret. For reaching this pass, as
well as that by the Col d'Arnas (which is far more difficult),
you turn from the valley of the Arc at Bessans, a place about
half-way between Lanslebourg and Bonreval, which is at the
foot of the ascent of Mont Isèran. These two passes send you
into one track on the Piémont side, near the sources of the
Chiara, which runs by Usseglio and Viu into the Stura above
Lanzo. The next track, by the Col du Colarin, also leaves the
Arc at Bessans, and carries you over to the source of one
chief contribuent to the Stura, and down the valley of Ala
to Lanzo. Higher up the Arc, from Vellet according to
Raymond's map, a pass over the Col d'Insea takes you to
another source of the Stura, and down the Val Forno to
Lanzo. And at the very glacier of the Arc there is a pass,
called by Mr. Brockedon Col Girard, which joins the one last
mentioned in that same valley at Gros Cavallo.

It must be by the Col du Lautaret, the easiest of all these,
that a well-known writer, M. Albanis Beaumont, has stated,
as his opinion, that the Carthaginians effected the invasion
of Italy. In his "Description des Alpes Grecques et Cottiennes," iii. 632, giving account of diverging tracks in the
Arc valley, and having said, " une branche pénétroit dans le
pays des Centrons," he proceeds thus : " L'autre se dirigeoit
" vers Lans-le-Bourg, Lans-le-Villard, et Bessan ; là elle
" commençoit à s'élever au-dessus de la chaine primitive des
" Alpes, qu'elle traversoit et venoit aboutir dans la vallée de
" Viu en Piémont, et ensuite à Turin : cette voie, qui n'est
" guère connue maintenant que par les contrebandiers, m'a
" parue, *lorsque je l'ai parcouru en* 1782, avoir été celle

" qu'avoit dû suivre Annibal pour pénétrer dans les plaines
" de Lombardie. La situation topographique de cette même
" voie, sa direction, la distance du sommet de cette chaîne de
" montagnes des vastes plaines de la Lombardie, un peu avant
" d'arriver à Roche-Melon, semblent venir à l'appui de ma
" supposition. Comme aucun historien n'a encore, à ma
" connaissance, fait mention de ce passage, il servit à désirer
" que ceux qui s'occupent de ces sortes de recherches, visitas-
" sent cette partie des Alpes, ce qui ne sauroit que tourner à
" l'avantage de l'histoire, et jeter des nouvelles lumières sur
" un sujet qui a occupé jusqu'à présent plusieurs hommes de
" lettres très distingués."

As M. Beaumont thought it so desirable that some one
should help us to a knowledge of this pass, and regretted that
nobody had done so, we also may regret that he has said
nothing about it himself, beyond the fact that he traversed it.
He could not have taught us less if he had stayed at home.
The curious thing is, that he should have offered to us both
the propositions : 1, that he crossed the pass himself ; 2, that
he thought it to be the pass of Hannibal. It is not easy to
accept them both.

The detailed account which Mr. Brockedon gives of his
journey over the Lautaret is most interesting and amusing.
For the subject of our speculations, the Carthaginian march,
this pass would be about as improbable as that of the Galèse :
perhaps not quite ; there is a story of its having once been
crossed by a patrol of French soldiers ; and we know for
certain that it has been traversed by a mule, which is a thing
that could hardly happen to the Galèse. One who takes
interest in Alpine things, will be amply repaid for a careful
attention to those pages of Mr. Brockedon which I have
mentioned. It is the number for January, 1836, in which
you may study the exploit of Garinot, Trag, and the mule,
over the crevasse on the Lautaret : let any one tax his

imagination for bringing upon that scene 30,000 men and a
troop of elephants, and weigh well, how far this route may
pretend to an improved accordance with the postulates of
Polybius.

I have taken this opportunity of pointing out the many
ways, practised by natives and open to pedestrians over the
great Alpine barrier, between the well-known passes of the
Little St. Bernard and the Mont Cenis : and what I have
adduced rests upon safe authority. These two ways have
supplied theories for our question : not so, any which are
between them. If Hannibal came up the Isère to Bourg St.
Maurice, he took for his onward course that which alone is
known to history. The course over the Graian Alp is the
recorded line from the Po to the Isère in the war against
Anthony : it was confirmed by the erection of a military way
under the empire : it is commemorated as a way to Lyons by
the geographer Strabo : and it is commended by the great
historian of the Alps, De Saussure, as the easiest pass of all
through the chain of those mountains. From the Mediterranean to the Adriatic there is no pass of Alps, where by so
short and practicable a mountain line you move from one
very fertile valley to another.

N.B. Though the Alps only are my proper subject, I hope
to be excused, if I shall add, in an appendix, a few comments
concerning the first movements made by Hannibal against
the Romans, being the sequel of the great enterprise which
we commemorate. For these also are distorted with doubt :
and unhappily I am driven to differ from the best friends of
our cause.

Of the many works written for contesting the question of
the Alpine track, there are but two, in which the line that I
follow has been maintained : the work of De Luc and the
Oxford Dissertation. In that question our agreement is

substantially unbroken. And yet, on the first conflict with a Roman army, Cramer differs from De Luc; and I am compelled to differ from both. Among the most celebrated men of our times, there is but one, who has positively sanctioned the Passage of Alps which is supported by us; the renowned Niebuhr. But in the early progress down the plain, I find occasion to dissent from his statements.

Thus I shall be tempted to transgress my proper subject : but it will be only so far as the Ticinus and the Trebia.

END OF VOL. I.

LONDON :
R. CLAY, SON, AND TAYLOR, PRINTERS,
BREAD STREET HILL.

For EU product safety concerns, contact us at Calle de José Abascal, 56–1°,
28003 Madrid, Spain or eugpsr@cambridge.org.

www.ingramcontent.com/pod-product-compliance
Ingram Content Group UK Ltd.
Pitfield, Milton Keynes, MK11 3LW, UK
UKHW010351140625
459647UK00010B/991